ENHANCING HUMAN PERFORMANCE VIA SIM...

# MODELING AND SIMULATIONS FOR LEARNING AND INSTRUCTION
Volume 3

*Series Editors*
**J. Michael Spector**
*Learning Systems Institute, Florida State University, Tallahassee, USA*
**Norbert M. Seel**
*University of Freiburg, Germany and Florida State University, Tallahassee, USA*
**Konrad Morgan**
*Human Computer Interaction, University of Bergen, Norway*

*Scope*
Models and simulations have become part and parcel of advanced learning environments, performance technologies and knowledge management systems.This book series will address the nature and types of models and simulations from multiple perspectives and in a variety of contexts in order to provide a foundation for their effective integration into teaching and learning. While much has been written about models and simulations, little has been written about the underlying instructional design principles and the varieties of ways for effective use of models and simulations in learning and instruction. This book series will provide a practical guide for designing and using models and simulations to support learning and to enhance performance and it will provide a comprehensive framework for conducting research on educational uses of models and simulations.

A unifying thread of this series is a view of models and simulations as learning and instructional objects. Conceptual and mathematical models and their uses will be described. Examples of different types of simulations, including discrete event and continuous process simulations, will be elaborated in various contexts. A rationale and methodology for the design of interactive models and simulations will be presented, along with a variety of uses ranging from assessment tools to simulation games. The key role of models and simulations in knowledge construction and representation will be described, and a rationale and strategy for their integration into knowledge management and performance support systems will provided.

*Audience*
The primary audience for this book series will be educators, developers and researchers involved in the design, implementation, use and evaluation of models and simulations to support learning and instruction. Instructors and students in educational technology, instructional research and technology-based learning will benefit from this series.

# Enhancing Human Performance Via Simulation-Based Training and Aiding

*A Guide to Design and Development*

*By*

Douglas M. Towne
*University of Southern California, St Helena, CA, USA*

SENSE PUBLISHERS
ROTTERDAM / TAIPEI

A C.I.P. record for this book is available from the Library of Congress.


ISBN 978-90-8790-201-8 (paperback)
ISBN 978-90-8790-202-5 (hardback)


Published by: Sense Publishers,
P.O. Box 21858, 3001 AW Rotterdam, The Netherlands
http://www.sensepublishers.com

*Printed on acid-free paper*

# TABLE OF CONTENTS

# PREFACE

This volume presents methodologies, designs, and applications developed over the past ten years in the pursuit of effective creation and use of simulations to support technical people in understanding, operating, and maintaining complex systems. While it does not intend to represent a survey of all the pertinent research in simulation-based training and performance support, citations are provided for the key research that either influenced the work or relates to it in some direct way.

While the focus of this volume is upon the design and function of development and delivery systems, some snippets of program code are sprinkled through the early chapters, in an effort to reflect the relative ease with which key processes are implemented when the design anticipates the needs. The workings of these code snippets are fully described in the text as well, so that those less intrigued with such matters can fully follow the discussions.

## On-line Examples

Many of the sample applications discussed here can be found and operated at the following Web site: http://www-rcf.usc.edu/~dtowne/.

Readers are encouraged to view and execute these on-line samples, since the static and monochromatic figures and accompanying text presented here cannot fully represent all the interactions to be experienced there.

# ACKNOWLEDGEMENTS

The majority of this work was supported by the Office of Naval Research (ONR), much of it administered by ONR and in later years by Naval Air Warfare Center, Training Systems Division (NAWCTSD), Orlando.

We are indebted to ONR for their support over the years, as well as other government funding agencies that supported earlier work, including USAF Armstrong Laboratories, Texas, and the Navy Personnel Research and Development Center (NPRDC), San Diego, CA.

We thank the many Navy technicians, training specialists, and site commanders who contributed their time and expertise to assisting us in developing and evaluating training and performance aiding systems in their midst.

The work in training fighting of high rise fires was made possible by the generous participation of members of the San Francisco Fire Department, the Los Angeles City Fire Department, and the Del Amo Financial Center, Torrance, CA. Quentin Pizzini and Donna Darling, of our organization, developed key parts of the training application.

We thank Merle Vogel (CSCWP, San Diego) for his substantial contributions to and support of the simulation of the aircraft nose wheel positioning system.

We thank the individuals, all of whom are cited by name in the various research reports referenced in this volume, without whose able contributions the practical applications could not have been produced and evaluated.

# INTRODUCTION

In recent years the tools and technology to produce and deliver realistic simulation-based systems for enhancing proficiency have become widely available at very reasonable costs. These proficiency enhancement resources include instructional systems, supportive practice environments, collaborative systems for aiding job performance, and interactive technical documentation. While it might be argued that resources that assist or support the individual in performing a task do not truly enhance proficiency, we consider such approaches as legitimate members of the family of methods that can improve the ultimate quality of job performance, and we include them in this volume.

Experience in employing these tools clearly indicates that effective applications can be produced at very reasonable costs, particularly when the simulation of the target system or problem environment is reused to serve more than one of the alternatives for improving performance.

### SCOPE OF THIS VOLUME

Some of the most critical questions that face the decision maker considering embarking on a simulation development program for training and/or performance aiding are:
− What sort of simulation methodology should be employed?
− What development tools and programming language are most appropriate and useful for this purpose?
− How may instructional content and processes be produced to work in association with simulation resources?
− How may simulation products be used to support both training and performance aiding requirements?
− What skills and previous experience are required to produce the simulation resources and the instructional application?

This volume will attempt to directly address these questions with detailed accounts of systems developed and applications produced.

### Terminology

The terms *model* and *simulation* will be used extensively and somewhat interchangeably throughout, however we will usually reserve *model* to refer to one or more emulations of identifiable hardware systems, while *simulation* is used

1

when discussing the emulation of a task environment consisting of system models as well as user interfaces for performing a task. In either case, the emphasis is on emulating the real world to the level of realism required to support learning and performance, rather than accomplishing engineering analysis or system design. While the model building methods presented here are certainly up to the task of creating such predictive simulations, the effort to do so is typically unwarranted when producing instructional and performance aiding applications.

## SYSTEM OVERVIEW

The family of development and delivery systems that will be covered in this volume is shown in Figure 1-1.

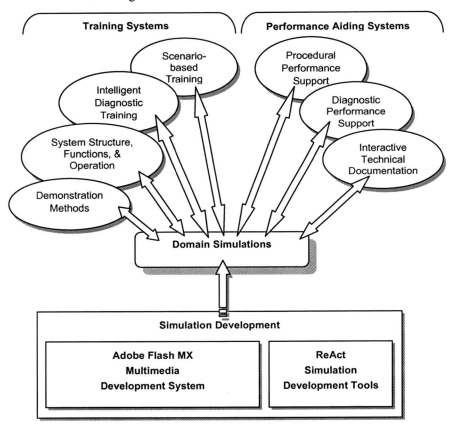

*Figure 1-1. Overview of Development Systems.*

The key elements of this architecture, starting from the bottom of the figure, are: 1) a simulation development system in which models are produced; 2) one or more models or simulations that emulate some real system or task environment; and 3) a number of domain-independent software systems, each designed to utilize and operate upon the domain-specific system models to deliver a particular kind of training or performance aiding activity.

Upon producing a model of a particular system or task environment, the developer interacts with one or more of the development systems to produce the particular types of training and/or performance aiding application desired. While one would rarely employ all seven systems to a particular domain or task, it is likely that two or more of the development systems would be used to produce complementary instructional, performance aiding, or technical support products for the domain. The final chapter presents an application involving five of the seven development systems shown.

*The Central Design Concept*

A key concept that the figure cannot adequately convey is that the domain-specific models remain as intact entities that serve as the representation of the real world when the various training and aiding systems interact with a learner/performer. With just one exception – scenario-based training – the models are not somehow customized by the developer to support the particular training or performance aiding application they will serve. Instead, the models are called upon and acted upon by the delivery systems in various ways that are specific to the particular training or aiding function being carried out.

*This is not to say that during model development we ignore the ultimate training and aiding processes we wish to carry out, but that the design of the basic elements of models is made sufficiently robust that the delivery systems have all the necessary control over the models to accomplish their functions.*

In a similar fashion, the training and aiding processes are not modified to deal with specific domain models. This approach to modularizing the content separately from the delivery processes is just one of the ways in which the methodology described here employs object oriented design, which will be elaborated below.

*The Exception: Scenario-based Training*

In the case of scenario-based training, discussed in Chapter 9, the simulation of the task environment is typically developed specifically to support that training requirement, and the simulation necessarily maintains some training-specific variables that reflect the proficiency with which the learner has performed various functions. Even in this case, however, the simulation of the problem environment could be used to serve another purpose, such as performance aiding, with little modification.

## OBJECT ORIENTED DESIGN

The principles of object oriented programming (OOP) and object oriented design (OOD) are central to all the systems and methods discussed in this volume, and the remainder of this chapter will briefly outline how these principles apply to the world of simulation-based instruction and simulation-enabled performance support. In the words of Booch (1991), object oriented design is

> ... built upon a sound engineering foundation, whose elements we collectively call the object model. The object model encompasses the principles of abstraction, encapsulation, modularity, hierarchy, typing, concurrency, and persistence. By themselves, none of these principles are new. What is important about the object model is that these elements are brought together in a synergistic way.

When these principles are applied to model development and instructional system development in a principled manner, the result is a system that offers increased transparency to inspection, ease of development and modification, and flexibility in reuse of elements.

These principles of object oriented design, or OOD, apply both to the models that are produced to support training and performance aiding and to the design of the software systems that rely upon those models to accomplish their objectives. Since entire volumes are required to even scratch the surface of all that OOD embodies, this section will only briefly consider the key elements of OOD and how they are evidenced in the system architecture that is the subject of this volume.

*Abstraction*

Abstraction refers to the process of representing more complex entities and systems in ways that reduce the apparent complexity through simplification of the representation. One objective of abstraction is to ease understanding by retaining the essential characteristics and processes that underlie the complex subject while omitting, combining, or further simplifying those aspects that can be so treated without materially altering the character of the system at the level being developed for use.

Simulations are, by definition, abstractions, for regardless of the level of detail presented, there are almost always more detailed ways to represent the elements that constitute the model. Even a highly detailed simulation of an electrical circuit involves abstraction, unless it happens to model the deepest known electrical phenomena at the quantum level, which is probably impossible.

When the intent of a simulation is to serve training and aiding purposes, the model is made as simple as will support the objectives of the application. Thus, if a model is constructed to teach a procedure on a front panel, there is no benefit derived from modeling the unseen elements that produce the effects that appear at the panel beyond that necessary to support the correct front panel responses. Instead, the observable behavior of the front panel elements can be expressed in terms of the states of the other observable elements. This is not to say that some functions of internal elements are never expressed in the model, for such functionality may be the essence of the transformation that occurs between the controls that are manipulated and the indicators that reflect change, but typically those internal functions can be highly simplified while still reproducing the correct system behavior.

A model of a device produced to support training in fault diagnosis, on the other hand, must involve some level of functional representation of the components of that system, so that faults can be produced and represented in an accurate fashion. These functional elements, however, can themselves often be massively simplified, so that the learner observes their normal and abnormal behaviors rather than the deep physical phenomena that produce those behaviors.

*Encapsulation*

While abstraction refers to the extent to which a model element is simplified, encapsulation refers to the process of hiding the implementation of that abstraction so that neither the developer nor other training/aiding software systems need be concerned with those details (except, of course, the original developer of the element). Once a model entity is constructed, and the abstraction of its function is encapsulated, the developer needs not again be concerned with how that functionality was produced.

As we shall see shortly, a key issue in the design of a simulation system is the manner in which domain-independent behaviors of model elements are separated from their domain-dependent behaviors, so that the former can be encapsulated and the latter can be specified each time the element is employed in a particular model.

A key aspect of the simulation development process that will be covered in Chapter 2 involves encapsulating the internal operation of model elements into well-defined functions with predefined names. Under the design of the ReAct simulation system, the function *setState* handles the graphical updating task for all model objects, regardless of type. Thus, once a particular type of control, for example, is constructed with a correct *setState* function, no future developer need spend time producing graphical updating functions when applying the object in a particular application. Of equal or more importance, other software systems, such as an instructional management system, can communicate with elements of models without having to be concerned with how the elements function. Thus those training and aiding systems can remain domain-independent rather than having to be customized to serve up the domain.

*Modularity*

Modularity is another possible manner of reducing complexity of a system representation, achieved by partitioning the overall system into individual elements that carry out functions that can be stated or described in a convenient way. Beginning programmers often produce programs composed of long sequences of

5

statements that reflect little of the structure of the problem at hand, even though the program might execute correctly. More advanced programmers tend to break down complex problems into modules (functions), each tackling a relatively concise sub-problem or represent an entity of a relatively narrow scope of operation.

Like abstraction, modularity enters into nearly all levels of simulations constructed to support training and performance aiding. At the lowest level of a system representation, it is both convenient and instructionally powerful to produce functional modules that carry out relatively simple functions that need not be represented or explained more deeply. These functional entities typically are physical entities in the real system, as well.

At higher levels in the system representation, a developer may, if the development environment permits, elect to produce a number of stand-alone simulations each handling some relatively well-defined and significant functions. Thus, a model of a radar system might be constructed of separate simulation modules representing the transmitter, the receiver, the signal processor, the display, and so on.

Finally, in the system architecture that will be outlined in this volume, there is significant modularity reflected in the very highest levels of system design. One module in a total training system is the simulation, another is the pedagogical content, and another is the training management system, and so on. By so separating the system model from the instructional content and the instructional management, the design permits reuse of the simulation to meet other purposes, and it greatly facilitates the division of labor during development and ease of maintenance when modifying or extending the application.

*Hierarchy*

As noted above, abstraction reduces the complexity of a system representation and encapsulation hides the internal details of the abstractions so that those details can essentially be ignored, once specified. Another opportunity for reducing the apparent complexity of a modeled system is to structure the representation hierarchically, thereby providing a structure for viewing the system at differing levels depending upon the need.

For example, by viewing an automobile as consisting of just a few basic functions, such as motive, braking, cooling, etc., the device seems more palatable and can be regarded as relatively simple. If the representation ended there, of course, the utility of the model would be highly limited. If, on the other hand, each subsystem is composed of another manageable layer of subsystems, and this decomposition continues to whatever level is required for the application, then nothing is lost by having grouped elements into families, and a great deal is gained.

The hierarchical structure of the automobile example is termed an *object structure*, or "part of" structure, in which a group of entities are part of another entity, or level. This means of viewing complex systems is so powerful it is employed in many complex example models given in this volume.

There is a second kind of hierarchy, called the class structure, or "kind of" structure, in which one entity is a kind of another entity. For example, we could group all operable controls into a group, or class, and say that they are all of one kind, since they all respond directly to user actions upon them. This exact type of hierarchical grouping is employed in the object model discussed in Chapter 2.

## Typing

The concept of *type* can be applied at very low levels of programming to define and restrict how different elements of data are to be interpreted and operated upon. At higher levels, and particularly in the context of simulation development, type plays an important role in distinguishing and specifying different kinds of model elements in a ways that permit processes to operate upon particular instances in useful ways since their type is warranted to be in conformance with some specification.

The discussions of Chapter 3, dealing with the development of reusable components, center heavily upon distinguishing among different kinds of model elements in generalized ways, which sets the stage for developing a hierarchy of model element types.

## Concurrency

Many simple device models involve apparently instantaneous changes in the states of elements. Switches are flipped from on to off with no apparent intermediate states, and lights change from red to green without perceivable delay or process time. In reality, all change involves the passage of time, but we customarily ignore those short transition times that are of little consequence to understanding, and we often artificially shorten longer transition times that need not be experienced in real time.

In many real world systems, however, there are not only continuous changes that occur over time in ways that should be represented accurately, there are also changes that occur concurrently. The simulation development system presented in the next few chapters, particularly in Chapter 5, provides methods especially produced for representing real-time processes either singly or concurrently. Importantly, the approach supports true simulation of multiple processes, in which other objects may respond to continuous changes, as opposed to multiple animations that do affect other elements of the model.

## Persistence

The last property of OOD discussed here is persistence, the preservation of object and system states from one time to another. Persistence of state is the assumed condition when running a single model, i.e., one expects that a change to object states will persist during a session. This does not necessarily mean that objects will not subsequently change from the state the user produced, as a result of some other cause or even the passage of time, but simply that a change of viewpoint to another section of a large model will not by itself cause objects to revert to some initialized condition, unless that is an explicit wish of the developer.

Persistence becomes an issue when large models composed of individual simulations are executed. Again, one expects that operations performed on any of the individual subsystems will persist even if the particular simulation is unused and out of view for an extended period of time, during a session. And, as a special case, a developer would hope that a development system would provide some means for recording and recovering the state of a complex system when a very complex simulation is resumed after an interruption. This capability is also essential when a training system wishes to set up the simulation for some instructional purpose, such as replaying a completed exercise or demonstrating an expert procedure.

Persistence is explicitly addressed by the developer in producing interactive technical documentation, as covered in Chapter 11, and the development system provides options for either maintaining a system state from one viewing to another or reinitializing it with each viewing. For example, suppose we wish to display a device model in a particular state when a particular "page" of a document (or screen) is viewed. If the accompanying text says "... here is system ABC in mode XYZ", then either the model should be made to not respond to user actions, which is possible, or it should be reinitialized to the stated mode each time that screen is viewed in a session.

## ORGANIZATION AND CONTENT OF THE VOLUME

Figure 1-1 also reflects the general organization of this volume, working from bottom to top. Chapter 2 will provide an overview of the basic Adobe Flash development system and the simulation development resource (ReAct) that works in conjunction with Flash to facilitate model development. Chapters 3 through 5 will focus upon the simulation development process, and they provide a number of example products of that process. Chapters 6 through 9 will detail the design and implementation of the training resources shown, viz., demonstration of system functions and basic concepts; instruction of system structure, functions and operation; intelligent diagnostic training; and scenario-based training. Chapter 10 will do the same for procedural and diagnostic performance support, and Chapter 11 addresses interactive technical documentation. The volume concludes in Chapter 12 with a brief example of a complete integrated system that provides training, aiding, and interactive technical documentation for a particular domain.

# RESOURCES FOR SIMULATION DEVELOPMENT

There are a number of commercially available development environments, each with their own programming language that could be used for simulation development and execution. These include MS Visual Basic, .NET, ToolBook, various Java development systems, and the Adobe Flash system. Of these, Adobe Flash was selected as the preferable approach for reasons that include these:

– Its graphics are vector based and can be easily scaled and rotated.
– It provides very high programmatic control over graphic elements.
– Its programming language, ActionScript, is ECMA-standard.
– Many users worldwide produce products, training, and support.
– Its no-cost run-time system is well integrated into most Web browsers.
– Its applications are compiled and execute on both PCs and Mac platforms.
– Its applications can be deployed via Internet, *without modification*.

All of the simulation applications and training and aiding delivery systems to be discussed are developed in Adobe Flash augmented with a set of Flash-based simulation development functions termed ReAct. This chapter will outline the capabilities of these two systems with particular emphasis upon the manner in which they adhere to the principles of object oriented design. The development resources added by the ReAct system will only be introduced in this chapter, and will be discussed in considerably more detail in later chapters, as various simulation development issues are addressed.

## ADOBE FLASH MX

Adobe Flash MX, hereafter termed Flash, is used worldwide by a vast number of developers to produce a wide range of multimedia applications. Primary among those applications are highly animated Web sites, the area in which Flash became a world leader. The system, however, is also fully capable of producing very sophisticated stand alone applications. Simulations can be developed and executed on both Windows-based PCs and Apple Macintosh platforms, ranging from tablet computers to desktops, and distributed applications require no modifications.

Importantly, Flash employs vector graphics as its graphical format, in which figures are composed of line segments. The great advantage of the vector graphic format is that figures can be scaled and rotated with virtually no loss in resolution or clarity, whereas the alternative graphical format, raster graphics, produces serious artifacts when scaled. Figure 2-1 illustrates the differences between a raster graphic and a vector graphic, both scaled to 200% from an original graphic.

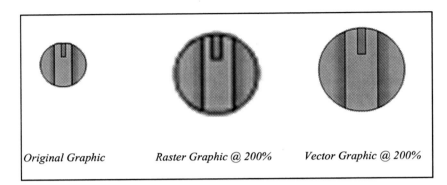

*Figure 2-1. Comparison of Raster Graphic and Vector Graphic, at 200% Scale.*

Like many of the more powerful authoring systems, the layout of tools and palettes can be managed by the user. The following diagram reflects the major parts of the Flash development system, in a typical configuration.

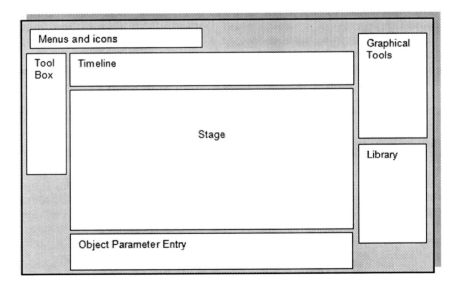

*Figure 2-2. Typical Flash Development Screen Configuration.*

*Main Work Area*

The main work area, consisting of the menus and icons, the timeline, the toolbox, and the stage is shown in Figure 2-3.

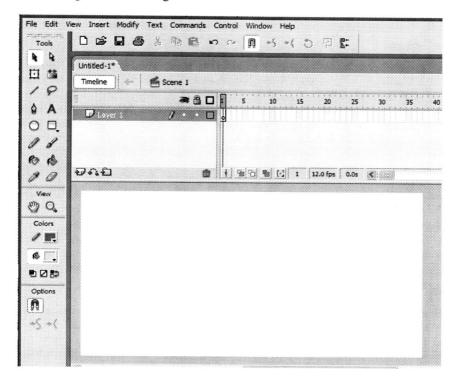

*Figure 2-3. The Main Work Area in the Flash Development System.*

This view reflects four of the main elements of the development environment: 1) menu items and icons, along the top, 2) the graphical toolbox for composing graphical elements, along the left side, 3) a *timeline* for setting the depth and time at which graphics appear, and 4) the *stage*, where graphics are produced.

*Menus and Icons*

The *menu items* (File, Edit, View, etc.), along the top are used to manage files and views, to format text, to initiate the creation of new graphical elements, and to accomplish other housekeeping functions. The graphical icons below that perform other common operations.

11

*Graphical ToolBox*

The graphical composition and editing tools are provided in a *toolbox*, along the left side. These are used for drawing, sizing, coloring, and otherwise manipulating graphics and text.

*The Timeline*

The *timeline* consists of numbered columns, termed *frames*, and rows, termed *layers*. The layers of the timeline represent the order in which graphic elements are ordered in the Z-axis, thus all graphics placed in the first layer appear over those in the second layer, and so on. In the original Flash system, only animations were produced, and virtually all graphical operations were done in the timeline. In simulation applications, the frames of the timeline provide a convenient mechanism for storing and showing different graphical views of an object or model, while the layers provide essential control over the layering of graphics in the third dimension.

The timeline also provides the capabilities to show and hide independent layers of the graphical composition (via the eye icon), and to lock and unlock independent layers of the graphical composition (via the padlock icon), so that changes made in one layer do not upset the contents of other layers. These options are only available during development and cannot be invoked programmatically.

*The Stage*

All graphics are initially produced on the stage. Prior to drawing out a new graphical figure on the stage, or bringing pre-constructed elements onto the stage, the developer selects a particular frame and layer in the timeline to which the element is assigned, thus the combination of the stage and timeline define a four-dimensional world of horizontal and vertical position, plus depth and time of existence.

*Example*

Figure 2-4 shows the timeline and stage during creation of a model of a simple front panel. As suggested by the names of the layers in the timeline, the panel knobs and dials reside in the uppermost graphical layer, the graphics for the static panel reside in the next layer down, and the scripting that resides outside the simulation elements is stored in the bottom layer. Thus, the operable elements all appear over the static background.

The timeline for this example involves just two frames; frame 1 is used to initialize the model, as will be explained later, and frame 2 contains the model. When this model is executed, Flash starts at frame 1, executes the initialization statements, then proceeds to frame 2 where it stops, showing the active panel.

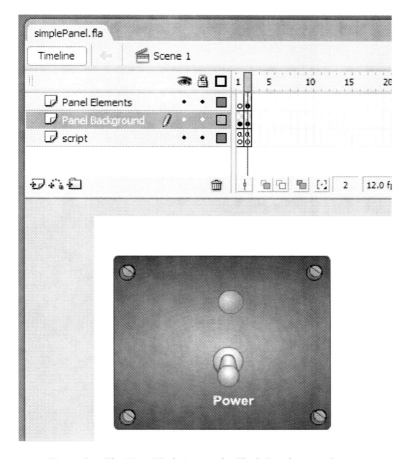

*Figure 2-4. The Main Work Area in the Flash Development System.*

## Additional Graphic Tools

Along the upper right side of the screen is a set of palettes for manipulating scale, color, transparency, rotation, and alignment of existing graphical elements.

Collectively, the graphical tools provide an impressive set of vector drawing capabilities, with both direct and programmatic control over such properties as visibility, position, rotation, scale, color, and transparency.

13

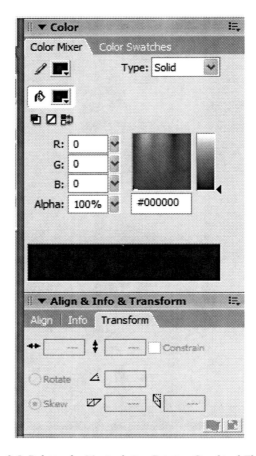

*Figure 2-5. Palettes for Manipulating Existing Graphical Elements.*

## The Library

Along the lower right side of the screen is the Library (Figure 2-6) that contains completed model elements. When an element in the Library is selected, it appears at the head of the Library for inspection, and may be dragged onto the stage.

Still called the *Symbol Library* by some, because of the historical origination of Flash as a tool for animating simple graphical symbols, the Library can actually store an extensive set of resources, including complex graphical elements, parameterized graphical elements termed *components* (examined in detail in Chapter 3), and even sound files.

While static background graphics are often drawn directly on the stage containing a simulation, virtually all operational simulation elements are created on an empty stage and then stored in the Library as components.

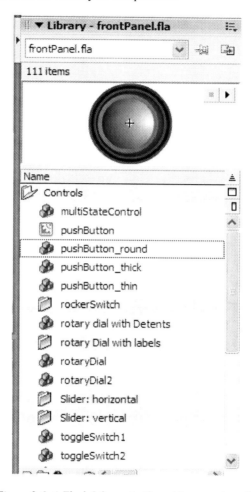

*Figure 2-6. A Flash Library (with pushbutton selected).*

*Scripting Component Behaviors*

The behavior of simulation objects is expressed in ActionScript (version 2.0), a full-fledged, object-oriented programming language based on the ECMA-262 standard, and thus very similar to JavaScript. This programming language provides all of the functionality required in both simulations and host training and aiding systems, including numerical manipulation, textual operations, logical processes, file input/output, and programmatic control of graphics. For completeness, this volume will present a few snippets of ActionScript for those familiar with the language, but each snippet is accompanied by a verbal interpretation of the code.

*Parameter Definition Table*

Upon completing the creation of a new component, the developer fills out a table listing the parameters that are to be associated with all instances created from it. This table, an example of which is shown here, lists the Name of each parameter as presented to the applicator when the component is instantiated, the Variable within the component behavior rules associated with this parameter, an initial default Value for the parameter, and the Type of parameter.

| Name | Variable | Value | Type |
|---|---|---|---|
| State Names | theNames | off,on | String |
| Sound | clickSound | TCHICK | String |
| Display Name | displayName | | String |
| Affected Objects | notify | | String |

*Figure 2-7. Component Parameter Definition Table.*

When presented to the applicator at the time an object is produced from a component, just the Name and Value columns are shown, as shown in the next section.

*Creating an Object Instance*

Dragging a component from the Library to the stage produces an instance of the component where dropped, with the original remaining in the Library, as shown in Figure 2-8.

When the newly created object is dropped on the screen, or is selected in the development mode at any time thereafter, a table appears automatically, listing the user-settable parameters for that object type, as seen in Figure 2-9.

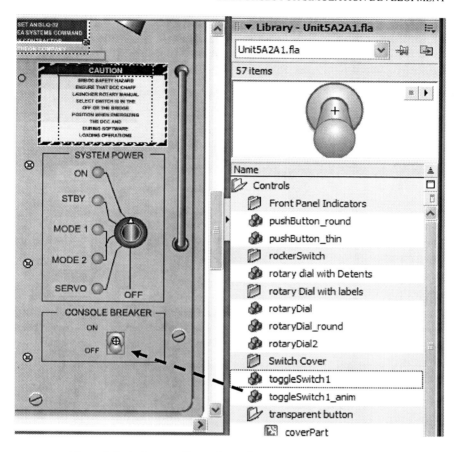

*Figure 2-8. An Instance Being Created From a Library Component.*

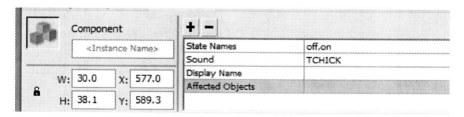

*Figure 2-9. The Component Parameter Value Entry Table as Initially Presented.*

The applicator then enters a name for the new element (in place of <Instance Name>) and values for the parameters. In this example two of the four parameters list default values, either of which may be left as is or overridden by the applicator. Following completion by the applicator, the table might look as follows:

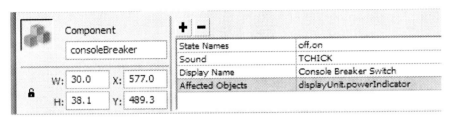

*Figure 2-10. The Component Parameter Value Entry Table after Completion.*

The use and meanings of these parameters will be covered in more detail in the next chapter.

*GUI and Multimedia Components*

The development system includes a number of GUI (graphical user interface) and multimedia management components, some of which are shown here (those labeled FLV manage presentation of Flash Video)

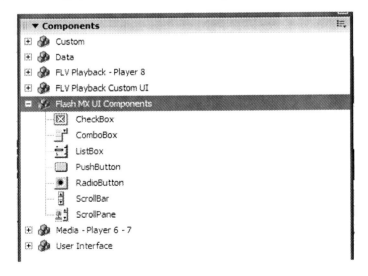

*Figure 2-11. Some Components Supplied in the Flash Development System.*

These elements are rarely used within device models, but are used heavily in training and aiding systems to provide user control over such aspects as instructional mode, topics, and learning choices. Like those elements produced by the developer, these interface elements may be included in any Flash application by dragging them to the stage, scaling them as required, and entering values for their parameters. For example, the following check box would allow a learner to indicate whether help is desired or not, during some instructional activity.

☐ Provide Help

This element would be produced by dragging the CheckBox element from the list of Flash UI Components and filling out the parameter table as follow:

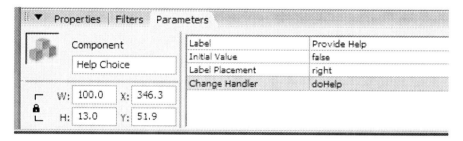

*Figure 2-12. Parameter Entry Table for a Flash Checkbox Element.*

## *Freeware and Third-party Resources*

As of this writing, a Google search for "Flash MX components" returns 1,320,000 results and searching for "Adobe Flash functions" returns 1,240,000 such sites, many of which provide extremely useful resources that can be downloaded, included in applications, and modified if necessary. The sites offer a wide assortment of both free and commercial third-party resources, including functions, graphical elements, video loops, sounds, 3D add-ons, text effects, and, most importantly, components. Table 2-1 lists a few such sites.

As might be expected, the great majority of the resources found on the Web are those that are of use to many users, such as user interface elements, text transformations, and animation functions. There are, however, a considerable number of more specialized components, as reflected in the samples of Table 2-2.

*Table 2-1. Some Web-based Flash Resources.*

| Site Address | Site Type | Content Available |
|---|---|---|
| flashloaded.com | Commercial resources | Multimedia content; Flash graphics functions; templates |
| flashcomponents.net | Free shareware | Graphical and GUI components; sound, video, and 3D media; utility functions |
| flashfoundry.com | Subscription based resources | Components, animations, templates |
| ActionScript.com | Adobe's Flash developer online community | Tutorials, forum, reviews, and free components |
| adobe.com/cfusion/exch ange/index | Adobe's central storehouse for free and fee-based components | Components |
| flashkit.com | Free shareware | Components |
| flash-db.com/Components/ | Free shareware with donations accepted | Components, tutorials, and applications |

*Table 2-2. Some Specialized Third-party Flash Resources*

| Component | Source |
|---|---|
| Rotating gears | FlashExtension.net |
| Operable stopwatch | FlashExtension.net |
| Convert 2D figures to 3D | Swift3D Xpress |
| A character animation that lip synchs to either a wave file or text file. | Digital Curiosity |
| LED alphanumeric readouts | Kaye and Castillo at http://www.flash-applets.com/tutorial/interactivesimulation.html |

This brief introduction to Flash will suffice for our present purposes. Many excellent resources exist that provide detailed guidance in developing Flash applications, including the Flash Help system itself as well as books by Bhangal (2004), Watrall and Herber (2004), Moock (2003), and Franklin and Makar (2004).

ALTERNATE SIMULATION METHODOLOGIES

There are many different simulation development systems, meeting a vast range of requirements. Some systems are more narrowly scoped, to meet a special simulation need, such as circuit analysis or structural design; some focus on time-related dynamic systems, such as process control; and others embody no aspect of time whatsoever.

In addition, there are great differences among simulation systems in the level of granularity that is represented. When the intent of a simulation is to test a provisional design or to analyze the behavior of a planned system, the system model is typically specified in the deepest possible level. Thus weather simulations and circuit simulations are cast in very deep physical terms so that the resulting system behavior can be observed experimentally with some reliability. In these cases the intent is to learn the behavior of the system under design based upon the known physical principles that underlie it.

When the intent is to model an existing system or phenomenon for training purposes, however, the domain expert already knows how the target system behaves and wishes to emulate that behavior with the least possible effort, consistent with the training objectives. In these cases a more superficial model may be far more appropriate and cost effective.

This volume will focus on a particular approach to simulation development and execution that lends itself well to representing a very wide range of domains and can serve higher-level training and aiding software with relative ease. To achieve this level of generality, no particular physical phenomena or principles are embodied within the simulation development system.

First, we will briefly examine and compare some alternate ways in which simulations might be developed. The five approaches to be discussed are: 1) a method that employs statecharts to represent the domain; 2) a method for combining predefined functional building blocks to represent system behaviors; 3) a constraint-based simulation system developed previously by our organization, 4) a system that employs user-developed components; and 5) an approach we will term the *direct* method, in which the simulation is composed of objects that directly communicate with one another rather than via an intermediary simulation engine process.

*Specifying Simulations via Statecharts*

Jonathan Kaye and David Castillo (2003) have adapted a technique, termed *statecharts* (Harel, 1987, 1997) for expressing the function of a complex system. Their approach makes a formal separation between the graphical characteristics of a model element, such as a toggle switch, and the domain-specific effects of that element, such as causing an indicator light to appear red if the switch is on.

Under this approach the graphical behaviors of model elements are fully encapsulated within the elements themselves, and the specific behaviors of model elements are initially specified in a graphical statechart form that is then converted to programmatic specifications. Thus, for example, a simple two-state indicator light is fully described within the light element, and the rules governing when it is on and when it is off are specified within the statechart for that application.

The basic elements of a statechart are current state, initial state (or start state), transition, and final state (or stop state) as shown here.

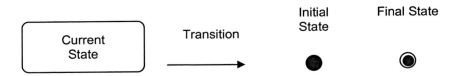

With these and other notations, statecharts are capable of representing such effects as discrete events, continuous processes, hierarchical states, history, concurrency, delays, and timeouts. As a very simple example, consider a simple device that can be in either a powered up or powered down condition. The statechart methodology might represent such a system as follows:

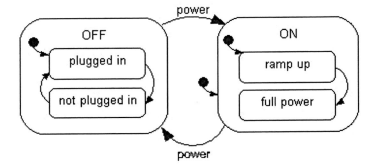

*Figure 2-13. Statechart Representation of a Two-state System (Kaye & Castillo, 2002).*

The rounded rectangles in this chart represent states, and the two main states each involve two sub states. The arrows represent possible transitions from one state to another, and the black dots with arrows express what sub state should be established first when the state that it appears in becomes activated.

*Developing Simulations from Statecharts*

When a statechart is completed that fully reflects the behaviors of the system, it is then expressed in event-action tables that are executable by a special processor written in ActionScript, the programming language of Adobe Flash. The developer of a statechart for a device requires extensive knowledge of this formalism, plus expertise in the domain being modeled, but little programming ability. And, *in theory*, the individual who then prepares the program statements to match the statechart needs to know how the statechart is represented in programmatic terms, but does not need to understand the domain.

## Advantages and Disadvantages of the Method

The statechart approach enjoys a number of significant benefits over methods that do not employ this manner of representation. First, the graphical elements that depict the real system in the model can be quite domain independent, since their model-specific functionality is expressed in the statechart rather than within the elements themselves. Secondly, the statechart representation provides a powerful and convenient mechanism for documenting the behavior of a system. If an error is found in the behavior of the resulting simulation, and one or more errors are almost always discovered regardless of the approach, the statechart provides a concise and explicit statement of the system behavior that can be analyzed apart from the programming code. If the statechart is deemed correct, then any misbehavior by the model must lie in the conversion of the statechart to program-readable code. And, importantly, the domain-specific code that expresses the statechart is highly centralized and easy to examine, as opposed to any method that would distribute program code across a large number of individual elements.

One possible disadvantage to this approach is that the statechart representation scheme presents an additional formalism that must be learned, understood, and correctly applied by the developer. One could imagine observing incorrect behavior in a simulation under development, yet having difficulty identifying the source of the problem owing to a conceptual error in developing the statechart. A second, somewhat speculative, consideration is whether or not the statechart formalism is indeed capable of expressing all the possible behaviors of complex systems. Even if it is, the statechart method appears to require considerably more skill and effort than is involved in coding system behaviors in more direct ways.

In summary, this approach is a most elegant approach, and it will be one that computer programmers will find appealing due to the explicit manner in which system functionality is expressed. Whether developers will be able to surmount the obstacle of learning this symbolic form of representation, and using it to communicate with domain experts, is an open question.

## SMISLE: Developing Simulations and Training

Unlike the other model development systems described in this section, the SMISLE (System for Multimedia Integrated Simulation Learning Environment) system (de Jong, van Joolingen, Scott, de Hoog, Lapied, & Valent, 1994) provides the tools for producing both the simulation of the domain and the instruction to accompany it, within the context of a structured discovery learning environment.

The simulation portion of SMISLE, however, is somewhat akin to the statechart method, in that the developer employs preexisting low-level (i.e., not highly domain-specific) functional blocks to construct representations of particular domains. Examples of functional blocks include adders, multipliers, and integrators.

The same advantages and disadvantages as the statechart method would seem to apply to this approach, particularly as concerns the ability of the method to

23

accommodate all possible simulation needs and to produce simulations that can be reused in multiple applications.

Like the statechart method just discussed, the executable model is generated automatically from a more abstract structure, here functional blocks, rather than being programmed directly. A major advantage of the overall SMISLE system is that one can produce a well-designed supported discovery learning system by producing the various necessary constituents, such as a learner model, an operational model (a model of operational expertise), and an instructional model.

We will revisit this system in Chapter 6 when discussing methods for supporting learners in discovery environments.

*RIDES: A Constraint Based System*

Quite a different approach to simulation is that employed in RIDES (Munro, 1994; Munro, Johnson, Pizzini, Surmon, & Wogulis, 1996) developed by our organization in the mid-1990's. RIDES is the third-generation of simulation systems we have developed, the first generation being GMTS (Generalized Maintenance Training System), (Rigney, Towne, Moran, & Mishler, 1978) produced in the LISP programming language, and the second being IMTS (Intelligent Maintenance Training System) (Towne & Munro, 1988; Towne, Munro, Pizzini, Surmon, & Wogulus, 1990). All of that work was influenced and inspired by the early STEAMER (Williams, Hollan, & Stevens, 1981; Hollan, Hutchins, & Weitzman, 1984) system, one of the first object-oriented simulation systems. Work by Forbus (1984) was also influential.

Through the years of development of GMTS and IMTS, and well into that of RIDES, the only commercial development systems that could support the kinds of simulation production and execution that were required to meet heavy-duty training needs were those of low-level programming languages, thus the graphics editing, model construction, and simulation rule parsing functionality of these systems was necessarily developed entirely in-house.

In RIDES, the domain-dependent behaviors of simulation elements are expressed within the elements themselves. Thus, the rule for a particular indicator light might declare that if a particular toggle switch is in the RADIATE state, then the light should be ON, and if the switch is in the OFF state, then the light should be OFF. When new indicator lights are required for an application, the RIDES developer copies one from an existing model and replaces the domain-specific portion.

RIDES is termed a constraint-based system because the properties of the elements, such as state, are expressed in stand-alone statements that are evaluated if and only if some constituent of the rule changes[1]. Thus, in the example of the

---

[1] This computation scheme is virtually identical to that used in spreadsheet systems such as Microsoft Excel, in which the statement within an Excel cell expresses the value of that cell.

indicator light above, the domain-specific rule for the state property looks something like this:

| Property Name | Property Value | Expression |
| --- | --- | --- |
| State | "OFF" | If toggleSwitch.state = "ON" then "RADIATE" else "OFF" |

Here, the Property Value column displays the current value of a property, and the Expression column holds the statement with which the property value is computed. Thus if the *state* property of the toggleSwitch element changes, the state property of the indicator light will be recomputed, yielding either RADIATE or OFF as its value. Any rules in other objects that refer to the state of the indicator light would then be reevaluated, and so on until all property rules are up to date.

Of course there must be another rule that specifies how the element is to appear in its possible states. Thus the indicator light might also carry a rule something like this:

| Property Name | Property Value | Expression |
| --- | --- | --- |
| FillColor | [1,0,0] | If State = "ON" then [1,0,0] else [0.75,0.75,0.75] |

Each entity in a RIDES model carries a table of such expressions, first listing the built-in properties (e.g., visibility, location, scale, and rotation) then any additional properties added by the developer (the order of listing properties has no affect upon the updating process). A more representative property data table for an entity like the indicator light is as shown here:

| Property Name | Property Value | Expression |
| --- | --- | --- |
| Visibility | true | |
| Location | [143,288] | |
| Scale | [1,1] | |
| Rotation | 0 | |
| State | "OFF" | If toggleSwitch.State = "ON" then "RADIATE" else "OFF" |

In this case, only the State property carries a value rule, one which sets the value of State to either "ON" or "OFF"

*Advantages and Disadvantages of the Constraint-based Approach*

The primary advantages of the constraint-based approach are that the properties of an object are explicitly listed in the Data Table, and simple expressions can be entered to that table relatively easily without confronting complex programming issues. In the example of the simple indicator, the applicator only needs to know that the light carries a State property that can be set to RADIATE and OFF and that two different colors are associated with these states. Furthermore, the applicator need not be concerned about the order in which property expressions are entered or evaluated, as the process that maintains the system model is sensitive to the priorities implicit in the value rules.

The flexibility and applicability of the constraint-based approach are hampered, however, by three limitations: 1) properties may not refer to themselves in their value rules[2]; 2) the developer has no control over sequence of evaluation; and 3) property value rules are recomputed whenever any property involved in the computation changes, whether that is appropriate or not.

*Self References.* The inability of a property to refer to itself prevents the constraint approach from incrementing counters and from computing new property values based on current values. For example, one cannot increment the number of shots fired by entering shotsFired + 1 for the shotsFired property. Also, if one wishes to increase the speed of a simulated aircraft by four percent, say, the correct expression for the speed property would be: *speed * 1.04,* but this mathematically correct expression is unacceptable to a constraint-based system.

*Sequence of Evaluation.* The inability to control sequence in which expressions are evaluated is usually not an issue, in those cases involving just property values of entities. If property A affects property B, and property B affects property C, then, if property A changes, the evaluation system will first update property B then property C, as it should. Difficulties arise, however, when some steps must be carried out in a prescribed order. Suppose, for example, that a model responds to a particular user action by: 1) reading in some data, 2) setting some property values from that source, and 3) displaying some of those data on the screen. While this sequence of operations could conceivably be produced by clever use of artificial properties, the constraint-based methodology does not provide a straightforward manner of listing these steps in order of intended execution.

*Recomputation.* Finally, there are situations when the automatic recomputation of a variable is not desired just because a term in its expression has changed. Suppose, for example, a property value depends on two others, but it should only be updated when one of those other properties changes. Consider the case shown below in which the state of object C (noted as C.state) changes only when object B changes state, and then it takes on the state value of object A multiplied by the state value of object B.

---

[2] This identical constraint is encountered in Excel when a circular reference is inadvertently entered. In this case, the system issues a warning that the expressions in a cell cannot refer to itself.

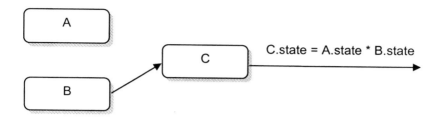

This is not an unusual condition in some electronic devices involving the setting up of some multiplying or amplifying value by one control, here object A, and then the triggering of the outputting function when some other object, here object B, changes state. In a constraint system, the rule for the state of object C would read: A.state * B.state which would yield a correct state value for C, but because object A is included in the computation, C's state would incorrectly update each time the state value of object A changes.

*Events*

In RIDES, the foregoing limitations were overcome by providing a second manner of expressing responses, termed the *event*. An *event* is a function that is executed when certain specified triggering conditions become true. Any number of events may be defined for an entity of a model.

While the event construct resolves the limitations of the constraint system, the relatively straightforward manner of hosting behavior rules in a table-based form is now compromised by the possible presence of other functions that also bear on the model behavior, thus the developer must be alert to multiple possible locations at which an element's behavior is expressed. The effort to create events when needed is not a real issue, but the ability to easily maintain existing applications and to locate the source of problems is affected.

*Limited Encapsulation*

A further weakness in the constraint-based format is that encapsulation of internal behavior expression is poor, since all the properties of an element reside in the property table. Thus, properties bearing on fixed internal behaviors are mixed in with those that are settable by the developer, exposing the element to inadvertent modifications and demanding that the developer sort through internal properties and domain-specific properties to locate those of interest.

*ReAct: A Component Based System*

Like RIDES, the ReAct system (Towne 1994, 2004) invokes a simulation engine to maintain model states, but ReAct packages domain-specific effects very distinctly, while avoiding the limitations of the constraint-based approach.

In ReAct, each instance of a component carries: 1) a function named *react* that expresses the domain-specific behavior of that entity, and 2) a list of objects that are affected by the object. When an object changes state, a built-in simulation engine automatically updates all affected objects, and all others indirectly affected. The *react* function is similar to a RIDES event, but because it carries a predetermined name and achieves a consistent outcome, the simulation engine always knows exactly how to update the condition of an object: simply call *react* on that object.

The kinds of statements entered into the *react* function are very similar to those that would be entered to an event or constraint rule in RIDES, but because affected objects are listed explicitly in ReAct, as opposed to the implicit approach of RIDES, the developer has complete control over the conditions that trigger evaluation.

Also, the list of affected objects carried by each model element in ReAct provides an explicit marching order to the simulation engine that maintains the model states. In those rare instances when the updating of the directly affected elements must be carried out in a particular order, the developer simply enters them in that sequence, otherwise the order of listing is arbitrary.

Chapter 3 will delve into the ReAct simulation system in considerable detail. There it will be seen that a small number of predefined properties are also specified, permitting one to create an external training or performance aiding system that can communicate easily with the simulation.

*The Direct Method*

Each of the four foregoing approaches to simulation development includes as a critical component some process that manages the maintenance of the model states as the user operates upon the model. Each of the approaches provides some way in which a change in one object can be communicated to those it affects.

Under the statechart approach of Kaye and Castillo, the domain-specific effects are expressed in the syntax of statechart entities and operations, and the program code that implements those relationships accomplishes the necessary maintenance of object states. Maintenance of SMISLE models is accomplished similarly. In the constraint-based approach of Rides, objects carry domain-specific rules that refer back to the elements that affect them, and a built-in simulation engine updates an affected object whenever a referenced object changes state. Finally, in the component-based approach of ReAct, model elements carry a list of elements they affect, and a simulation engine updates affected objects as necessary.

One might reasonably wonder why a statechart formalism or simulation engine should even be used. Why not, instead, simply embed program code into each model object so that when one changes state it directly calls the objects it affects so that they can update themselves? Thus, if a toggle switch is actuated, as determined by the mouse event that recognizes such activity, why not just update the toggle graphic then also call an update function on each of the affected indicators? Using good programming technique, this could be accomplished in a way that avoids combinatorial explosion of cases, as each object would take care of notifying just those it affects. Furthermore, the program code that carries out the updating within each object could be encapsulated in a predefined function so that software maintainers would not have difficulty in identifying it at a later time. And, finally, the golden rule of object oriented programming – "No object shall operate directly upon another" – is not violated since each object would still be responsible for updating itself.

The simple answer to this question is that indeed one could probably implement this method relatively successfully, particularly if an experienced and disciplined programmer were to implement the simulation. The major drawbacks of this approach are that 1) considerably more programming skill is required to design and implement a direct system than to apply a simulation management system that provides the object model and updating process, 2) much greater control over the simulation is achieved when the state updating process is centralized rather than distributed, and 3) some centralized mechanism for maintaining time-based changes would still have to be provided.

The first of these drawbacks might be considerably alleviated if a system programmer were to adopt some or all of the object design presented in Chapter 3 of this volume. The second drawback arises if one wishes to manipulate a model from some external system such as a training program. There are cases when such systems must establish the states of various model elements in very specific ways, an objective that is only achieved by first disabling the simulation engine so that it does not propagate effects from one object to another. This could be accomplished under the direct approach by providing a test of some global variable within each object to determine if propagation is wanted or not, but this just adds to the complexity of each object. Each time such a new requirement arises, in the course of producing other training and performance aiding systems, one could be forced to go back and modify all the objects in the model to satisfy the newly realized requirement. Finally, the direct approach only addresses inter-object cause-effect relationships, and does not deal with time-related effects. As a result, the design would either have to embed time-based computations within each object whose behavior is time-based, or else a centralized process would have to be provided to handle these situations.

## INTRODUCTION TO REACT

ReAct is a set of functions, properties, and objects designed to extend the capabilities of Flash to facilitate the development and execution of complex simulations. The key elements of this system are: 1) a well-defined object specification, or object model in OOD terminology, that provides a framework with which to produce new components; 2) a set of functions that serve common and critical simulation execution purposes; 3) a simulation engine[3] that automatically maintains a model as a user manipulates it, and 4) a set of components that can be used as is or adapted to produce functional cousins.

Of these, only the component set is visible to the developer, as a Library (see Figure 2-8, above) that can be imported into any application being developed. The functions, the simulation engine, and the properties within ReAct are loaded automatically into a Flash application at compile time via a single ActionScript statement[4] that directs the compiler to load the ReAct functions into the current application. Once this statement is executed, any objects or other model processes that employ the functions and properties provided within ReAct are fully operational. Furthermore, any model that includes this statement and conforms to the object model outlined in the next chapter will automatically update in response to any user action on the model and to the passage of time, if appropriate.

*Built-in Functions*

The functions provided by ReAct perform a relatively wide range of simulation-specific tasks, a few of which are listed in Table 2-3.

*Table 2-3. Some Built-in ReAct Functions.*

| Function | Result |
| --- | --- |
| broadcast | Notify the simulation engine that an object has changed state. |
| register | Record the type of the calling object for use by any training or aiding system. |
| drawTicks | Draw a number of lines of specified length, width, color and distance from the calling object about the calling object (used around rotary dials). |
| hDrag | Drag the calling object horizontally between given limits and return the Value between given maximum and minimum values. |
| loadJPG | Load a given JPG file then call a specified function. |
| cycle | Set the property of an object to a specified value and hold for a specified time, and then proceed to a second value and hold, and so on. |
| change | Change the specified property of the specified object to the given value over a specified period of time, either linearly or non-linearly. |
| stopChange | Stop changing the specified property of the calling object. |
| angle | Return the angle between two given objects, relative to a point. |

This table is only provided to introduce the kinds of services the ReAct functions provide, and will not be further elaborated here. It can be seen, however, that the

---

[3] The simulation engine is also a function, one triggered from within each object when it changes state.
[4] loadMovieNum("react.swf",999);

functions include responding to both discrete and continuous user actions in various ways, performing some complex drawing operations, reading files[5], and carrying out repetitive or continuous operations over a time period. Furthermore, the functions in ReAct focus on the presentation of simulations, leaving management of training and performance aiding functions to those specialized processes, as outlined in later chapters.

Chapter 3 will continue the discussion of ReAct, outlining the rationale and structure of the ReAct object model including the properties that its objects maintain.

---

[5] Since files are read into Flash asynchronously, a programmer cannot simply enter one statement to load a JPG file then follow that with a statement to, say, scale it. The ReAct function loadJPG takes care of this asynchronicity by continuously monitoring the progress of file loading, then calling the onComplete function, supplied in the calling function, when the file is fully loaded.

# DESIGN OF SIMULATION COMPONENTS

The design of model components presented in this chapter is not the only way to structure such elements, but it does support all the demands we have placed on interactive models in supporting instruction, practice, proficiency assessment, and performance support. In addition, and importantly, this design also supports surprisingly rapid development, not only of the simulation itself but also of the instruction and performance support applications developed later.

## GENERAL ISSUES

The general-purpose authoring environment of Flash provides all the tools required to produce *components*, the graphical and functional elements of which system simulations are composed. The term *component* refers to a parameterized functional and graphical element representing a type of entity from which specific instances are created at simulation authoring time. Example components include toggle switches, meters, airplanes, and forest fires.

While the Flash development system places no constraints on the structure or operation of components, it is extremely useful to specify some particular properties and functions that simulation components will indeed support. For example, if all components in any specific model are known to support a function named *highlight*, then any training or aiding program can easily highlight a list of model elements by simply calling the highlight function on each member of the list, without regard for the particular manner in which each member accomplishes this function. The specification of components for uses in simulations is central to the ReAct model development system.

Producing components that meet the specifications in no way increases the simulation development workload. In fact, having such a reference on hand avoids the necessities to design components from the ground up and to consider all the things a component should do. Furthermore, as we will see later in this chapter, a developer will rarely be required to produce new components without any possibility of adapting an existing element that already embodies some if not most of the desired functionality. It is the very essence of the object-oriented approach that permits one to build highly domain-specific elements as adaptations of ones previously produced.

Understanding the general specifications for simulation components, then, accomplishes two objectives: 1) it allows the developer to easily adapt an existing component to new requirements, and 2) it enables the developer to exploit the functionality of components from within higher-level training and aiding systems.

Furthermore, the particular component design presented here allows simulations to be produced as stand-alone resources that contain no embedded training or performance aiding content or functions, thereby facilitating the use of the simulation in a multitude of higher-level systems that carry out those activities.

Most examples in this chapter will refer to simple front-panel elements such as knobs, dials, and indicator lights, since these are so simple and generally understood. More complex and diverse examples will be provided in later chapters.

*Terminology*

*Components and Objects.* It is important to distinguish between an *object* and a *component.* As used here, a *component* is a complete implementation of a particular kind of simulation element, while an *object* is a specific case, or instance[6], of a component. In object-oriented parlance, a component is a *class definition.* Typically a component carries a number of parameters that may vary from one specific instance to another and a number of functions that carry out operations specific to that type of element.

*Parameters and Properties.* While *parameters* and *properties* are nearly identical, the term parameter is preferable when describing those properties that are directly set by the applicator to shape the appearance or behavior of an object. A later section will show that parameters are set in a table that appears for each object. Properties, on the other hand, are set by functions.

*Models and simulations.* Models and simulations are composed of objects, each having been instantiated from its parent component and each carrying specific values for each of the parameters associated with that particular type of element.

*Applying and Adapting.* Finally, when we speak of *applying* a particular component, we mean that we create an instance and assign particular parameter values, whereas when we *adapt* a component, we mean that we actually make changes to a copy of the element, thereby producing another, slightly different, component.

*Simulation Engine.* This chapter will also refer to the *simulation engine,* which is the widely-used term for a process that maintains the states of elements within a model as the model is manipulated. This function, a key part of the ReAct simulation system, notifies all model elements that are affected when a particular object changes its state. Each of those objects may then respond as appropriate and will cause the objects they affect to be notified in turn. This process normally continues until all affected objects have been updated, except in the special case of a feedback loop that will be discussed in Chapter 4.

---

[6] In Flash terms, each instance is termed a movie clip, a term of historical derivation that now belies its true power and flexibility.

As we shall soon see, the construction of simulation components in accordance with good object-oriented design principles greatly facilitates the production and execution of complex models as well as their use in training and performance aiding modules.

## On Efficiency

Exploiting the component construct permits remarkable efficiency in terms of computer resources required to execute simulations. Even if a particular application is composed of a large number of instances of some relatively complicated component, the application itself will remain surprisingly compact, since instances are nothing more than simple pointers back to the prototype definition plus the values of the properties and parameters of the instance. All of the program code that defines the prototype is only carried in the application one time. Thus, for example, one could create an application with hundreds of individual aircraft, each being an instance of a single, very complicated, component, yet the application would be just slightly larger than one with only a few such instances.

## Requirements

The requirements that training and performance aiding systems might place on components of simulations are much different, and less obvious, than those related to supporting simulation. Those requirements must be taken into consideration before investing time developing and applying simulation components so that instruction and aiding systems can be produced in a straightforward manner and offer all the functionality desired. In general, external systems must be able to both *control* the simulation and *extract information* from it. This section will outline these requirements, and later sections will complete the discussion of how those requirements are met.

*Supporting Extraction of Information from Models.* Most instructional and performance aiding systems require the ability to automatically construct a list of all the objects used in a simulation, and from that source also determine the location of each element. This basic requirement is easily satisfied via a few lines of ActionScript, thus component design is not an issue in regard to these needs.

Four additional types of information are required to support instruction and aiding that are not automatically supported, and therefore do impact component design. As shown in Table 3-1, external systems may need to access the full names of components, determine their current states, recognize their type (in order to deal selectively with different kinds of simulation elements), and determine what the current failure condition of a model is, if any.

*Table 3-1. Information Extraction Requirements That Affect Component Design.*

| Required Information | Use |
| --- | --- |
| Full name of objects | Refer to objects by full name |
| Object states | Assess and discuss object conditions |
| Object types | Identify indicators, controls, test points, and replaceable units in the model |
| Object failure conditions | Refer to failure conditions of objects |

Consequently four properties, named *displayName, state, type,* and *failureMode.* will be provided in each object, in order to 1) refer to objects by their complete names; 2) refer to the states of objects in meaningful terms; 3) identify those objects that can be manipulated, interpreted via direct observation, and read with test equipment; and 4) refer to object fault conditions.

*Supporting Control of Models.* External systems must be able to 1) set any object to any of its states; 2) detect and capture object selections when made by the user; and 3) highlight objects selected either by the user or by the external system. Table 3-2 lists these requirements.

*Table 3-2. Control Requirements That Affect Component Design.*

| Action | Use |
| --- | --- |
| Set object states | Establish and/or demonstrate system operations. |
| Detect object selections | Capture user responses. |
| Highlight objects | Support showing or selecting subsets |

To permit external modules to set object states, components must carry a state-setting function, that we call *setState.* Thus, for example, instructional software could establish some operational mode by setting the states of the controls, even though those controls also respond to mouse actions by the student.

The need to capture a user selection of an object in the simulation demands that each object carry a mouse function that will report back – to whatever module is administering the instruction or aiding process – that the object was selected. For components that are normally moused by the user, the mouse function must respond differentially to its selection, depending upon the particular interactive mode in progress. When the user is operating the simulation, controls should respond to mouse actions by changing state, however when the user is identifying one or more objects by selection, the object must send a reference of itself to the module in control of the instruction or aiding process.

Finally, instructional and aiding systems must be able to highlight and unhighlight objects at any time, regardless of the form or structure of the objects. This requirement arises from the common need to emphasize a subset of objects in the model, either to support the student when selecting a subset, or to instruct the student about that set of elements.

## CHARACTERISTICS OF REACT COMPONENTS

There are no limits to the functional complexity or graphical extent of a component. One component might be produced to represent simple toggle switches, and another might represent entire aircrafts. One component might appear as a simple graphic while another might include many moving parts as well as text fields, sounds, and other elements. One component might involve only simple discrete changes from one state to the next while another might involve continuous changes over time in one or more parts of the component.

Most components include both a graphical part and a functional part; however the graphics and function are fully separate entities, thereby allowing an applicator to create a cousin of an existing component by first duplicating the original then only changing the graphical portion or just the functional portion of the duplicate.

Many components, such as knobs, dials, and indicators, exhibit their internal states graphically, but not all do. For example, a functional model of a digital circuit might involve elements representing AND, NOR, and NOT gates. In some practice environments, such as troubleshooting exercises, the developer may wish for these elements to not exhibit their internal states, similarly to the real world. In this usage, the user must perform explicit testing operations in order to determine the state of the elements. In other conditions, it may be highly useful for such elements to clearly exhibit their current states, so the learner can more easily understand why the circuit produces the outputs it does. Later we will examine a model (digital adder) in which the training application manages the display of the object states to suit the training objectives.

### Properties Predefined in Flash

The Flash system automatically supports a number of predefined properties that can be used to customize any component or object. The names of these properties all begin with underscore (_), to denote that they are the built-in ones as opposed to properties added by the developer. Table 3-3 lists those used most often in modeling and simulation.

*Table 3-3. Some Object Properties Predefined in Flash.*

| Property Name | Characteristic |
| --- | --- |
| _alpha | Transparency (0 is totally transparent, 100 is totally opaque) |
| _height & _width | Pixel height & width of object |
| _name | Object name |
| _parent | The object that contains the current object |
| _rotation | Degrees to which an object is rotated |
| _visible | Whether object is visible (true) or not (false) |
| _x & _y | Pixels to the right of reference point and below reference point |
| _xmouse & _ymouse | Horizontal & vertical position of mouse from reference point |
| _xscale & _yscale | Horizontal & vertical scaling of the object (100 = full scale) |

The _name property listed in Table 3-3 is of particular importance, as simulation objects refer to each other via this property. Typically, the names assigned to objects are abbreviated and contain no special characters, e.g., *powerSwitch*, *frequencyMeter*, or *panelLight*. As will be elaborated below, a different property, displayName, is used to contain the full name of an object, including special characters if need be.

## User Defined Properties

In addition to the built-in properties carried by all objects, the developer may create any other properties that are useful within an object. A very small set of such properties has been created specifically to support execution of models, and these properties form the foundation of ReAct components as described in the next few sections.

## Creating Components for Simulation

In the following sections we will develop a simple hierarchy of component types, starting with the most general specification of a simulation element, termed the *base class*, then proceeding to more specific kinds of elements. This section will refer to the functions within an object as *method*s, which is the more specific term for a function within an object that manipulates object properties.

### THE BASE CLASS SIMULATION OBJECT

In accordance with object oriented programming methodology, we begin by specifying the methods and properties that are common to all simulation components, and thus to all objects produced from those components. While one of the methods – setState -- carries no content at this highest level of definition, this specification establishes just what activities a particular simulation element will perform.

The properties, parameters and methods common to all simulation objects in the ReAct system are as shown in the center of Figure 3-1, with external software systems and human entities shown at the sides to indicate how the object relates to the rest of the environment. The outside influences shown in the figure come into play at different times. The applicator sets the parameter values for an object when the object is created from the component and modifies these values at any time thereafter. The state setting method is triggered when a training or performance aiding activity needs to manage the object for instructional purposes. The mouse down method notifies external training and aiding systems that the object has been selected if, and only if, an object selection process is in progress as indicated by a particular global variable discussed later. And finally, the state setting method triggers the simulation engine whenever the object changes state.

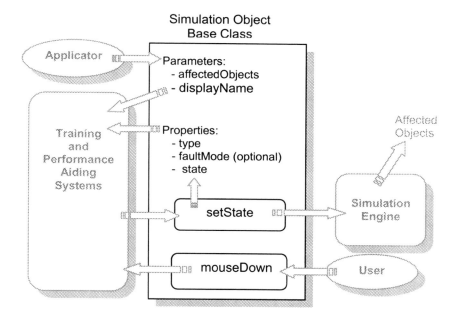

*Figure 3-1. Base Class of ReAct Objects (with External Entities).*

## The Object Parameters

*affectedObjects.* The *affectedObjects* parameter is a list of zero or more names of objects directly[7] affected by the listing object. The setState method within each object triggers the simulation engine after updating the object state if the model is in simulation mode, according to the global variable *userMode.* By setting the userMode variable to anything other than *simulate*, external systems can manipulate individual objects with the simulation engine effectively disabled, a critical requirement in some training situations.

*displayName.* Unlike the _name property supported by the Flash system, the *displayName* property is not referred to by other objects in the model. This property is used to fully describe an element for presentation to a user by any

---

[7] Directness is relative to the level of granularity being expressed in the particular simulation application. For example, if we are simulating a front panel we might say that the power switch directly affects the power light, even though there are certainly intervening connections and components between them.

external training or aiding system. For example, a particular switch might be assigned the _name of powerSwitch, so other objects can refer to it easily, yet carry the *displayName* of "Main 12V. +/- Power Switch" so a training system can present a complete descriptor. The special characters in this displayName value would be invalid if used in the built-in _name property.

*Method setState*

The *setState* method makes the graphical changes necessary to render the object in the state it is given as an argument, it sets the *state* property of the object, and it notifies the simulation engine that it has changed. The manner in which it accomplishes the graphical changes is specific to the type of object, and will be described below. This method also produces a sound when an object changes state if, and only if, there is a sound specified as a parameter for that object type, and if the global variable *playSound* is TRUE. External software systems can set playSound to FALSE in order to set controls silently.

An object state may be a numerical value, a text value, a color value, a Boolean value, or a list of values.

*Method mouseDown*

The *mouseDown* method built into the base class permits objects to respond to user selections when training and performance aiding activities are in progress. For controls that normally respond to mouse actions, the mouseDown function checks the value of the global variable *userMode* before responding. If that variable is set to *simulate*, then mouseDown responds to the mouse action normally, but if userMode is not *simulate*, then mouseDown notifies the training function running the interaction that the user selected it. This design completely relieves the developer from having to anticipate what possible training and aiding functions objects might need to support. A new function can be added to an external training system long after the simulation has been constructed, and no changes need be made to support that new function. Specific examples of this capability will be provided in a later chapter.

Notice that at this top level of the object hierarchy the mouse down method does not trigger the state setting method, and only notifies any external training/aiding systems that the object has been selected. The reason for this is that the behavior of the mouse down function is very specific to the type of object in which it resides, thus the full functionality is only complete when we develop specific objects, as we soon shall.

Even at this highest possible level in the object hierarchy, however, nearly all the methods and properties that are used within specific objects are declared. All simulation objects accept values for the two parameters *affectedObjects* and *displayName*; they all carry the properties *state*, *type*, and *highlighted*, and optionally *faultMode*; and they all implement the methods *setState* and *mouseDown*. Furthermore, a few global variables, not shown, are accessed by all objects in a model to determine the high level conditions in which the model is being operated. The uses of these parameters, object properties, and methods are as described next.

*Other Object Properties*

Two other properties are maintained within each simulation object: 1) *type*, reflecting the general nature of the object, and 2) *faultMode*, reflecting the possible failure state of the object.

*type.* Each component carries a list of one or more *type* values that designates inherent characteristics of the component that are important to external training and aiding systems. Since type is specified within a component, the value is passed down to all instances created from the component and need not be changed by the applicator.

The four possible values of component type are 1) *control*, 2) *indicator*, 3) *ru*, for replaceable unit, and 4) *tp*, for test point. The *control* type value indicates that the user can manipulate the element; the *indicator* type indicates that the state of the element can be directly seen by the user; the *ru* value indicates an element that can be replaced if it is suspected as being faulty, and the *tp* value indicates that the state of the element can be read by some (simulated) test equipment. As examples, the type list for a toggle switch is *control, ru*; that of a meter is *indicator, ru*.

Table 3-4 indicates some ways in which the different type values are used within training and performance aiding systems.

*Table 3-4. Example Uses of Component Type Values.*

| Type Value | Use Within Training/Aiding Systems |
| --- | --- |
| control | Automatically generate a list of controls to summarize their states. |
| indicator | Detect what symptom information a user can see when diagnosing the condition of a model that may contain simulated faults. |
| ru (replaceable unit) | Automatically generate a list of model elements that can be replaced when practicing troubleshooters have diagnosed a fault. |
| tp (test point) | Automatically determine when a test probe is at such a location that the value at that test point can be transferred to the (simulated) test equipment, for display. |

*faultMode.* The *faultMode* property, an optional property used only if an application will be simulating faulty system elements, gives the current failure condition of an object. When the value for this property is *none* or *undefined*, the object functions normally. If some external system such as a troubleshooting exercise program has assigned a value to this property, such as *burnedOut*, then the behavior rules within the object will cause it to operate according to that fault condition. This chapter concludes with a more detailed discussion of modeling faults in systems.

41

*Highlighting Objects*

One method for emphasizing a single element is to display a pointing hand, as shown here.

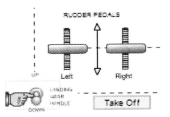

This approach will be seen in a later chapter in which elements of a model are explained one at a time. When a set of elements is to be selected or emphasized, however, we prefer highlighting the elements, rather than displaying multiple pointing hands. In ReAct, each component provides a built-in graphic named *highlight* that overlies the object as suggested here.

Initially, the transparency (the _alpha property in Flash) of this element is set to 1%, so it is effectively invisible (importantly, it is invisible in development mode as well). To highlight an object, then, it is only necessary to set the _alpha property of the highlight graphic to 50%, thereby allowing the state of the object, if any, to show, yet clearly setting the object apart from those not highlighted. So, if the element shown above is named L3, then it could be highlighted with the statement

```
L3.highlight._alpha = 50;
```

In most instructional and aiding processes, however, the name of the element to be highlighted is not used, but rather a variable name stands for the affected object. This more typical condition is reflected in the complete function for managing highlighting (when objects are selected by the user) shown here:

```
highlighting = function (whoGotClicked) {
  // Toggle the highlighting of the selected object.
  if (whoGotClicked.highlight._alpha > 1)
      whoGotClicked.highlight._alpha = 1;
      else whoGotClicked.highlight._alpha = 50;
}
```

This function is called whenever the user is selecting objects, and it highlights the selected object – whoGotClicked -- if it is currently not highlighted, else it restores the selected object to its normal unhighlighted condition. This toggling action permits the user to click on objects until the desired set of objects is highlighted (then the user selects on OK button that is always presented when multiple objects are to be selected).

## THE TWO BASIC COMPONENT TYPES: CONTROLS AND REACTORS

There are two basic kinds of simulation components: 1) *controls*, which respond to actions by the user; and 2) *reactors*, which respond to changes in other objects or to changes in time elapsed since some action took place. Most components are of one or the other of these two types, but some components function as both controls and reactors.

A simple example of a control is a toggle switch; an example of a reactor is a meter; and an example of an element with combined behavior is a circuit breaker, capable of being set manually as well as being tripped by excess current in the circuit model in which it is placed.

Note from Figure 3-1 that all components carry the *mouseDown* method to support user selection, thus the presence of this mouse function does not imply that the object is necessarily a *control*.

## THE CONTROL COMPONENT TYPE

Control components respond directly to user actions, the most common of which are various mouse manipulations such as clicking down on the object (mouseDown), releasing the mouse on the object (mouseUp), and moving the mouse while holding the mouse button down (mouseMove). While mouse actions are the most common, any other type of user action is allowed, and one may certainly define controls that respond to keyboard entry, voice, joystick movement, or even movement of the user's eyes, given the required hardware and software utilities.

In retrospect, there probably is a better term for simulation objects that respond to user actions than *control*, since the term is so commonly used to signify front panel elements. Certainly all such operable elements meet the definition of a ReAct control, but the reader is cautioned to realize that a ReAct control is more general than a common, real-world front panel control. In a later section, for example, we will examine the *aircraft* object, a simulation element that is both a control and a reactor. It is a control because the user can affect it with the mouse, and it is a reactor since it also responds to actions by other elements in the simulation.

### *Properties of the Control Component*

Like all simulation components described here, control components carry the properties and parameters shown in Figure 3-1. The author of a component may, and usually does, add additional properties to support the behavior of the particular object type. Note that *state* is not a parameter to be set by the user, because *state* is automatically initialized within the component definition itself (and possibly overridden by initialization performed by a training system or aiding system). In addition, there is no property required to express an object's highlighting condition, as explained next.

### Functions and Structure of the Control Component

We now turn to an examination of how the functionality of controls is achieved. As seen in Figure 3-2, the structure and content of control components are nearly identical to that of the base class, the only differences being that 1) additional mouse functions are defined, if appropriate; 2) the mouse functions now trigger the setState function as well as notifying external software modules of a selection; and 3) a third parameter, *sound*, is used to specify what sound the control makes when it changes state (sound may also be specified for reactors, but it is not built in to the general reactor class).

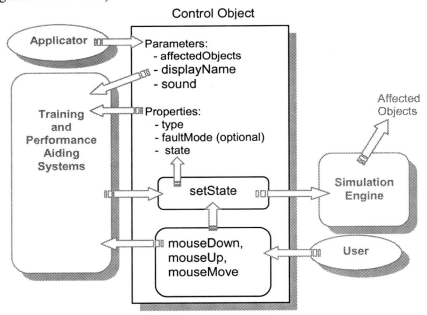

*Figure 3-2. Base Class of ReAct Control (with External Entities).*

As seen in the figure, the state of a control can be affected by two alternate external sources: 1) the user, via the mouse or other input medium; and 2) external training functions that command controls to move into particular states, possibly to demonstrate the resulting symptoms or to exhibit the device model in a particular configuration.

Another key difference between this more specific object type and the general simulation object specified previously is that the *setState* method is now fully defined within each control component, according to the nature of the particular element. Because the action of a particular type of control component is fully specified within the methods, controls rarely require any additional programming attention to fully apply them in a particular model. The applicator only needs to modify appearance and set parameters that govern behavior to apply controls in specific applications.

Each control component definition carries one or more mouse response functions particular to that class. For example, a two-state discrete control simply responds to a mouse-down action, whereas a discrete radial control, or dial, responds to three different mouse actions: 1) mouse down, to begin the continuous tracking of the mouse position; 2) mouse movement which causes the dial to rotate about its center; and 3) the mouse-up action that terminates the tracking and releases the knob graphic to snap to the nearest detent.

## *Operations Performed to Reflect State*

Whether an instance is being manipulated by the user or configured by external mode-setting functions, the state-setting method is called to establish the particular graphical rendering that matches the state value that it is handed. The operations performed by this method include:
- displaying the graphical representation associated with the user's mouse actions;
- setting the *state* property value of the instance to correspond with the graphic;
- playing the sound that is associated with the state change, if any;
- notifying the simulation engine that the instance has changed state, so that all affected objects can be notified and updated as well; and
- calling a function, *userAction*, not defined in ReAct, but possibly defined in an instructional or aiding system that is recording actions performed.

## *Graphical Construct*

The particular manner in which the graphic of a specific control type is changed to represent a change in state depends upon the nature of the control. Controls with multiple discrete states are typically constructed of a static background part and two or more state-dependent foreground parts. The simplest possible example is a two-state toggle switch, shown here in its two discrete states.

The graphics and behavior of this two-state entity is easily produced by placing the background graphic on one layer of the timeline and each of the two state graphics in a layer above that, with each state graphic appearing in a different frame, as shown here.

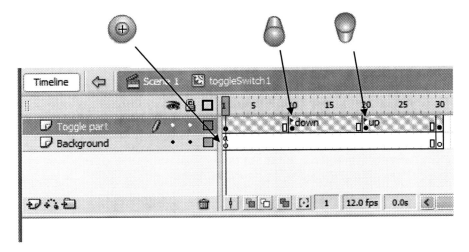

*Figure 3-3. Layout of a Two-state Entity.*

While the timeline is also used to produce animation, here it simply provides a convenient home for the three graphic pieces, and it furthermore accomplishes a separation between a background graphic and the two foreground parts. The two rows (or layers), labeled "Toggle Part' and 'Background' contain the graphics for the variable and fixed part of this component respectively.

The numbered frames containing black circles are *keyframes*, frames that may be labeled and at which unique graphics appear. In this component, as with most, the background graphic is present in all frames.

Note that this component could have been constructed using just three frames: frame 1 could hold the component initialization statements, as it does above, frame 2 could hold the down graphic, and frame 3 could hold the up graphic. We elected instead to place the down graphic in frame 10 and the up graphic in frame 20, which in no way impacts the behavior, performance, or storage requirements of the element. The advantage of spreading out the placement of the graphics in this manner is that this layout provides sufficient room to display the labels 'down' and 'up' assigned to the two keyframes, a very useful way of indicating what the contents of each key frame are for later reference.

Now, when either the developer or a program statement commands the object to show itself at frame 10, the switch appears in the down state, while showing frame

20 produces the up state appearance. In Figure 3-4, the developer has selected frame 10.

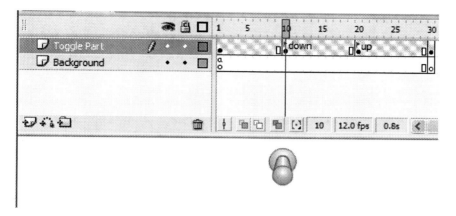

*Figure 3-4. Relationship of Frame Content to Displayed State.*

Of course the graphics of this control could have been implemented in other ways, two of which are: 1) by simply providing a single graphic of the toggle part, and rotating that graphic 180 degrees to accomplish an up or down state, or 2) putting the entire down graphic in frame 10 and the entire up graphic in frame 20, that is, foregoing the background/foreground construct. The approach described above is preferred, however, since it is consistent with the general approach to rendering more complex elements, including those possessing three or more discrete states.

Additionally, we might choose to implement a different behavior for this control type. Rather than producing two discrete states, we might instead cause the toggle to change continuously from its current state to its new state. This approach, implemented as a little animation sequence, has been done, and will be explained fully in chapter 5.

*Determining State Values*

While the simple operation of going to frame 10 or 20 accomplishes the desired graphical effect, the *setState* method must still determine a meaningful state value, here a name, to assign to the element. It might seem that the state names are already determined, as "down" and "up", but these terms only have meaning within the control component itself, and have little use when we author behavior rules for other objects. In the following panel segment, for example, a toggle switch is used to set the system into a High Power mode or a Low Power mode, and those are the natural names for state.

**High Power**

**Low Power**

Thus, *setState* should set the state of this element to "Low Power" when the element is shown down, at frame 10, and to "High Power" when shown at frame 20.

To provide a mapping between the internal graphical states and the external state names, all discrete-state controls carry an additional parameter, *stateNames*, in which the applicator lists the domain-specific names that correspond with each graphical state. The list is a simple comma-delimited string, such as "Low Power, High Power". Then, after *setState* selects the graphic to display it sets the state value to the corresponding name in the *stateNames* list.

A second example should suffice to make clear how graphical updating and state value setting is accomplished in general. Consider the simple rotary dial, one that rotates with the mouse, not snapping into a discrete detent when released, but physically limited to some minimum and maximum rotation in the real world.

The graphics for this element are simply what is shown here, i.e., there are no discrete states. As the user drags the mouse about the center of this dial, *setState* computes the rotation value of the mouse cursor and rotates the graphic correspondingly (within limits, as discussed next).

To determine state value, controls such as this carry two additional parameters, one that lists the minimum and maximum degrees of rotation that the control permits, and a second that lists the minimum and maximum value corresponding with the minimum and maximum rotation.

In the example shown below, the dial can be rotated from 0 to 180 degrees, and as the panel markings[8] make clear, the minimum and maximum values associated with these rotations are 0 and 50 (Hz), respectively.

---

[8] The panel markings would be part of the panel background, i.e., the control would not be modified for this specific application.

The value for the rotation parameter of this control is therefore: "0,180" while that for the value parameter is "0,50". As the user drags the mouse about the center of this element, the state setting method rotates the graphic to the same orientation, within the limits of 0 and 180 degrees. As long as the mouse is down in the control, the object continues to rotate and compute a state value as a function of rotation according to these expressions:

State value = minimum value + value range x (current rotation/rotation range)

where value range = maximum value – minimum value
and
rotation range = maximum rotation – minimum rotation

In the case shown below, the dial is rotated to 40 degrees.

In this case the dial value is 11.1, computed as 0 + 50 x (40/180).

*Basic Control Components*

In addition to a number of relatively specific control components, the ReAct Component Library provides eight very basic components, defined according to the type of mouse action that manipulates them. These eight control classes are shown in Table 3-5.

49

*Table 3-5. Eight Fundamental Control Components.*

| Control Class | Example Instances |
|---|---|
| Two-state positive | Toggle switch, latching push button |
| Two-state momentary | Spring-back push button |
| n-state | 3-position toggle switch |
| Discrete rotary | Radial dial with detents |
| Continuous horizontal | Horizontal slider w/o detents |
| Continuous vertical | Vertical slider w/o detents |
| Continuous rotary | Radial control w/o detents |
| Invisible | For special control purposes |

These eight fundamental components have served to implement a very wide range of control elements with very little additional development effort.

*Additional Mouse Manipulation Functions*

To the basic mouse functions provided in the ActionScript programming language, ReAct adds the mouse manipulation functions shown in Table 3-6 for use by the developer:

*Table 3-6. ReAct Mouse Manipulation Functions (Towne, 2004).*

| ReAct Function | Example | Result |
|---|---|---|
| drag (left, top, right, bottom) | drag (10, 30, 200, 450) | Object follows mouse vertically and horizontally within the specified bounds. |
| vDrag ( top, bottom) | vDrag (20,84); | Object follows mouse vertically from 20 to 84. |
| hDrag (left, right) | hDrag (0,500) | Object follows mouse horizontally, between 0 and 500 pixels. |
| rotate (CWDegrees) | rotate (180) | Object rotates clockwise with mouse, between 0 and 180 degrees. |
| hold () | hold () | The object's *state is updated* as long as the mouse is down. |

In addition to providing mouse actions not built into Flash, these ReAct functions automatically call the simulation engine during mouse activity, thereby permitting other objects in the device model to respond synchronously.

*Semi-transparent Controls as User Buttons*

Invisible, or nearly-invisible, controls serve several critical functions in simulation presentation and usage. In this usage we would term these controls 'buttons' since they facilitate a user interaction rather than representing an operable part of the model. To make clear to the user what areas are selectable, it is usually desirable to make such buttons nearly transparent, rather than fully invisible. In this manner the user is made aware of the selectable covers, yet the underlying graphics are clearly visible. In Flash, degree of transparency may be established when a graphic is created, or it can be manipulated programmatically via the _alpha property.

One highly useful application of the semi-transparent button is as a mechanism for providing selectable segments of large systems that are represented in a simplified form. Typically, in these cases, the graphics underlying the overlays are not operable components, but instead represent some part of the total system. When any of the buttons is selected, the user is given a complete model of that section of the system. An example of this usage is presented in Chapter 4.

Buttons of this type also provide a convenient way of responding to user mouse actions on sections of a model that are not ordinarily considered operable, as described next.

*A Complex Control Component Designed for Usability*

Issues of usability arise at every level of simulation development from the lowest component design task to high level instructional and aiding processes. A crucial objective in designing the control elements of models is to provide representations that look and respond sufficiently like the real system elements that the actions required to operate them are obvious to the user. Since the model elements are manipulated by actions that differ from those used in the real world, considerable attention must be paid to making the element responses those that most people would anticipate, thereby obviating the need to instruct the user in operating the elements of the model and avoiding responses that surprise or puzzle the user.

In most cases, pressing the mouse down when the cursor is over a control corresponds to pressing or taking hold of the real object with the hand and fingers; dragging a control with the mouse corresponds to moving or rotating an object; and releasing the mouse button corresponds to releasing the object. For some objects, this correspondence is extremely close and natural. The pushbutton component, for example, is operated by mouse almost identically to the way a real pushbutton is: the user 'reaches' with the arm or mouse cursor to the button, presses the mouse button or real button, and releases the mouse button or real button.

Elements as simple as the two-state toggle switch, however, begin to introduce some uncertainty about how the model element is to be manipulated. When users operate a simulated toggle switch, do they expect that they must simply click it, so that it responds to the mouse down or mouse up action, or will they expect that they must drag it, more like the way a real switch is moved to its alternate setting? The question is somewhat academic for such a simple element, because the user is virtually certain to discover upon first use how the element is to be operated by mouse; if the simulated toggle switch responds immediately upon clicking or releasing, then the user learns what action is required almost subconsciously, and if the toggle refuses to budge unless the mouse is dragged, then this behavior is also learned, although we would seriously debate the wisdom of that design[9].

While experience indicates that virtually anyone who knows how to use a mouse will easily discover the behavior of a simulated toggle switch, whatever its implementation, the issue of designing for usability becomes considerably more serious and less obvious with more complex elements. Consider this five-position rotary control with five associated indicator lights and six associated labels (note that two of the settings, *Mode 1* and *Mode 2*, are tied together):

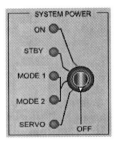

In the real system the control is rotated so that it points at, or near, one of the five discrete settings and released. Because of internal springs and detents, the dial then pops into the closest detent. When set to any position except OFF, either one, two, or three indicator lights illuminate as shown here:

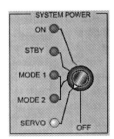 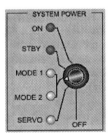 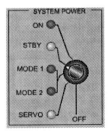 

*Figure 3-5. The Four Energized Settings of the System Power Switch.*

While the particular lights that illuminate in each setting might be a surprise to a technician not familiar with this equipment, the usability issue has to do with how this control should be implemented so the user need not guess at how it is actuated

---

[9] It is interesting that the design we favor – a simple mouse up action producing the toggling response – corresponds less with the real world than does a dragging action.

via the mouse. There are several alternative designs for achieving correct behavior, the simplest of which is to carry on with the approach recommended for a toggle switch, and have each of the six labels and five indicator lights respond to a mouse up action. By this design, the user simply clicks where the dial is to be positioned, and it responds as it should. While this behavior is consistent with the toggle switch design, it fails to support those users who expect to drag the dial, an action that is absolutely required to position rotating dials that do not have labeled settings.

Alternatively, the dial can be designed to only rotate when dragged, just like the continuous rotary dial must be, but this may surprise and confuse those who expect to just click on the desired discrete setting. The solution we have taken is to support both selection of settings and rotation of the dial itself. The implementation of this design is considerably more complex than either of the two alternatives, but the resulting usability seems well worth the trouble, especially since the labor is only expended one time in producing the component. This one element has served well in representing all rotary controls with discrete settings.

The desired behavior is achieved by placing totally transparent controls over the five areas of labels that are to be mouse-sensitive, as shown here (the invisible buttons are outlined here for explanatory purposes).

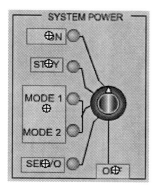

Each of these five buttons calls out the rotary dial as its affected object, so when a user clicks on one of them the simulation engine notifies the dial, which then sets itself to the correct setting.

To serve those who would drag the dial, the dial component carries exactly the same radial dragging functionality as a continuous rotary dial, via: 1) a function that responds to mouse down, to initiate dragging, 2) a function that continues to modify the rotation of the dial as the dial is dragged about its center with the mouse, and 3) a function that determines the nearest detent when the mouse is released, and snaps the dial to that setting.

Chapter 4 will present a simulation application involving this component.

## THE REACTOR COMPONENT TYPE

The second distinct type of simulation component is the *reactor*. Reactor components are constructed and employed exactly as are control components as described above, i.e., they are built in the Flash development environment, stored in the Component Library, and used to create objects by instantiation and setting of parameters. As seen in Figure 3-6, reactor component are also very close ancestors of the base class of all simulation objects.

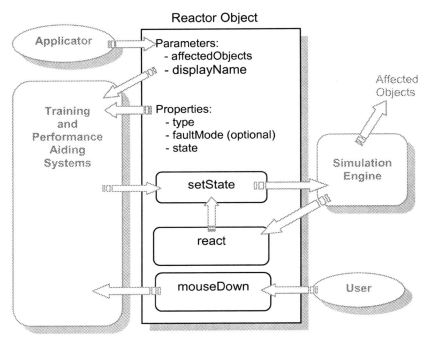

*Figure 3-6. Structure of Reactor Classes.*

The two primary differences between reactors and controls are that 1) a reactor responds to changes in other objects (via the simulation engine) rather than to mouse actions, and 2) the *react* method is responsible for determining what state the object should assume, typically based upon the states of some other objects in the model. Thus, the *react* function is model-specific and is produced for each reactor object in a model. Since the *react* method determines the object's state value, the *setState* method within reactors is only concerned with establishing the graphical changes necessary to render a reactor in the state it is handed.

Note that the chain of effect updating does not go on endlessly, as might be inferred from the three arrows passing from the simulation engine to the *react* method to the *setState* method and back to the simulation engine, in the figure.

A reactor is first activated when the simulation engine notifies it that one or more objects that affect it have changed state. The object's *react* function then determines what state the object should assume and passes this value to *setState*. The *setState* method carries out its duties then calls the simulation engine into action which notifies all affected objects. Only in very special cases involving feedback loops, as covered in Chapter 4, does this updating process loop back to the original reactor object without some intervening action on the part of the user.

## The React Function

The shell of the react function is provided in the reactor component and therefore passes to all the instances created. This method is completed by the developer after an instance is created. For programmers, the construct of the react function shell is as follows:

```
react = function (whoChanged, newState) {

}
```

The simulation engine calls this function, passing it the name of the object that changed, which becomes *whoChanged* in this function, and what new state this other object attained, which becomes *newState*. Now the programmer only needs to enter statements to determine the reactor state based on these values, and sometimes on values of other object states as well.

Suppose we have a simple two-state indicator light that has the states named "ON" and "OFF", and that this particular light is ON when some toggle switch is ON, and OFF when the toggle switch state is OFF. In this simplest of cases, the toggle switch names the indicator light as its single affected object, and just one statement needs be entered in the *react* function of the light, resulting in this completed function:

```
react = function (whoChanged, newState) {
        setState (newState);
}
```

In words, whenever called, set the state of this indicator light to match the state of the affecting object. Note that the function need not identify what object changed, since in this case only one object lists this reactor as its affected object. More typically, an *if* statement is used to set the state of a reactor, since the state of the reactor and the state of the affecting object usually do not correspond, and sometimes the *if* statement may involve the states of objects that have not just changed.

A few additional examples are given next, primarily to indicate the manner in which reactors are brought to life in a particular domain model.

*Example*

In the segment of a panel model shown here, the TEST MODE indicator is a simple light that is red when the switch just below it, the TEST switch, is ON, otherwise it is gray.

The TEST switch calls out the TEST MODE indicator as its only affected object, and the react function for the indicator light is as follows:

```
react = function (whoChanged, newState) {
        if (newState == "on")
                setState ("red");
                else setState ("gray");
}
```

In words, if the new state of the affecting object, the TEST switch, is "on", then set the state of the indicator to "red", otherwise set it to "gray". As before, the value of *whoChanged* is not used, since only one object affects the light, but all affected objects have access to the object that has changed in case that information is required within the function.

A slightly more interesting example involves a meter needle that reflects the speed of some speedy automobile. The meter below features a rotatable needle, a standard reactor, superimposed over a digitized meter face.

In this application, then, the react method for the meter needle is simply:

```
react = function (whoChanged, mph) {
        setState (mph);
}
```

(Since we know that the state value handed to the needle is *mph*, we increase readability of the function by replacing *newState* with *mph*).

The work of the needle's setState method is to set the needle's state value to the mph value it was handed and to rotate the needle to correspond to that value. The needle was originally drawn facing directly downward, so at 0 mph it should rotate to 45 degrees, and at 160 mph it should rotate to 270 degrees. The statement for needle rotation, in degrees, as a function of mph, is therefore:

_rotation = 45 + mph * (270/160);

which may be simplified to:

_rotation = 45 + 1.69 * mph;

## Basic Reactor Components

Just five basic reactor types are defined, although many hundreds of specific reactors have been constructed. Examples of the instances associated with these five reactor classes are shown in the following table.

*Table 3-7. Typical Instances of the Basic Reactor Classes. (Towne, 2004)*

| Reactor Class | Example Instance |
|---|---|
| Discrete graphic reflects state | Fuse |
| Color reflects state | Indicator light |
| No evidence of state | AND[10] gate |
| Continuous graphic reflects state | Meter needle |
| Text | Digital read-out |

## Other Component Examples

The specifications provided previously are sufficient to guide the production of new components, but it cannot be overstated that almost all new components are produced by adapting existing components that have functional similarity to that desired.

Having said that, let us consider four components that are somewhat different than the simple front panel elements that served as introductory examples: 1) a circuit breaker that functions as both a control and reactor; 2) logical elements, such as AND, NOR, and XOR gates; 3) a wire that displays its condition, and 4) a 'blip' symbol representing an aircraft appearing on a military air traffic control radar system. Complete simulations involving these components are presented in the following chapter.

---

[10] Note that we might choose to have elements such as AND gates reflect their status, for instructional purposes, in which case the first class would apply.

*A Component with Control and Reactor Behaviors*

Although a circuit breaker component already exists in the ReAct Component Library, we will ignore that, to demonstrate how a component is constructed to function both as a control and a reactor. We will begin by constructing a 20-ampere breaker, and then get smarter and generalize our element to deal with any load value.

First, we duplicate a simple two-state toggle switch, and modify the background graphic and the two state-dependent graphic states to produce the following two appearances.

With no further change, this component functions manually like any other two-state control. Now, we add a *react* method to the breaker component to give it the ability to trip when the circuit current is excessive. The function to do that is as follow:

```
react = function (whoChanged, current) {
        if (current > 20 && state == "on") setState ("off");
}
```

In words, the *react* function says that if the value of current handed to this breaker exceeds 20 and the breaker is currently in the *on* state, then set the breaker to the *off* state. It is tempting to put an *else* clause at the end of the *if* statement that sets the state of the breaker to *on*, when the current is less than 20 (amperes) but upon testing such a specification we would find that the breaker magically resets itself as soon as the current is reduced below the trip point. This is certainly not the behavior we want to specify, at least for this simple breaker which must be manually reset.

Since circuit breakers come in a variety of capacities, we realize it would be wise to generalize the specification of the element so that it could represent a range of breakers. First, we add a new parameter to the component, and assign it the variable name *breakerCapacity*. Next, we change the text field that currently contains "20" to be a named field whose value can be set programmatically. We'll call that field "*capacityValue*". Third, in *setState*, we add a statement that sets the text value of the capacityValue field to the value of *breakerCapacity*. And, finally, we modify the react function as follows:

```
react = function (whoChanged, current) {
        if (current > breakerCapacity && state == "on") setState ("off");
}
```

Now, the component will serve as the prototype for any breaker, regardless of the value at which it trips. If some model involves breakers that look different than this one, but behave similarly, we can simply duplicate this one and modify the graphics.

## Logical Elements

We turn now to some components that are actually exceedingly simple, but are somewhat different than those discussed above. Suppose we wish to develop components for seven of the most common logical elements: OR, NOR, AND, NOT, NAND, X-OR, X-NOR. Here we will consider how these elements were produced.

The drawing task is exceedingly simple, since the AND gate and NAND gate are very similar:

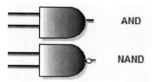

The OR and NOR are similar:

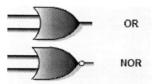

Adding an arc gives us an X-OR and X-NOR:

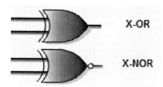

Finally, a simple triangle with a circle represents a NOT:

Now all that remains is to enter a statement to each of the *react* methods for these seven elements. Because each element determines its output entirely in terms of its input(s), we can complete the react function in the *component* definition for each, and never have to make domain-specific changes within the objects produced from them. For example, the expression that determines the state of an AND gate is simply:

input1&& input2

where input1 and input2 are the two inputs to the AND gate, and the "&&" symbol is the logical AND operator in ActionScript. The two input values are automatically set when a ReAct model starts up, determined from the two components that list the component in their *affectedObjects* parameter value.

Similar statements are entered for each of the seven logical components, as shown in Table 3-8[11]:

*Table 3-8. Statements in the React Method for Seven Logical Elements.*

| Logical Element | Statement in react Function |
|---|---|
| AND | setState (input1 && input2) |
| NAND | setState (! (input1 && input2)) |
| OR | setState (input1 ‖ input2) |
| NOR | setState (! (input1‖ input2)) |
| X-OR | setState ((input1 ‖ input2) && ! (input1 && input2)) |
| X-NOR | setState (input1 == input2) |
| NOT | setState (! input1) |

Since these elements do not display their states graphically, there is no further work to be done. If, in a training application, we wish to display the states of such elements, we can easily place text reactors near each output, to display a 0 or 1.

This approach can be observed in the following simple demonstration of the seven logical elements. Here, the user can select the element type to study via the seven radio buttons. When an element type is selected, that logical element appears along with its truth table. Then, the user can set the input(s) as desired, and view the output of the element as well as the condition that applies in the truth table.

In the figure the user has selected the OR element and set the switches to states of 1 and 0, which highlights the third row in the truth table and produces an output of 1 (true).

---

[11] In ActionScript, && is AND; ! is NOT; ‖ is OR; and == is equal to.

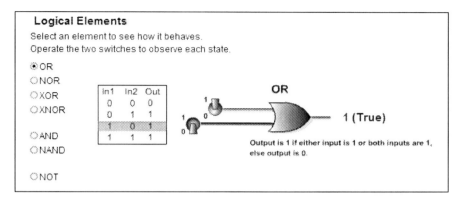

*Figure 3-7. A Model to Demonstrate the Behaviors of Logical Elements.*

While possibly not apparent in this black-and-white form, the wires connecting the switches to the logical elements display in black when they carry a 0 (or low), and in red when they carry a 1 (or high). The next section will cover these components in more detail.

This somewhat instructional model is structured as seven keyframes, each containing one of the seven logical elements along with its truth table values and behavior rule statement. Below the seven keyframes is a common background layer containing the seven radio buttons, the truth table with its overlaid highlighting bar, the two switches and wires, and the output indicator that reads either "1 (True)" or "0 (False)" depending upon the state of the logical element.

The react function for the text display object is simply

```
react = function (whoChanged, theState) {
      if (theState) text = "1 (True)" else text = "0 (False)";
}
```

In words, if the state of the logical element that governs this text display field is TRUE, then display "1 (True)", else display "0 (False)".

*Wires*

In the previous example, a learner gains little from observing the state of the wires connecting the switches to the logical elements, but in other models of digital systems the graphical portrayal of state can be a very powerful aid to tracing through the high and low values, and thereby understanding the behavior of the system.

From a behavioral standpoint, wires are nearly identical to simple two-state indicator lights that display black when off and red when on. They are constructed on the Flash timeline as shown in Figure 3-8 to appear black at keyframe 10 and red at keyframe 20, identically to the two-state elements seen previously.

61

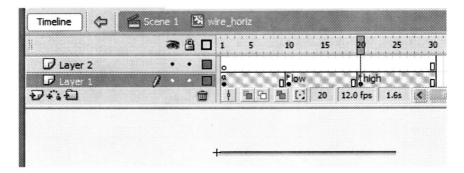

*Figure 3-8. Setup of a Wire Component.*

Now, whenever the wire carries a 0, its state-setting method shows the wire in black, and when it carries a 1 it is shown red (on-screen, the wire shown in Figure 3-8 is red).

There are two such graphical wires defined, a horizontal wire and a vertical wire. Each of these can be stretched to the desired length via the Flash Free Transform tool while avoiding an unwanted scaling of wire width.

## Modeling Faulty Behaviors

In all of the foregoing, components were given rules that specify how they behave when in good working order, and all objects created from those components inherit that good behavior. If one wishes to simulate failures in a system, however, the prototypes of the objects involved in the model must also be capable of acting in various failed conditions. Although the added effort to enrich components with bad behaviors is normally very modest, developers may elect to skip this aspect if they are sure that there will never be a need to induce failures into their system model. If that assumption ever proves to be false, the components involved can be readily extended with abnormal behaviors.

As noted above, each object carries a property *faultMode*, which names the failure that is currently induced into it. If *faultMode* is none or is undefined, then the normal behavior rules are used to simulate the element. If some external system, such as a diagnostic training system, has set the *faultMode* of an object to some value, say *burnedOut*, then there must be rules within the prototype component that specify that behavior.

As a simple example, the two-state toggle switch carries the following two statements to specify how it behaves when failed:

```
if (failureMode == "open") state = stateNames[0];
if (failureMode == "closed") state = stateNames[1];
```

The first statement sets the state of the switch to the first state defined for it, which happens to be the off (open) state if the failureMode is equal to "open". That is, if the open fault is being simulated, then the switch will act off regardless of its setting. Similarly the second statement causes the switch to act closed if it is failed in a closed, or shorted, condition.

In a similar fashion each of the logical components shown previously carries statements that simulate four possible fault modes: 1) outputs a 0, regardless of inputs; 2) outputs a 1, regardless of inputs; 3) outputs the value of input1; and 4) outputs the value of input2.

Chapters 7 and 8 continue the discussion of instructing and aiding the diagnostic skills and knowledge associated with fault diagnosis.

# MODEL BUILDING

The process of constructing a model can be surprisingly rapid and satisfying. Even if new versions of some components must be produced to accurately emulate the real system, this process is typically very straightforward, although like all development undertakings, the time to finish off all the little details is typically underestimated. This chapter will outline the basic steps necessary to produce a working model and then consider some of the issues that arise when developing more complex simulations, including dealing with real time effects, ongoing processes, and modeling faulty systems.

At its very simplest view, simulation development consists of three steps: 1) as necessary, constructing new components or modifying existing ones to look and act the way the current simulation requires; 2) assembling background graphics and existing components into a domain-specific representation, and 3) specifying how each component in a particular simulation affects others.

## A FIVE MINUTE MODEL

We will now go through all the steps of building a complete, but very simple, model. In fact, this first model, consisting of just one toggle switch and a single two-state indicator light, will be the simplest possible model that involves model state maintenance via the simulation engine.

*Step 1*

We open the Flash file *reactTemplate*, rename it *fiveMinuteModel* and save it. This template file is simply a Flash file that already contains the single statement to load the react functionality, along with three layers of graphics named *foreground*, *background*, and *script*, a good default beginning.

*Step 2*

Into the *background* layer, we draw a simple panel and add four panel screws from the Library. The panel screw element, while not a true parameterized component, is in the Library for our use. We add the text label *Power*, and have the simple background shown here.

65

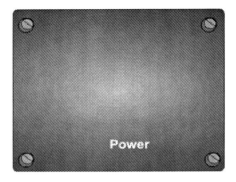

*Step 3*

Into the *foreground* layer, we drag a toggle switch and a two-state indicator from the Library. We position and scale these two elements to produce the configuration shown here.

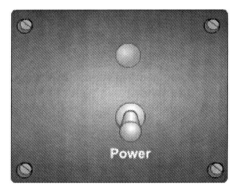

The particular indicator light we used appears green when in state "on", otherwise it appears gray. If we want to change these colors, we key in different values to the Parameter table that appears.

*Step 4*

We select the toggle switch and assign it the name powerSwitch, we set the Display Name[12] parameter to *Power Switch* and the Affected Objects parameter to

---

[12] Note that the Parameter table calls this variable "Display Name", which is more readable than the true, internal, variable displayName, to which it is associated.

*powerLight* (which has not yet been named). The Parameters display area for the switch now appears as follows:

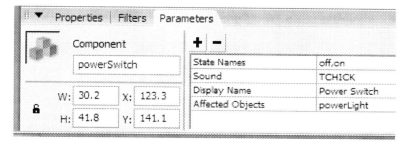

## Step 5

We select the indicator light and assign it the name *powerLight*. Then we enter the following react function for the Power Light:

```
react = function (whoChanged, newState) {
        setState (newState);
}
```

which says to set the state of the powerLight element to match the state it is handed. More typically, the state names of an affected object do not match those of an affecting object, a case that will be shown later. This simple model is now complete. Upon running the model, the switch responds to our mouse clicks, we hear the switch click when it changes state, and the light responds to the switch state

In addition to working as we would wish, the elements in the model all carry property values that are crucial to any other program that might wish to conduct training or support of job performance.

All models are built using this same basic process, with the usual additions that 1) most applications involve producing some new components, or at least some modified component graphics, and 2) the *react* method of some elements may be considerably more complex than the example.

## A REAL FRONT PANEL

Now that we have looked at the simplest possible model, let's consider the other end of the continuum, in which we wish to construct relatively complex simulations using objects unlike anything we've ever produced before and involving continuous changes in addition to the simple discrete actions discussed above. The remainder of this chapter will outline how these more realistic requirements are met, and the following chapter will address applications that involve complex real-time processes.

The panel shown in Figure 4-1 is a completed operational simulation of one unit in a real Electronic Warfare (EW) system (Towne, 2005a). This panel will be seen in many future chapters as well as we discuss simulations of hardware systems.

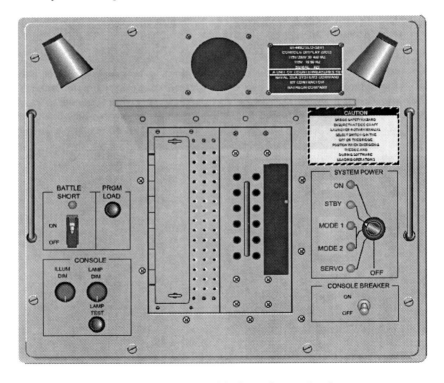

*Figure 4-1. A Model of a Real Front Panel.*

The only difference in development methodology between this simulation and our five-minute model is that one of the components, the cover over the Battle Short Switch, did not already exist in the graphical form required and was therefore produced from an existing component.

The cover is simply a physical barrier that must be raised in order to actuate the Battle Short Switch, as a precaution against inadvertent actuation. For our purposes, this cover acts almost exactly[13] like a toggle switch, one that happens to have no impact on other objects. All that is required, therefore, is to duplicate any one of the toggle switch components, and substitute a different graphic for the two states, as shown here.

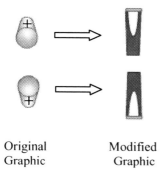

Original        Modified
Graphic         Graphic

The System Power Switch is an instance of the discrete-state rotary control discussed in detail in Chapter 3. The initial parameter table for this element, as presented to the applicator, is shown here.

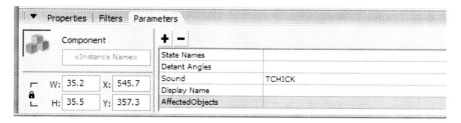

The developer now enters the name *power* for this object and values for the parameters that govern this object's behavior. In this case, one of the five parameters, *Sound*, happens to carry a default value, *TCHICK* which is left as is.

---

[13] On the real equipment, the operator holds the Battle Short cover up while throwing the toggle switch underneath it, but in the simulation the user simply clicks on the cover and it flips to its up position. This difference in behavior seems entirely acceptable, as simulating the true behavior of the cover would require significantly more complex actions by the user.

In the following, the developer has entered values to fully specify this particular rotary dial.

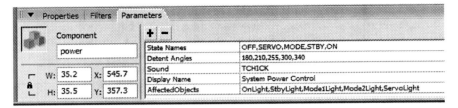

The dial, now named *power*, will act as follows:
- It can be rotated from 180 to 340 degrees (see the minimum and maximum angle values entered for *Detent Angles*, the second parameter);
- Its knob will automatically snap into detents at 180, 210, 255, 300, and 340 degrees when released;
- It will assume the associated state names listed on the first line (for example, at the second detent angle, 210 degrees, this dial assumes the second state in the *State Names* list, *SERVO*);
- It will emit the sound named *TCHICK* when the mouse is released and the dial snaps into a detent; and
- It will be referred to as *System Power Control* by any system presenting training or aiding content to a learner or performer.

All that remains is to assign behaviors to each of the five indicator lights surrounding the Power Switch. Whenever the switch snaps into its final detent position, the five associated indicator lights are notified so that they can reset their state as appropriate. The following rule, associated with the light next to the STBY (standby) setting of the System Power Switch, is typical of the rules for the indicator lights:

```
react = function (whoChanged, whatState) {
    if (whatState == "STBY")
        setState ("on");              // orange
        else setState ("off");        // gray
}
```

This rule simply states that if the state (of the Power Switch) is STBY, then the light is on (orange), otherwise it is off (gray).

This completes the development of these elements. The remaining active elements are simple rotary controls and pushbuttons that are instantiated directly from elements in the Library and a small indicator that will be discussed later.

## SIMULATING UNSEEN FUNCTIONS

The models and components presented above all portray front panel elements as they appear in the real world, i.e., they are models of those physical elements actually seen and handled by the system operator. These models can effectively support instructing and aiding the performance of procedures and the assessment of front panel indications, but they are not particularly useful for explicating the inner workings of a complex system. For that purpose we turn to the modeling of functions that are not easily seen in the real world.

Between the controls that the operator manipulates and the indicators that the operator observes to assess the condition of the system are numerous internal elements that do all the work. This classification of elements into those at the user interface versus those 'inside' the system is a relatively general and useful one, since it applies to a very wide range of domains we might wish to simulate, such as air traffic control environments, managing the fighting of a forest fire, or steering an aircraft on the ground. In all cases, the user has access to a number of elements that can be seen and/or manipulated in some manner, while the task environment includes a number of other elements that cannot be directly seen or manipulated.

### Simulating A System With No Internal Moving Parts

While real world digital circuits provide virtually no evidence of their internal conditions, a simple simulation such as that of Figure 4-2 can be instructive in several ways.

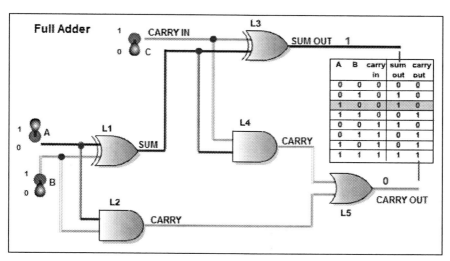

| A | B | carry in | sum out | carry out |
|---|---|----------|---------|-----------|
| 0 | 0 | 0 | 0 | 0 |
| 0 | 1 | 0 | 1 | 0 |
| 1 | 0 | 0 | 1 | 0 |
| 1 | 1 | 0 | 0 | 1 |
| 0 | 0 | 1 | 1 | 0 |
| 0 | 1 | 1 | 0 | 1 |
| 1 | 0 | 1 | 0 | 1 |
| 1 | 1 | 1 | 1 | 1 |

*Figure 4-2. A Model of a Digital Adder Circuit.*

71

In this simulation the user is able to manipulate the inputs to the circuit via three toggle switches, observe which leads are in high and low states, and see how the circuit output produces the sum of two binary inputs with an optional carry input[14].

In the figure, the user has set the inputs at A and B to 1 and 0 respectively, with no carry input at C, and the circuit has responded to those inputs by outputting a sum of 1 with a carry of 0.

Rather than simply displaying the output of the circuit, the model provides a number of visual aids to facilitate the tracing and mental simulation of the circuit. The highlighting of the leads allows the user to trace the high and low values from one element to another, the digital outputs of 1 and 0 indicate the SUM OUT and CARRY OUT outputs of the circuit, and the highlighted row in the table makes clear what condition is being simulated at any time.

The model consists of three toggle switches, five logical elements (two ANDs, two X-ORs, and one OR), two text indicators that can read 1 or 0, a number of wires that may be highlighted or not, and a bar that positions vertically to highlight the current circuit condition in the table. The switches supply inputs to two of the logical elements, their outputs pass to the remaining three elements, and the states of the SUM OUT and CARRY OUT signals are reflected in the values of the two indicators. These behaviors are achieved simply by specifying the affected objects of the elements.

All that remains is to position the bar, a reactor that is a simple semi-transparent rectangle whose vertical position is reset any time a switch is thrown. First, the appropriate row number (starting at row 0) is computed via the statement:

```
rowNum = d2  + 2 * d1 + 4 * d3;
```

where    d1 is the state of switch A (0 or 1),
         d2 is the state of switch B (0 or 1),
and      d3 is the state of the switch C (0 or 1).

Then, the _y location of the bar is computed with the statement:

```
_y = _parent.dataTable._y + 29 + 12.9 * rowNum;
```

In words, the _y value of the bar is equal to the _y value of the top of the table plus 29 pixels (to get down to row 0) plus 12.9 pixels per row number. The values of 29 and 12.9 were obtained in the Flash development mode by simply moving the mouse and reading the vertical coordinates at the top and bottom of the table and dividing the difference by 7.

---

[14] The CARRY OUT output from one adder can be connected to the CARRY IN of a following adder circuit, to achieve addition of larger numbers.

## SIMULATING A SYSTEM WITH INTERNAL MOVING PARTS

One system that involves many working elements not normally seen by the operator is that which allows a pilot to steer an aircraft while on the ground and also assures that the steering mechanism assumes a locked and centered position when in the air. This system of electrical, hydraulic, and mechanical elements is distributed among a number of sections in the aircraft, and, since many are hydraulic in nature, their internal states are difficult or impossible to observe.

The nose wheel, consisting of hydraulic and mechanical components, is shown here.

*Figure 4-3. Aircraft Nose Wheel Steering Mechanism.*

The functional model of this subsystem was constructed by first producing a bitmap image of the main system diagram from the technical manual, placing this image in a dedicated layer of the model, then overlaying simulation elements atop this diagram until the static background was no longer useful. Then that layer was deleted and some additional objects and notations were added.

The result, shown in Figure 4-4, closely resembles the static diagram from the technical manual, however the controls shown in the lower left were added to complete the functionality of the system (Towne, 2001, 2002a).

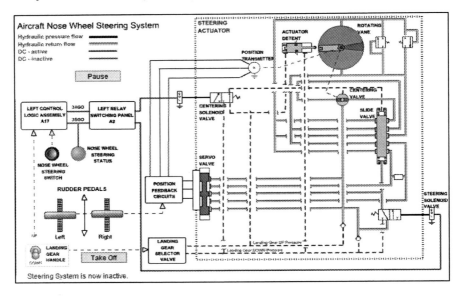

*Figure 4-4. Functional Model of Aircraft Nose Wheel Steering System.*

The working elements in this model include: 1) the user-operable elements in the cockpit, as physical representations; 2) the functional elements that respond to the cockpit controls, ultimately moving or locking the nose wheel; and 3) two artificial buttons (*Take Off* and *Pause*) that allow the user to manage the simulation conditions.

*The User-Operable Elements*

The user-operable elements in the model, shown in more detail in Figure 4-5, are 1) a Nose Wheel Steering Switch, a pushbutton; 2) the Nose Wheel Steering Status Light, a two-state indicator; 3) the Landing Gear Handle, a toggle switch; and 4) the two Rudder Pedals.

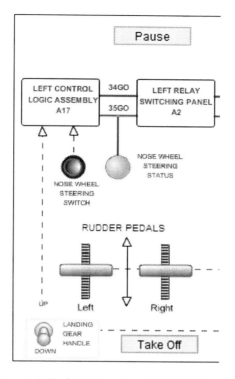

*Figure 4-5. Cockpit Elements and Artificial Controls.*

### Artificial Controls

The two artificial controls, buttons provided to allow user control over the simulation, are also seen in Figure 4-5. The *Pause* button allows the learner to temporarily halt any continuous, real-time changes that are in progress, to better observe the system model during those phases. When the *Pause* button is clicked, its label changes to *Resume*, permitting the resumption of the simulation. The *Take Off* button is a simple way for the user to get the aircraft into the air, to observe how the system behaves in that condition. Of course the model could include all the elements necessary to virtually take off, but such complication seems unwarranted for present purposes.

### The Internal Elements

The internal elements seen in Figure 4-4 include electrical wires, electrical components, hydraulic lines, and hydraulic/mechanical parts. The color coding of the hydraulic lines, not evident in these black and white figures, differentiates the lines carrying working pressure from those carrying the hydraulic fluid back to the reservoir at lower pressure. The Rotating Vane is geared directly to the aircraft nose wheel. When the vane is pointing directly to the left, in the figures, the aircraft nose wheel is pointed straight ahead; when the vane is positioned below the Actuator Detent, the aircraft steers left; and when above, it steers to the right.

*Activating the Steering System*

To activate the steering system, with the aircraft on the ground, the user presses and releases the Nose Wheel Steering Switch and observes the Nose Wheel Steering Status light come on. Then, if the user drags either Rudder Pedal down below its neutral position, the other pedal rises, a number of valves change state, many of the pressure lines change their condition, and in short order the Rotating Vane begins to rotate. Figure 4-6 shows the steering system activated and steering left because of high pressure directed to the top of the vane element.

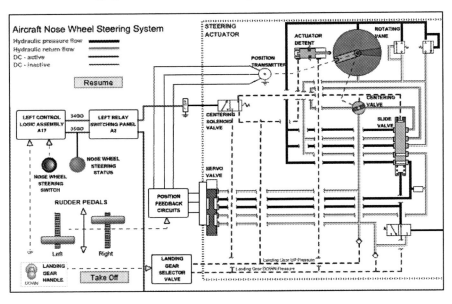

*Figure 4-6. Rotating Vane and Associated Elements.*

After a few seconds, if the rudder pedals are not moved again, some of the valves change state again because feedback circuits have detected that the vane rotation has reached the proper orientation in relation to the rudder pedal positions, the high pressure lines return to normal, and the vane stops rotating. At this point, the aircraft would continue to steer to one side or the other, until the pilot centers the rudder pedals, causing the vane to return to its neutral position.

The following table summarizes the main functional elements used in this model, all of which change graphically to reflect state.

*Table 4-1. Hydraulic/Mechanical Components in Nose Wheel Steering Simulation.*

| Component | Graphic Example | States | Behavior / Graphics |
|---|---|---|---|
| Actuator Detent | | Three discrete states: 1) retracted, 2) extended, and 3) extended and locked. | Internal mechanism slides against spring, according to pressure difference at two input ports. |
| Servo Valve | | Three different flow routes can be produced (see below) | Internal mechanism slides proportionately to electrical inputs. |
| Slide Valve | | Three discrete states: 1) fully left, 2) centered, and 3) fully right. | Internal mechanism slides against springs according to hydraulic pressures at end. |
| Solenoid Valve | | Two discrete states select from two possible hydraulic flows. | Internal mechanism slides under magnetic force against spring resistance to either of two positions. |
| Rotating Vane | | Rotates clock wise or counter clock wise, at fixed rate, until stopped. | Direction of rotation determined by pressure difference on sides. Stops rotating when pressures are equal or mechanically stopped. |
| Hydraulic Line | | High pressure or Low pressure | Appears red when under high pressure, blue under low (return) pressure. |

The behaviors of these mechanical/hydraulic elements are all relatively simple; some of them change state in response to electrical inputs, others to hydraulic pressures. Additionally, some (the Servo Valve and the Rotating Vane) are continuous in nature and others assume discrete states.

The Servo Valve, for example, receives electrical inputs that cause its internal part to move, thereby altering the flows of fluid through it. In the real system, this valve is continuous, i.e., the internal part can assume any position from fully left (as seen in the table) to fully right. In the model, however, we have defined this object as having three discrete states, in order to facilitate observing its state and thereby understanding the resulting fluid flow. When observing the model in action, this element almost appears to be operating as a continuous element, and we feel the user will not come away with any misconceptions about the element.

As modeled, this valve produces three distinctly different fluid flow conditions by blocking or opening flow between adjacent ports.

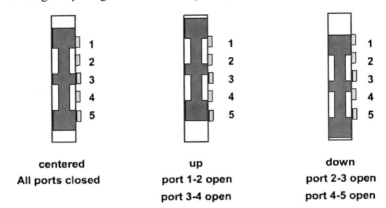

|   centered   |      up       |      down      |
|--------------|---------------|----------------|
| All ports closed | port 1-2 open | port 2-3 open |
|              | port 3-4 open | port 4-5 open  |

*Figure 4-7. Three of the Possible Configurations of the Servo Valve.*

While the discrete state parts act upon one another as the model diagram would suggest, two features of this steering system lead to considerable complexity in behavior: first, the amount of rotation of the rotating vane is governed by a feedback loop, and secondly, the rotating vane rotates over real time, rather than snapping into a discrete graphical position. Some discussion of these two issues is in order.

*Modeling the Feedback Loop*

The Position Feedback Circuits shown in Figure 4-6 constantly compare the current position of the rotating vane, as measured by the Position Transmitter shown out to the left of the Rotating Vane, to the amount of rudder pedal displacement, and they send a voltage to the Servo Valve that is proportional to that difference. This input causes the Servo Valve to adjust its state, thereby modifying the amount of pressure reaching the Rotating Vane.

One approach to modeling the feedback process would be to model the detailed operation of the Position Feedback Circuits, so that as the rudders move these circuits output a signal that correctly drives the Servo Valve. An easier approach, however, is to have the rudder pedals notify the Servo Valve when they move, and have the Servo Valve make the determination of how far, and in which direction, it should move. Since the details of the Position Feedback Circuits were not the subject of the instruction, and were not represented within the model, this more direct approach was taken. Whenever the Servo Valve moves, it updates the status of the hydraulic lines connected to it, these in turn affect the Slide Valve, and ultimately pressures reach the Rotating Vane via the lines coming into the top and bottom of the vane object.

## Real-time Rotation

The rotation of the vane over time is accomplished by a simple technique in which the vane continually compares its current rotation to target rotation toward which it is heading. If there is a difference, the vane rotates one degree in the direction required, thereby producing rotation at a rate of 30 degrees per second, until the vane rotation is consistent with the positions of the rudder pedals. This approach will be more fully described in Chapter 5.

## User Options

The Pause and Resume functions are easily implemented by simply having the vane check to see if the model is in a Paused condition prior to updating its position. If so, it does nothing. As soon as the user returns the model to a resumed condition, the vane continues on its way to its destination rotation.

If the user actuates the Take Off button, some of the electrical elements are notified, which prepares the Actuating Detent to extend and ride on the vane as it rotates toward its centered orientation. Simultaneously, the Servo Valve directs pressure to one side of the rotating vane, and the vane's target rotation is set so that it stops rotating when it is pointing directly left in the figure. When the vane reaches this position, the Actuating Detent snaps into the notch of the vane, so that the vane, and hence the nose wheel, cannot move while in flight.

The foregoing gives an abbreviated account of the overall system logic of both the real system and the model. This surprisingly complex system performs a number of different functions depending upon the control settings established by the pilot/user and whether the aircraft is on the ground or in the air.

Two interesting conclusions can be drawn from the experience of producing this model: 1) the simulation model developer need not have the skills possessed by the original system designer, but must understand the basic function of the system being modeled, and 2) while the real system functions from electrical voltages and hydraulic pressures, the model can be made to behave very realistically without dealing with these phenomena at their basic levels.

One final note might be of interest. When this model was first developed it, of course, did not function correctly, as bugs are virtually unavoidable in such complex undertakings. After all apparent bugs were exterminated, however, the model still did not function according to the textual descriptions in the technical manual (in fact, the developer did not fully understand those descriptions until after the model was made operational and could be observed).

To resolve the problem, the developer consulted with maintainers who were experts in the behavior of the system, and they discovered a critical error in the system diagram which had previously gone undetected. That is, the system could not have worked as described in the manual, as the system was represented in the manual's system diagram. Upon making this correction to the model, it did function correctly.

## MODULARIZING LARGE MODELS

Chapter 3 introduced the notion of using semi-transparent buttons to overlay simplified representations of large models, in order to select detailed models for those sections. The following figure demonstrates this usage applied to a military system constructed of four major sections.

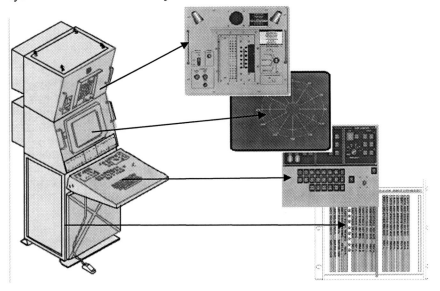

*Figure 4-8. Semi-transparent Buttons Leading to Detailed Models.*

Each of the four shaded areas on the drawing at the left is a semi- transparent button that calls up the associated section model shown at much reduced size on the right. The top section of this system is seen to be that shown in Figure 4-1.

This application illustrates an object-oriented capability that is crucial to managing complexity through modularization. Each of the four models shown above is a completely separate simulation file that can be executed alone or by any other application.

## MODELS WITH VIRTUAL AGENTS AND UNKNOWNS

Many real world task environments involve more than just a hardware system to be operated or maintained by the user. While large, distributed, and complex hardware systems may be an important part of many such environments, there may also be other personnel carrying out their functions, there may be environmental conditions that materially affect the difficulty and the character of the task, and there may be unknowns to be considered. Such environments, in which the unknowns include uncertainties about the intentions of others, characterize many military tasks.

One such task is that of monitoring air traffic in the area of one's ship and taking actions to protect the ship from possibly hostile forces. In general, the task involves attempting to identify all aircraft that are near the ship, and advise any that are in a potentially threatening posture (heading toward ship, high speed, and low altitude) to change course.

This task, performed in the Combat Information Center (CIC) of the ship, involves operating a radar display, receiving information from external sources, and issuing requests, warnings, and orders to others. Aircraft are displayed as computer-generated blips on the radar screen, with one's own ship at the center of the display, a simulation of which as shown in Figure 4-9 (Towne, 1995, 1997b).

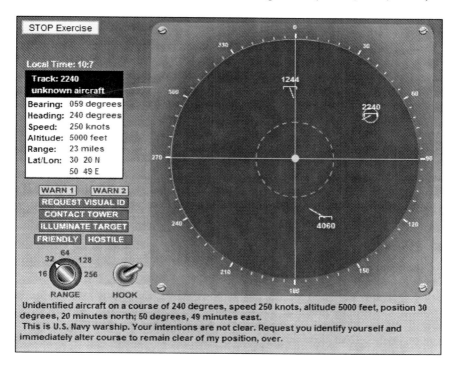

*Figure 4-9. An Air Traffic Control Simulation (CIC).*

At the instant this screen was captured, the aircraft designated as track 2240 (at a bearing of 059 degrees) had been selected (hooked), and a warning had been issued to that craft, as seen in the text area at the bottom.

In the real task environment this warning, as well as all requests, commands, and aircraft responses, are spoken, but in this model we substitute text display for the spoken word, realizing that this alters the skills required of the user somewhat. To eliminate the artificial buttons that currently evoke textual messages would require use of very sophisticated speech recognition software, and would involve extremely difficult and somewhat unreliable assessment of what the user actually said. The voicing of the returned radio responses, on the other hand, could have been accomplished with one of the better text to speech utilities, with very satisfactory results, but this has not been done.

It is important to realize, therefore, that the user of this model will not master the skill of formulating verbal requests and orders, and will have to learn this in some other way.

## ELEMENTS OF THE CIC USER INTERFACE

*Radar Blip*

As will be explained fully in Chapter 5, the simulated radar produces a new picture of the world every second, which is exactly what the real system does. At each second, each blip 1) updates the values of its own position, speed, heading, and altitude properties; 2) displays its velocity leader to correspond with its heading and speed; and 3) positions itself on the screen at a location consistent with the current setting of the radar Range control (*the settings of the Range control in this simulation are artificial and do not match those of the real system*)

There are three different parts to a blip's graphical appearance: 1) its *threat level* symbol, representing the operator's classification of the aircraft (unknown, friendly, or hostile); 2) its *velocity leader*, a straight line that points in the aircraft's heading and is sized to reflect its speed; and 3) its track number, a 4-digit number unique to each blip on the screen, displayed in a text field within the blip symbol.

The three threat level symbols are as shown here:

unknown     friendly     hostile

Initially, all aircraft blips appear in the unknown status. The operator may move the joystick, near the bottom of the screen, to position a circular cursor over any of the aircraft. When the joystick is pressed, the aircraft under the cursor becomes the currently selected, or 'hooked', aircraft, and all subsequent actions pertain to that aircraft until another aircraft is selected.

The actions that can be taken on the hooked aircraft include: 1) reclassifying its threat level, 2) issuing warnings to it; and 3) carrying out actions aboard ship to identify and/or deter the aircraft. The aircraft blip responds to changes in time and to a number of other actions taken by the air traffic controller at the radar display console. Some of the reactions are as listed in Table 4-2.

*Table 4-2. Some of the Responses of an Aircraft Blip.*

| Action Affecting Blip | Response of Blip (condensed) |
|---|---|
| Time passes | Update position, speed, heading, altitude |
| Threat assessment made | Display blip symbol to reflect assessment |
| Ship beams signal | If aircraft is military & not hostile, head away from ship |
| Ship issues warning | If friendly, and receiver working, respond & change course |
| Warning shot fired | If not hostile, change course |

The three states of a blip are defined almost identically to those of a two-state control, with the third state being 10 frames further to the right, as shown here.

When an exercise starts, all blips appear in the unknown state, and the operator may then reclassify any as more information is obtained.

The velocity leader is simply a straight line, oriented to match the heading of the particular aircraft, and sized to reflect its speed. Here is an aircraft that has been classified as friendly, proceeding in a north-easterly direction at moderate speed:

The track number is assigned to a blip when it first appears on the radar screen, and it does not change after that. Here is blip 3127, judged to be hostile, traveling at high speed in a northerly direction.

**3127**

*Properties.* The blip component carries the properties listed here, the first four of which are updated continuously for each instance, as the simulation proceeds:

– location, expressed as the longitude and latitude within a 50-mile square air space
– altitude, in feet
– speed, in knots
– heading, in degrees
– type of aircraft, e.g., military, commercial jet, rotary wing, etc.

– communication channels being monitored (military or commercial)
– intentions (friendly and cooperative, uncooperative, hostile)

In addition, for the properties of altitude, speed, and heading, each blip carries two associated properties that express the rate of change in the property and the limit value for the property. If an aircraft is proceeding at a fixed heading, for example, the two additional heading maneuver properties are 0. If directed to change course, however, one of the two associated properties reflects the rate of change in direction and the other reflects the new heading when the maneuver is complete. When the maneuver is completed, the two associated properties are reset to 0.

*Artificial Buttons*

The button at the upper left of Figure 4-9 permits the user to start, pause, and abort exercises prior to their normal conclusion. Another button appears when a scenario is in progress, which brings up instructional material, as covered in a later chapter.

*The Character Read Out (CRO)*

When selected by the user, a blip copies the values of its position, heading, speed, and other properties to a table on the radar screen called the Character Readout, or CRO, shown here.

| Track: 2240 unknown aircraft | |
| --- | --- |
| Bearing: | 059 degrees |
| Heading: | 240 degrees |
| Speed: | 250 knots |
| Altitude: | 5000 feet |
| Range: | 21 miles |
| Lat/Lon: | 30 19 N |
| | 50 48 E |

Two of the properties appearing in the CRO – range and bearing – are computed from the blip's current position, specifically for the CRO presentation and are not properties carried by the blip itself. The values in this table are then updated every second to reflect changes in status as time passes.

Any commands issued by the air controller to an aircraft are now directed to this most recently selected one. If directed to change course, for example, and certain other conditions are true, the aircraft will change course after a simulated delay. Or, if the controller directs the crew to attempt to identify the aircraft visually, their response will depend upon the true nature of the aircraft as well as visibility conditions that apply at the time.

*Warnings to the Hooked Aircraft*

Two buttons are provided with which the operator issues warnings to the hooked aircraft. Figure 4-9 shows the wording of Warning level 1, which is the statement usually issued initially to an aircraft that appears possibly threatening.

The second warning level is worded with greater gravity, advising the selected aircraft to immediately change course or be subject to defensive action by the ship. A typical Warning level 2 appears as follows:

> Unidentified aircraft on a course of 160 degrees, speed 300 knots, altitude 10000 feet, position 30 degrees, 21 minutes north; 50 degrees, 36 minutes east.
>
> This is U.S. Navy warship. Your intentions are not clear. You will be fired upon if you do not immediately clear the area, over.

Each of these two warnings is automatically constructed by the simulation by filling in the actual course, speed, altitude, and position of the hooked aircraft into a skeleton statement.

*Issuing Requests and Orders*

The three buttons below the warning buttons are used to issue requests and orders to others than the hooked aircraft. As with the warnings, all messages are displayed in the bottom section of the display. The first of these, Request Visual ID, issues a request to the crew to perform a visual identification of an aircraft. A typical request is as follows:

> Bridge, can you make a visual ID of aircraft at bearing 22 degrees, altitude 10000 feet, range about 14 miles?

The Contact Tower button issues a request to a land-based airport tower to assist in identifying a nearby aircraft. A typical request to the tower is as shown here:

> Tower, are you controlling a commercial aircraft at altitude 10000 feet, heading 160 degrees; position 30 degrees, 21 minutes north; 50 degrees, 37 minutes east?

The Illuminate Target button issues a command to the crew to emit a radar signal aimed at the hooked aircraft, which is also an action taken in preparation to firing upon the aircraft.

> Illuminate aircraft at bearing 22 degrees; altitude 10000 feet.

If the aircraft being so 'illuminated' is a military aircraft, the on-board electronics will warn the pilot that this is being done.

*Friendly/Hostile Buttons*

The Friendly and Hostile buttons are used by the operator to classify the hooked aircraft. Upon selecting either button, the hooked aircraft blip changes to reflect the classification. The accuracy of these classifications is evaluated at the end of each exercise.

*Responses to Simulated Radio Messages*

In the simulation, all responses from aircraft and others are displayed in the text area at the bottom of the display. For realism, each response type carries a fixed time delay. As examples, a simulated visual ID requires 20 seconds, and a confirmation that the designated aircraft has been illuminated involves a 10-second delay. Responses from aircraft also involve delays, however these are somewhat shorter. One could easily extend the realism of the response delays to involve random variation in duration.

The wording of each response depends upon a host of variables that hold in the current exercise. Responses from warned aircraft depend upon the nature of the aircraft; a friendly aircraft will always agree to change course as directed if it actually receives the warning, as shown here:

| U.S. Navy Warship: This is Royal Air Force fighter en-route to fleet exercises. Changing course as requested, over. |
| --- |

It is possible to establish conditions in which a friendly aircraft has an equipment malfunction or is not monitoring the correct radio channel, and does not therefore receive and heed the warning.

In a similar way, a request for a visual ID will produce an accurate description of the hooked aircraft if it is within range of the optical sighting equipment on board, considering the current visibility conditions. These in turn depend upon the time of day or night at which the exercise is supposed to be happening and the current weather conditions. Similarly, under poor visibility or long range conditions, the (virtual) crew will report their inability to make an identification.

Chapter 5 will describe the process of updating blips periodically over time, updating the CRO, and managing the timing of responses to commands to individual aircraft in the simulation.

# SIMULATING REAL-TIME PROCESSES

Most of the behaviors discussed until now have been discrete-state, i.e., the state changes are carried out as rapidly as the computer resources can manipulate the graphics and update any property values. Of course, all changes in the real world (possibly excepting the quantum level) require some finite time to complete, but when that time period is so brief that it cannot be perceived by the human eye, there is usually little benefit gained from simulating these brief state transitions as continuous processes.

Many, if not most, real world systems, however, involve some state transitions that are perceivable as continuous processes over a period of a second or more. In most of these cases it is instructionally useful or essential to portray these transitions with relatively high time fidelity. In this chapter, therefore, we will explore a number of ways in which continuous state transitions may be simulated. More specifically, four different methods for simulating real-time, continuous, changes will be presented: 1) methods for animation, 2) a flexible function for specifying and executing real-time changes, 3) continuous monitoring of an object's input conditions, and 4) an approach for simulating passage of time throughout the presentation of a simulation application. Each of these four methods is useful, effective, and preferred in particular conditions that will be described.

## ANIMATION METHODS

Portraying continuous graphical changes over time via animation methods is appropriate when the change always occurs in one fixed way that never needs to be halted during its course of action. Generally, such changes are quite brief, and may even be just marginally essential to the simulation as a whole. In all the simulation applications undertaken so far by the author, the only use of animation made was that of showing a two-state control, such as a toggle switch, change state in a continuous manner, and this was done only to enhance the realism of the control's response to the user.

In Flash, animations are set up by placing each of the intermediate graphical states along the timeline, starting with the initial state, ending with the final graphical state, with all the graphics in between representing intermediate appearances. The animation effect is produced by jumping to the first frame of the sequence, and it continues automatically, at a constant rate, until the final frame is shown. An attractive feature of Flash is that it automatically passes through the timeline at a rate that is selected, typically 30 frames per second.

While some animations could be so computationally complex that the particular computer process cannot keep up with that specified rate, Flash still controls the presentation so that the total elapsed time is as desired.

Animation of the two-state toggle switch is done by simply adding three additional graphical elements. Recall that in ReAct a two-state control is constructed of a background part, here two circles with some gradient fill, over which appears either of two possible toggle parts, one up and one down, and the state setting function simply selects which of the two toggle parts to display.

By adding just three intermediate graphics, as shown here, the switch can be made to change in a seemingly continuous manner from its down state to its up state (with the fixed background included here for clarity):

The effort to produce the three intermediate graphical states is extremely minor, since the second and fourth cells are mirror images, and the middle state is easily drawn. These five graphics are then placed into the Flash timeline in two sets, one set showing the switch going from down to up (frames 10 through 14 below), and one sequence showing up to down (frames 20 through 24 below).

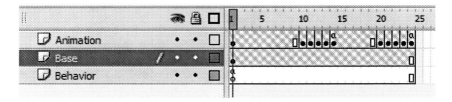

As with the discrete-state configuration, the setState function within the toggle switch jumps to frame 10 to produce the up state and to 20 to produce the down state, the only difference being that here five graphical states are shown in rapid succession, until a Stop statement is encountered at the end of the five-cell animation.

This approach to animation provides considerable flexibility in producing just the desired graphical effect, but there are virtually no opportunities to adjust the effect, stop the process, or produce effects on other parts of the model programmatically.

*Automatic Generation of Tweened Graphics*

The Flash development environment provides the capability to tween two graphics automatically, i.e., to generate all the intermediate graphical elements between two given end state graphics. After entering the terminal up and down graphics to the Flash timeline the developer selects a menu item that produces the intermediate graphics that morph the initial graphic to the final one.

The problem with using automatically generated intermediate graphics, as any Flash user can easily confirm, is that the result is not as good as manually drawn elements. The following sequence shows the same terminal graphics with three intermediate graphics as produced by this automatic capability.

Considering the ease with which we can manually produce intermediate graphics, the built-in tweening process is not preferred, although it must be said that when played at 30 frames per second the automatically generated morphing is nearly indistinguishable from the hand crafter version.

*The Built-in Tween Function*

The most recent version of Flash, version MX 2004, provides a function named *tween* that may be useful in producing some limited types of animations. Unlike the graphical tweening shown above, in which one graphic seems to morph into another along the timeline, the built-in *tween* function supports animating just three object properties: position, size, and transparency. While limited to just these three object properties, the *tween* function is powerful in that arguments can be added that call for non-linear changes, thus simulating acceleration or deceleration of the change. Excellent documentation and examples of the use of this function can be found at http://www.adobe.com/devnet/flash/articles/tweening.html.

Another approach that might seem preferable in achieving changes over time is to simply program the change desired. While it is difficult to see what function would produce the intermediate toggle switch graphics, other changes involving graphical and numerical properties might be better accomplished programmatically than via animation on the timeline. In fact, the next section will describe in detail a very powerful function for doing just that.

*A Tween Function for Simulation Applications*

The ReAct *change* function, described below, is a very powerful function for changing object properties over time in a well managed manner that supports simulation requirements. Before considering this approach, however, it is important to outline the limitations of less generalized programmatic approaches. Suppose, for example, we simply wish to move an object from its initial location, signified by the _x property, to one 600 pixels to the right, over some specified time period. Those unfamiliar with Flash might think that we could insert a simple function into the object that would do this. The following snippet of pseudo-code applies this method:

```
set time of starting the move, in milliseconds
for (some variable going from 0 to a large number) {
    determine the elapsed time since starting, in milliseconds
    compute _x as a function of elapsed time and total desired change in _x
    if computed _x is greater than or equal to goal, set object _x to goal and exit
    else continue
}
```

This simple loop increments the _x property of an object by the correct number of pixels with each pass through the loop, until the object attains its goal horizontal position. Upon implementing this code, however, we discover that the object jumps virtually instantaneously from its initial position to a final position that is 600 pixels to the right, for the simple reason that Flash does not update screen graphics until a new frame has been entered (there is a function, *updateAfterEvent*, that will force a screen update, however this function is somewhat limited in the way it can be applied).

Overcoming this problem is easily done in Flash by simply embedding the function within the built-in *onEnterFrame* function, one that is automatically called 30 times per second, if that is the specified update rate for the application. The approach of writing various special purpose functions such as this one, however, is poor. First, considerably more code will ultimately have to be added to deal with stopping the change before the goal value is reached, a necessary option in many cases. Further code will have to be produced if there is ever a delay desired in starting the process. And finally, each such special function will have to ensure that it calls the simulation engine, so that the affected objects are kept apprised of the current property value.

## A FLEXIBLE FUNCTION FOR CHANGING PROPERTIES OVER TIME

A much more effective method for accomplishing real time change is to employ a single function that addresses a wide range of possible simulation needs. Such a function, termed *change*, in provided in ReAct to manage the time-dependent change of any property of an object over a specified duration, to attain a specified goal value, with the options of calling for a delay before the change begins and for specifying non-linear changes.

The formal syntax of the basic *change* function is:

```
change (property, goalValue, duration);
```

where:

*property* is the property of the calling object to be changed;
*goalValue* is the value of property to be attained, if not stopped externally;
*duration* is the time, in seconds, in which to accomplish the change;

While duration is expressed in seconds, all underlying actions of the change function operate in milliseconds, thus one can provide a duration of 12.58 and observe a change that is indeed very close to 12.6 seconds in length.

Typically, the change function is called by an object to modify one of its own properties over time. A typical call might be:

```
change (_rotation, 90, 3.5);
```

This would cause the _rotation property of the calling object to change from its current value to 90 degrees over a 3.5-second duration. Note that if the object started at a rotation of 85 degrees, the result change would appear quite slow, but if the initial value were 10 degrees it would progress much faster. Ways to achieve a fixed rate are given below.

Alternatively, external elements, including other objects, can trigger a change in an object by simply referencing the object in the call, as shown here:

```
meterNeedle.change (_rotation, 180, 9);
```

which specifies that the _rotation property of the meterNeedle object is to change over time. Object oriented programming purists may blanch at the thought of one object starting a change in another object, which is considered bad form. Still, sometimes it is very convenient for one object to do just that, so this function permits us to be unprincipled.

There is no general limit to the number of simultaneous real time changes that may be ongoing. If a very large number of continuous changes are initiated, however, and those changes involve considerable computer processing resources, then one could possibly observe jerkiness of movement, as the update process exceeds the compute time available in each cycle. The durations of the various changes, however, would remain accurate, at least to a small fraction of a second.

## Using Variable Arguments in the Change

While the examples above are illustrative, they are not very typical, in that most calls to the *change* function supply variables for one or more of the arguments rather than constants. In the case of the meter needle, we would more typically compute the *goalValue*, in degrees, from some value being measured, probably the property of some other object. Thus, if the meter were set to Voltage, our behavior rule for the needle would first compute the *goalValue* as a function of 1) the voltage at the test point currently being touched by the probe, 2) the current setting of the Voltage Range control, and 3) the total range of the meter needle, in degrees.

If we compute this value and call it *theDegrees*, then the call to change would be:

```
change (_rotation, theDegrees, 3);
```

The developer will also want to consider whether or not it is realistic to specify a constant duration in any particular change process, realizing that when the difference between the goal value and the initial value is large, the rate of change will be large, otherwise it will be small. In some situations, this effect is very realistic, but in others the rate of change is relatively constant and it is the duration that contracts or expands to satisfy the total amount of change involved. In those cases, the change statement is preceded by one that computes the duration as a function of the amount of change involved and the rate at which it occurs, and this duration variable is supplied in the call.

### Delaying the Start of Changes

The literal value "delay", followed by a number in seconds, can be supplied as arguments to the *change* function to specify a delay before commencing the real time process. For example

```
change (temperature, 340, 200, "delay", 60);
```

would change the temperature property of an object to 340 over a 200-second duration, but not starting for 60 seconds after the call is executed. This is a more convenient way to schedule a delayed process than starting a timer and then executing the change when the timer expires.

### Producing Non-linear Changes

The default behavior of the change function is to update the given property evenly over the duration of the process, i.e., in a linear fashion. In the example above, the temperature would increase at a constant rate of 1.70 (degrees) per second, derived as 340/200. Many real world effects do not occur in a linear fashion, however. Hydraulic components, for example, typically begin moving at a slow rate and speed up as inertia is overcome. Other changes slow down as they approach their goal value. Objects often display this effect when under the control of some feedback mechanism that is producing an impetus to change that is proportional to the difference between the goal value and the current value.

To produce a non-linear change with minimal effort by the applicator, the change function also accepts the literal arguments "easeIn", 'easeOut", and "easeInOut". The first of these – easeIn – produces small initial rates of change that gradually increase over the life of the process. The second – easeOut – works in reverse, i.e., it begins with larger rates of change that diminish as the process approaches its terminal value. The third – easeInOut – produces change rates that start and end at lower values and achieve maximum values at the midpoint.

An example call to produce a non-linear change might be

```
change (_y, 800, 5, "easeIn");
```

This will change the _y property (vertical position) of an object to a value of 800 pixels from the reference point over a period of 5 seconds, starting slowly and accelerating over time.

*Comparison*

It is informative to compare the amount of change that occurs over the course of a linear change to one that is quadratic, as obtained by adding one of the easing options. Suppose we have a meter needle sitting at 0 degrees rotation that we wish to change to 90 degrees rotation over a 3 second (3000 ms) period.

The straight line in Figure 5-1 reflects the constant rate of change produced by executing

```
change (_rotation, 90, 3);
```

whereas the curved line below it corresponds to a call with "easeIn" appended, and the curved line above it corresponds to a call with "easeOut" appended.

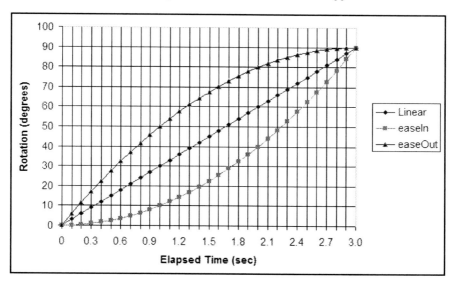

*Figure 5-1. Comparison of Linear and Quadratic Changes.*

In all three cases the rotation of the meter needle is 90 degrees after 3000 ms, but the quadratic easing accelerates the rate of change at the beginning or end.

*Controlling Concurrency*

The only limitation in applying the change function is that sequential calls involving the same property must be separated in time so that they do not conflict. Suppose, for example, we wish to rotate a meter needle to 90 degrees over 3 seconds and then have it fall back to 85 degrees over 2 seconds. It might seem that the following two calls to *change* will accomplish this sequence of real time changes:

```
change (_rotation, 90, 3);
change (_rotation, 85, 2);
```

In fact, each of the two changes will be initiated and maintained over time, so for the first two seconds the meter needle will be jumping erratically as it attempts to satisfy both calls. The easiest way to resolve this problem is to specify a delay on the second phase of the meter action, as follows:

```
change (_rotation, 90, 3);
change (_rotation, 85, 2, "delay", 3);
```

*Inside the Change Function*

The real time change process is started when the change function is first executed and is carried out over time by another function that is called 30 times per second. When the *change* function is first called, it adds a (numerical) vector to an array that contains all ongoing, or scheduled, real-time changes. The vector, an array itself, lists the object involved, the property to be changed, the time at which the change should begin, and the amount of change per millisecond, if no easing options are supplied.

'Then, every 1/30 of a second the process maintenance function updates all ongoing processes listed in this array that are either ready to begin or are in progress. Each such property is updated by computing the time since the last update, then computing the current value according to the linear or quadratic formula. For linear changes, i.e., no easing specified, the statement for current value is simply:

```
current value = initial value + deltaVal * deltaT;
```

where deltaVal is the change in value, per millisecond, computed as:

(goalValue – initialValue) / duration, in milliseconds

and deltaT = current time – time since last update, in milliseconds.

If easing is specified, then the current value is obtained by a quadratic expression, which for easeIn is:

current value = initial value + (goalValue - initialValue) * $deltaT^2$/ $duration^2$

where *deltaT* is as above, and duration is the total specified time for the change, in milliseconds.

## Stopping Real-time Changes

Most processes run their course once started, however some processes must be aborted when certain conditions obtain. Along with the *change* function, therefore, are two functions, *stopChange* and *stopAll*, for stopping ongoing processes before they reach their designated targets. The former function stops an ongoing change to a specified object property, leaving the value of that property at its current level, whatever that is. The latter function stops all ongoing real time processes in the same manner. We might use the stopChange function to abort a simulation of filling a tire with air if the air pressure holds at its latest value when pumping is aborted.

The stopAll function is used in those cases when all ongoing changes should cease, either because the model has been put into such a state that no such processes would continue or because some training/aiding activity assumes control and wants to stop any changes in progress.

Of course, the stopChange or stopAll function may not be sufficient to bring some changes to an end in a realistic manner. Suppose a user moves a simulated meter probe away from a test point of a simulated circuit that is was formerly reading. Since we know that the meter needle may have been in the process of changing to reflect the value at that point, we must first kill that process and then return the meter needle back to zero in a realistic way. In this case we might follow the call to stopChange with another real time process to return the needle back to zero, with the call:

```
change (_rotation, 0, 0.5);
```

## CONTINUOUS MONITORING OF CONDITIONS

The simulation of an aircraft nose wheel steering system presented in Chapter 4 includes a vane that rotates if there is more pressure on one side than the other and if the vane is not locked into a centered position. The vane is shown in Figure 5-2, on the left rotating clockwise due to more pressure at the lower hydraulic port than the upper one, and on the right rotating counter clockwise due to higher pressure at the top port (on-screen, the low pressure lines are displayed in blue and the high pressure lines are in red).

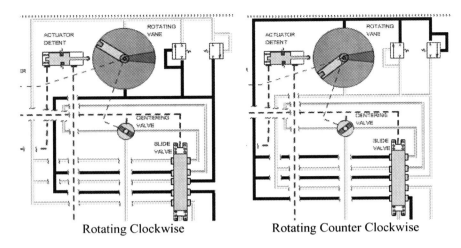

Rotating Clockwise           Rotating Counter Clockwise

*Figure 5-2. Nose Wheel Steering Vane Rotation.*

When that model was initially developed, this vane rotation was implemented using the *change* function just described. Because the limit value of vane rotation changes with each miniscule movement of the rudder pedal, however, the graphical behavior of the vane was not smooth. This jerkiness was the result of stopping any ongoing rotation and starting a new change process, with each detected movement of the rudder pedals.

An alternate approach was therefore implemented, and the result was both simpler code and smooth vane rotation even under conditions of frequent and rapid movement of the rudder pedals. Under this approach, the vane continuously compares its current rotation to that which it should attain, according to the state of the Servo Valve. If the vane is not at its rotation target, it rotates by 1 degree toward the side imposing the lower pressure. This process continues at a rate of 30 times per second, and produces a steady rotational rate regardless of the amount of rotation that is required to satisfy the Servo Valve. Anytime the vane reaches its target rotation, it notifies the Servo Valve, and that valve returns to its centered position, thereby transmitting equal pressure to both sides of the vane.

The primary reason this approach works so well is that the user can fiddle with the rudder pedals at will without materially affecting the vane. The only impact of pedal movement on the vane is to change the vane's target rotation value. Even if the rudder pedals are moved in a manner that requires the vane to reverse direction of rotation, the vane's simple behavior rule stays the same: rotate 1 degree toward the lower pressure and notify the Servo Valve if the current target rotation is attained.

This approach should perform well in any condition where an object responds in a manner that is closely linked to some external events that are relatively rapid and continual, such as user 'tracking' actions or random events.

## PERIODIC MODEL UPDATING

The last method for dealing with real time is one that is very effective when simulating a task environment involving some ongoing process, such as a forest fire, aircraft maneuvering about, or a hostage situation. The technique is similar to that just described, but instead of having an object update its own status over time, we create an object that updates all the elements in the model at regular intervals.

There are a number of different ways to accomplish this ongoing update process in Flash ActionScript, including: 1) using the powerful *setInterval* function; 2) using the simple *enterFrame* function; and 3) setting up a loop on the timeline. The *setInterval* function, once called, will execute a given function repeatedly, at the given time interval, in milliseconds. The *enterFrame* construct executes with each change in frame, so an object carrying this function can easily execute the model update process each time an internal counter reaches a specific value.

Finally, the timeline loop is easily created, and executed. Since Flash automatically runs through frames on the timeline at a specified speed, within limits, regardless of the particular computer processor hardware being used, we can create a timeline that loops endlessly and triggers an update to the simulation with each pass.

The following simple setup provides a mechanism carrying out a periodic update every ½ second.

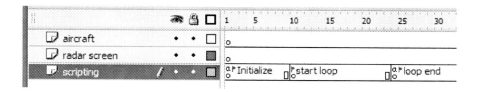

Here frame 1 contains code to initialize the model, possibly to set up some particular scenario; the looping process begins at frame 10 and ends at frame 24; and the code at frame 24 updates the world model then jumps back to frame 10. Since the loop is 15 frames in length, the update process will be executed every ½ second, with the Flash execution system set to run at 30 frames per second.

## THE CIC SIMULATION

The CIC Simulation presented in Chapter 4 is structured as a timeline loop as shown above. The updating code at the terminal frame of the loop performs three simulation functions: 1) it updates the position, status, and display of all the blips by executing each blip's *update* function (defined one time in the blip component), 2) it updates the Character Readout (CRO) to reflect the properties of the currently hooked blip; and 3) it presents responses when they are ready to be delivered to the operator.

The delayed-action responses are managed by maintaining an array of pending responses, sorted in ascending order of the time when each should be presented. When a visual ID is requested, for example, the response is constructed, the time at which it becomes due is determined, the new response and its due time are appended to the array, and the array is sorted by due times.

Thus, the update loop needs only check the due time of the first response in the array. If that earliest response is ready to be issued, it is presented to the operator and removed from the list. If the first entry is not ready, there is nothing further to do.

If it happens that multiple scheduled responses become ready simultaneously, just one is presented with each cycle. Currently, there are no provisions for avoiding two responses coming up in such time proximity that they cannot be distinguished by the user. This can easily be done by ensuring that no other response is within, say, 5 seconds of the one being appended to the pending response list.

In addition to the three simulation functions outlined above, the updating code also makes some determinations that may be required by an instructional/aiding system. One of the most important of these is the minimum distance approached by an unknown or hostile aircraft during an exercise. This measure is very useful in assessing the learner's proficiency, as will be discussed in a later chapter.

# DEMONSTRATING BEHAVIORS AND CONCEPTS

Simulations may be executed by instructors and learners alike to produce instructive illustrations of system behaviors and complex processes. Whether the target systems are real world hardware entities or fundamental concepts, demonstrations can provide powerful insights into the expected observable behaviors as well as unseen phenomena that produce those responses.

The discussion of this chapter will start with uses of simulations in conventional classroom instruction, then proceed to a generally applicable method for demonstrating fundamental concepts, and conclude with a design for augmenting simulations with text and graphics in a loosely coupled manner. This progression also works from applications in which the student participation is minimal to those in which the student is engaged in producing the effects of interest, reporting the observation of those effects, and predicting outcomes in various alternative conditions.

## USE OF SIMULATIONS IN THE CLASSROOM

Some training environments are able to provide either a real, operational, unit of the target system to be learned or a very realistic hardware-based simulator of the real system. Sometimes, such units are called "trainers", although they rarely qualify as such unless one includes the instructor in the configuration.

Typically, in these training environments, just one or two students can operate or practice at one time, and they must be monitored relatively closely to ensure their safety and that of the hardware. Additionally, instructor-led demonstrations may be hampered by high ambient noise levels as well as limitations in the number of people that can observe the instructor's actions and the system's responses. Still, a real system or hardware simulator can be a real asset if it can be kept running and used safely under close instructor guidance, for it is the real thing that will be encountered when the students complete their training.

Whether or not such a hardware unit is available, an instructor can employ a software-based simulation to great benefit in the classroom to address a number of related training requirements including familiarization of system organization and structure, demonstration of operating procedures, explanation of internal system functions, and demonstrations of diagnostic strategies. Using overhead projection, the instructor can work through such demonstrations and explanations in a way that all can see and hear and even replicate at their own workspace if provided with the necessary delivery resources.

In addition to informally narrating the presentation of simulations in classroom lectures and demonstrations, some instructors may wish to produce training materials to be presented in the context of the simulation, thereby exploiting their instructional expertise as well as their knowledge of local conditions and of the student population. There are at least three systems that permit a non-programmer to rapidly create presentations in which existing simulations are augmented with additional text and graphics: 1) MS PowerPoint, with which many instructors are already familiar, 2) PKS, a system developed specifically for the development and presentation of training and documentation materials in association with simulations, and 3) the Flash Slide Presentation System, available in the Professional 8 version of Adobe Flash.

*Embedding Simulations in PowerPoint Presentations*

Any simulation developed as described in this volume may be included as a working element of an MS PowerPoint presentation. The resulting file could provide any kind of instruction or guidance, from leading students through the performance of some task on the simulation or stepping through a demonstration that illustrates the functionality of a modeled system. Figure 6-1 shows one slide in a sample PowerPoint application, after the user has actuated the model.

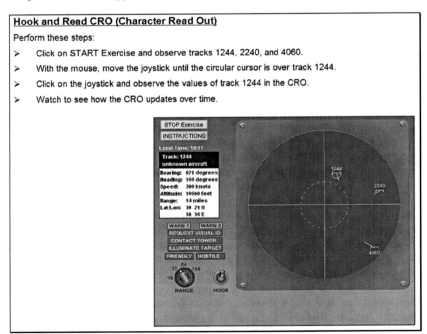

*Figure 6-1. An MS PowerPoint Slide Containing a Working Simulation.*

For clarity in this figure, the font size was made much larger than is necessary under normal display. A full-screen PowerPoint slide provides sufficient space on which to present a considerable amount of accompanying text.

*Implementation.* The embedding of Flash simulations in PowerPoint is accomplished via an ActiveX control named Shockwave Flash Object. If this element is not already installed on the presentation system, it is easily downloaded from the Adobe Web site[15]. Detailed instructions for bringing compiled Flash simulations into a PowerPoint presentation may be found at:

http://www.indezine.com/products/powerpoint/ppflash3.html.

*Issues and Limitations.* Several limitations apply to models presented within PowerPoint. First, the ActiveX control is not supported by the PowerPoint Viewer or by Macintosh versions of PowerPoint. Secondly, system states created in one slide do not carry over to other slides, i.e., if the same system is shown on another slide, it will act independently of any others (however system states established on a particular slide will persist across multiple viewings in the same session). Third, models within PowerPoint do not start running when the slide is first shown[16], so some means must be provided to start execution. Finally, to navigate forward and backward, after an embedded simulation is operated in any way, the presenter must first click outside the simulation area to return keyboard focus to PowerPoint.

If these limitations are understood, and can be tolerated, PowerPoint represents an easy way for instructors to add their own content related to simulations used in the classroom and possibly outside the classroom as well.

### Embedding Simulations in the Personal Knowledge Source (PKS)

The Personal Knowledge Source, or PKS ((Towne, 2002b), is a system designed specifically to facilitate the development and delivery of simulation-centered presentations and documentation. While PKS screens can be presented sequentially as in a slide presentation, its paradigm is that of pages in a document. PKS provides a selectable table of contents, as seen in the example of Figure 6-2, with which one may more easily navigate to particular topics.

As in PowerPoint, external simulations are brought into PKS screens, then scaled and moved as desired, however the process is more direct in that the developer simply selects the simulation to be embedded from a list then drags and scales it directly. In addition, PKS provides an extensive set of tools for adding text and graphics to the presentation screens, as well as tools to control the behavior of the model on the screen. Another advantage of PKS over PowerPoint is that it runs on both PC and Mac platforms. PKS will be more fully described in Chapter 11.

---

[15] http://www.adobe.com/cfusion/knowledgebase/index.cfm?id=tn_14235
[16] This bug in PowerPoint may be removed in PowerPoint 2007, but that version was not available for evaluation as of this writing.

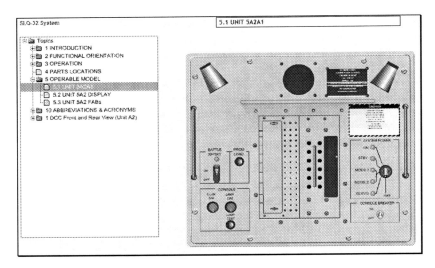

*Figure 6-2. A PKS Screen with a Working Simulation and Table of Contents.*

*Embedding Simulations in the Flash Slide Presentation System*

Finally, the Flash Slide Presentation System, shown in Figure 6-3, may be used to develop simulation-enabled presentations.

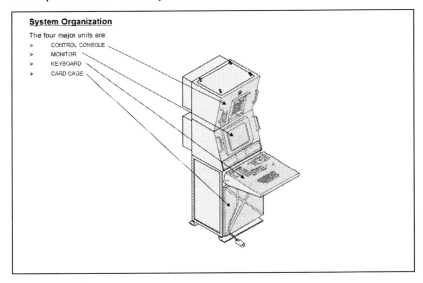

*Figure 6-3. A Simulation in the Flash Slide Presentation System.*

Like PowerPoint, this system employs the slide paradigm, thus navigation is primarily sequential, although hyperlinks can be employed.

*Recap*

In summary, all three systems described above accommodate the augmentation of existing simulations with ad-hoc text and graphics via direct manipulation of the GUI rather than via programming. The process of doing so in PowerPoint is very limited and clumsy, but the software is ubiquitous and familiar to most. The features in PKS far exceed those of PowerPoint or the Flash Slide environment, but the software is only now becoming available commercially. Finally, the Flash Slide Presentation system offers a possible alternative to PowerPoint that offers considerable control over the result.

These methods yield text and graphics that are either not integrated at all with the simulation, as with PowerPoint and the Flash Slide Presentation system, or somewhat loosely integrated with the simulation, as with PKS. This low level of integration is the price paid for methods that involve very modest time, effort, and skills to carry out, and that price may be quite acceptable if the desire is to produce something quickly that incorporates instructor content.

## DEMONSTRATION OF BASIC CONCEPTS

Simulations can be extremely powerful in demonstrating various basic concepts, such as the flow of electrical current, hydraulic fundamentals, or operation of basic electrical circuits. Since such principles are so unique, however, we develop the simulation and the demonstration as one, rather than employing a domain-general development system to operate upon a simulation of the phenomenon, as is done in Chapters 7 through 9.

In general, applications concerning basic concepts can be structured in two phases: 1) an observation phase in which the learner operates the simulation and observes the effects, and 2) a predictive phase in which the simulation of the concept is presented in various conditions and the learner predicts how it will behave. Particular attention must be paid to the design of the observation phase to provide the guidance and control essential to effective progress and learning, as discussed next.

*Avoiding the Pitfalls of Unstructured Discovery Learning*

Some of the earliest uses of simulations were found in what is termed (unstructured) *discovery learning environments*, in which the learner is allowed or required to experiment with a simulation of the phenomenon of interest and to discover the underlying principles that govern its operation. The expectation was that principles learned by conducting the scientific method of discovery by experimentation are more powerful and memorable than those that are simply presented as facts to be memorized. For example, a learner might be given a simulation of a simple electrical circuit, and advised to adjust the voltage and resistance to determine how they affect current flow, i.e., to discover Ohm's Law.

While the experimental results do not contradict the notion that discovered truths are more memorable than dictated facts, they do reflect a nearly universal problem that the unstructured discovery environment presents a learning environment that most learners cannot exploit effectively. Typically, a small proportion of students happily and successfully complete such experiments, but the majority of students are not effective in carrying out such investigation on their own. As suggested by de Jong, van Joolingen, Scott, de Hoog, Lapied, & Valent (1994):

> The reason for the possible ineffectiveness of computer simulations is that learners, while interacting with a simulation, encounter difficulties which they cannot overcome on their own.

They go on to propose that the difficulties arise from problems in formulating hypotheses, switching between hypotheses and experiments, and monitoring their own performance. Much more success is achieved when structured guidance is provided in the conduct of the experiment and the interpretation of observations, as is done in the SMISLE system (de Jong, van Joolingen, Scott, de Hoog, Lapied, & Valent, 1994).

SMISLE

The SMISLE system design features five model types and two basic approaches to instruction. The model types are 1) a *runnable model*, the executable model of the domain, 2) a *cognitive model* that represents the domain for training purposes, 3) an *instructional model* that manages instructional support, 4) a *learner model* that reflects the hypothesized knowledge state of the learner, and 5) and an *interface model* that represents the domain to the learner. Thus, this system, like the $D^3M$ system for scenario training discussed in Chapter 9, integrates the instructional functions with the simulation functions.

The two instructional approaches in SMISLE are 1) *model progression* (White & Frederiksen, 1989, 1990), in which a succession of domain representations are used, progressing from simplified to more complete, and 2) *cognitive apprenticeship* (Collins, Brown, & Newman, 1989), which works to prevent faults in student understanding.

*The Informal Principles of Assured Discovery*

For our purposes, we have employed a simpler, admittedly less robust, approach – one we term "assured discovery" – that performs well when the instruction concerns a particular phenomenon to be observed. The simple and informal guidelines of assured discovery are to design the observation phase so that 1) the chance of not observing the desired effect is virtually zero, 2) the student time to correct an erroneous observation is extremely brief, and 3) the introduction of mathematical formality is either deferred or avoided.

In the case of demonstrating how current flow is affected by voltage (presuming that the prerequisite concepts have been introduced), the learner is first directed to vary voltage and observe current as shown in Figure 6-4. This initial screen involves no algebraic terms, no formulas, and no quantities; the learner is only asked to determine if current increases or decreases when voltage increases.

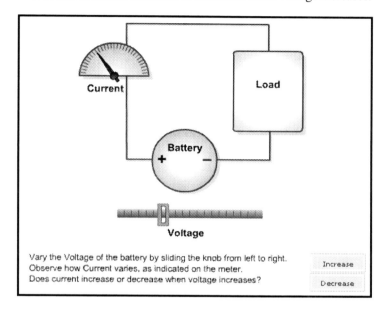

*Figure 6-4. A Qualitative Simulation of Current as a Function of Voltage.*

After the direction of change is successfully indicated, the circuit is presented as shown in Figure 6-5, and the learner is asked if current varies proportionately with voltage or not. When the learner correctly responds that the change in current is proportional to the change in voltage, two similar screens are presented that address resistance, arriving at the conclusion that current varies reciprocally with resistance.

Now, algebraic terms could be introduced, if desired, leading to the formula for Ohm's law, although this significant increase in formality and mathematical rigor may not be required. Work by Forbus and Whalley (1994) and Forbus (1984) in qualitative physics is most instructive in considering non-quantitative approaches.

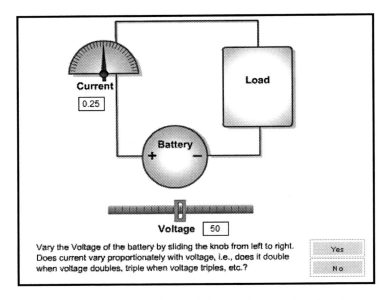

*Figure 6-5. A Quantitative Simulation of Current Flow as a Function of Voltage.*

### The Predictive Phase

Following the observation phase, the application presents the simulation in a number of different, randomly generated, conditions and asks the learner to indicate certain values. For the voltage-current relationship, the simulation is shown with various voltage and current values (Figure 6-6), and the learner predicts the current at a different voltage. In the case shown, if the source is increased to 45 volts, a current of 0.88 amperes would result (note that the correct answer can be determined with a simple proportion calculation, thus the resistance value need not be used).

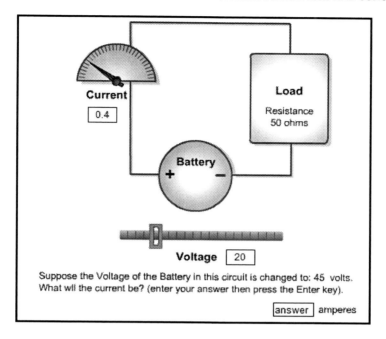

*Figure 6-6. A Quantitative Prediction Item.*

## DEMONSTRATING AND EXPLICATING COMPLEX SUBJECT MATTER

Possibly the greatest return for the investment in simulation development is obtained when instructional demonstrations and explanations are coupled with the simulation in a more principled fashion. Such coupling does not mean that the instructional developer modifies the simulation in any way, but instead brings the simulation and the instructional material and interactions into a unified entity, thereby greatly facilitating the development of the instruction as well as producing a stand alone instructional resource.

As a prelude to the following discussion, it is important to acknowledge that the explanation and demonstration capabilities discussed below do not directly assess learner progress or proficiency, and they do not enforce a high level of user participation. These capabilities instead offer effective means for illustrating and explaining complex systems and complex tasks, instructional phases that are necessary but not sufficient for complete instructional administration. Chapter 7 will deal with methods for supporting practice and assessing individual understanding and performance in a much more controlled environment.

*Example*

We will begin by examining a completed demonstration application, then work backward to see how that application is produced. Figure 6-7 shows the aircraft nose wheel steering system simulation at start-up, with meta-instructions displayed.

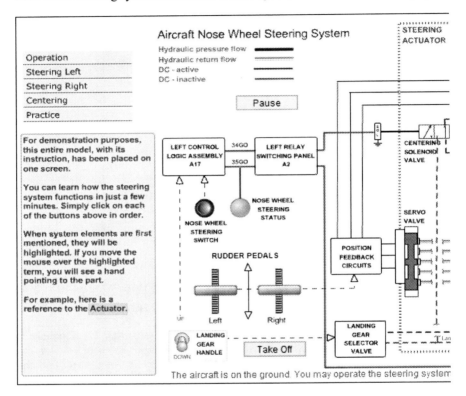

*Figure 6-7. Meta-Instruction for a Particular Simulation.*

*Meta-Instruction*

When first started, the application displays instructions concerning its use. The guidance given here also explains one of the interactive elements used throughout: the object highlighter. This element is a semi-transparent rectangle that can be placed over any text, as seen over the term "Actuator". When the user moves the mouse cursor over this box, a beep sounds and a hand appears, pointing at the named element. This element is used throughout the presentation to facilitate identifying elements in the simulation that are mentioned in the text.

*Demonstrations and Explanations*

In this application, the first four buttons present demonstrations and explanations of various system functions. Figure 6-8 shows the application immediately after selecting the Operation button (i.e., prior to any actions taken by the learner).

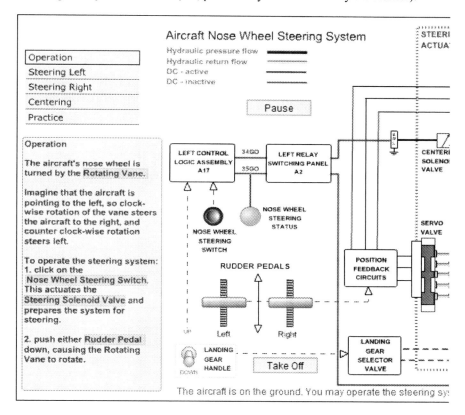

*Figure 6-8. Initial Explanation of System Operation.*

Now, the user may read and study the text, locate the highlighted elements mentioned in the description, follow the directions to operate the model, and observe the response of the system model. In Figure 6-9, the learner has carried out the recommended steps, and the system is responding.

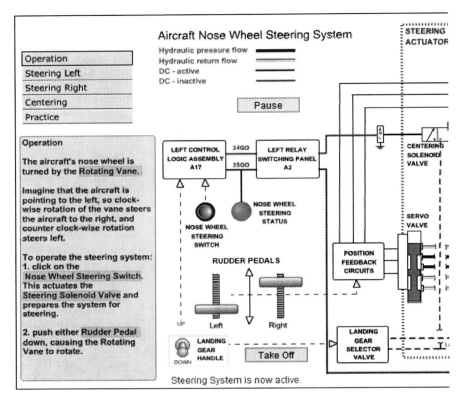

*Figure 6-9. Simulation Responding to User's Actions.*

When the learner selects the Steering Left button the discussion turns to that facet of system behavior, and so on through the Centering mode. Importantly, the instructional interface permits substantial control by the user. The user may repeat a topic as many times as desired and may jump forward or backward at will. Such freedom is essential if the learner is to observe and understand the differences and similarities among the different functions the simulated system performs.

*Free Practice*

At any time[17], the user may select the Practice button which provides guidance in utilizing the model for further study (Figure 6-10).

---

[17] For those instructional designers feeling uneasy about this level of user control, the Practice mode could easily be restricted to those learners who have at least visited the four instructional topics.

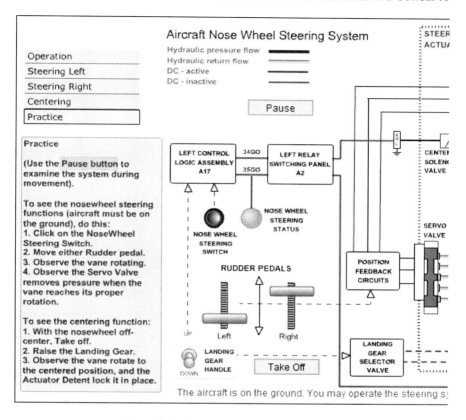

*Figure 6-10 The Application in Practice Mode.*

This practice section presents no new information, but instead summarizes the procedures used to place the system into its two main modes of operation, viz., steering mode and centering mode. The learner can therefore operate the system with this guidance on screen, returning to the previous sections whenever the more detailed explanations are needed.

*Implementation*

Very little programming is required to produce an application like that shown above, utilizing an existing simulation. The simple *setState* function call described in Chapter 4 places any of the model elements into a desired state, and the value of the *state* variable for an element gives the status of that element.

For example, to demonstrate the steering system in the process of steering left requires two statements to initialize the aircraft as being on the ground with the steering system enabled, one to set the rotating vane to a fully clock-wise rotation (steering hard right), one to set the centering valve to its steering state, and one to set the left rudder to fully down. Now, all the other elements in the model respond according to their behavior rules, and the learner sees the nose wheel turning counter clockwise, as explained in the text. Because the vane was initialized steering hard right, the learner is able to see the transition to steering left over the longest possible time interval.

*Instructing a Complex Task*

A similar design was used to introduce and demonstrate performance of the CIC air traffic control task. This application also starts with the presentation of meta-instruction, as shown in Figure 6-11.

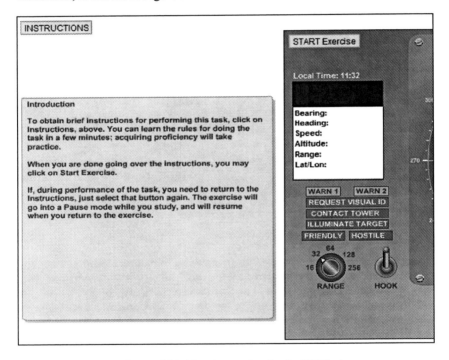

*Figure 6-11. Meta-instruction for the CIC Task.*

Upon selecting the INSTRUCTIONS button in the upper left corner, the user sees the four options shown in Figure 6-12, which serve to:
- demonstrate various aspects of the task;
- introduce elements of the operator panel;
- explain the hooking process and permit the user to practice this sub task; and
- demonstrate and explain the other actions required of the decision maker.

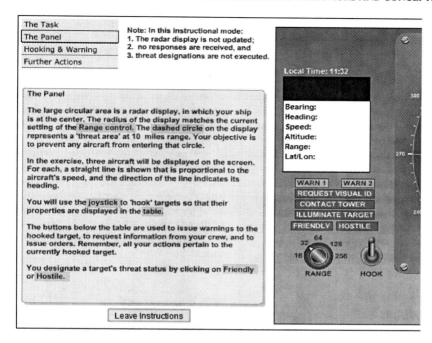

*Figure 6-12 Demonstration of the CIC Task.*

Figure 6-13 shows the user is practicing the task, with instructions available if needed.

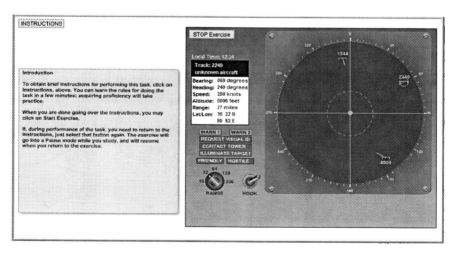

*Figure 6-13. Practicing the CIC Task.*

The user may select INSTRUCTIONS at any time, to freeze the current simulation while reviewing the instructions.

## RECAP OF DEMONSTRATION METHODS

The demonstration methods involve differing levels of development effort, instructional power, and flexibility. Presenting simulations within a general-purpose presentation system, such as MS PowerPoint, PKS, or the Flash Slide Presentation System, permits very rapid production of a resource that can have value to the instructor in the classroom as well as to students wishing to review or study the presentation further, however user involvement is typically low or absent. Demonstrations of concepts can illustrate effects that are difficult to visualize otherwise and can involve the learner in making predictions that require application of the concept. Finally, coupling a simulation with a relatively general-purpose user interface, such as that shown for demonstrating the aircraft nose wheel steering system and the CIC task, can put a simulation through its paces so that all of the instructive system behaviors are presented.

Table 6-1 summarizes some of the important advantages of each approach.

*Table 6-1. Comparison of Demonstration Methods.*

| Demonstration Method | Level of Student Participation | Development Effort | Instructional Flexibility & Power | Primary Advantage |
|---|---|---|---|---|
| PowerPoint host | Low | Low | Very low | Widespread availability |
| PKS host | Low | Low to moderate | Low to moderate | Extensive tailoring options |
| Flash Slide host | Low | Low to moderate | Low to moderate | Good integration |
| Assured discovery | Moderate | Moderate | Moderate | Some learner engagement |
| Coupled simulation | Moderate | Moderate | Moderate to high | Can fully exploit simulation |

# MODEL-BASED INSTRUCTION

This chapter will deal with possibly the most universal kinds of instructional requirements associated with real world systems: those that address understanding how complex systems function, how they are operated, and why they behave and misbehave as they do. The discussion will consider methodologies for developing and delivering instruction that is closely coupled with the domain model.

## STRUCTURED EXERCISES FOR INCREASING AND ASSESSING PROFICIENCY

The methods described in Chapter 6 can deliver instructionally powerful demonstrations that may be critically important to conveying a sound technical understanding of system behavior, but they lack the capacity to manage instructional delivery and to assess learner proficiency. For these requirements, we employ a content development process that supports the instructional developer in assembling the content via direct manipulation of the simulation and delivers that content in a relatively structured manner involving similar item types.

In spite of the simple content data structure used, a wide range of skills and abilities can be addressed with this approach, including:
- familiarization of equipment panels;
- performance of complex procedures;
- understanding functions of internal system elements;
- predicting failure effects, and
- tracing signal flows.

The system architecture of the structured approach is shown in Figure 7-1. Via direct manipulation of the simulation, and entry of explanatory and prompting text, the instructional developer produces a set of instructional *items* which collectively constitute an *exercise* and one or more instructional delivery specifications that can be applied to any exercise. Both the exercise and the instructional delivery specifications are saved as reusable data files. Any one combination of exercise and instructional delivery specification forms a *lesson*, also saved as a data file.

The learner then interacts with the domain model, under the direction of the lesson. Depending upon the particular specifications for instructional delivery, a lesson can be presented in three possible modes: 1) a walk-through mode that presents the content that is to be learned, 2) a practice mode in which the learner performs the exercise with assistance and remediation as required, and 3) a test mode that assesses the individual's proficiency.

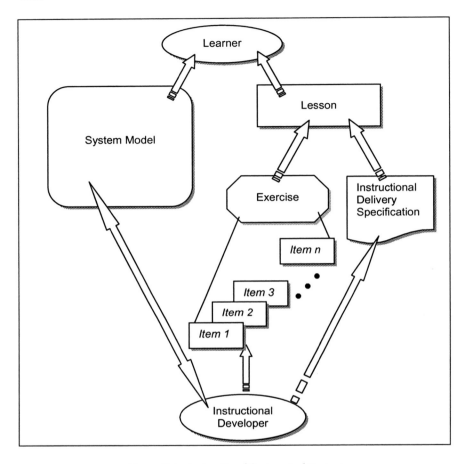

*Figure 7-1. Instructional System Architecture.*

*Creating a New Exercise*

New exercises are created in the Instructional Development System, a three screen user interface that can be used to produce many different kinds of simulation-based instructional exercises. The initial example application of this section will instruct the operation of the aircraft nose wheel steering system in Centering Mode, and a later section will elaborate on many of the other types of topics that may be addressed with this system.

*Exercise Setup.* A new exercise is set up on the first screen of the instructional development system, shown in Figure 7-2 as initially presented to the developer.

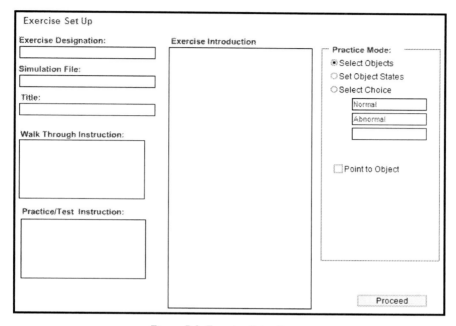

*Figure 7-2. Exercise Setup Screen.*

The entries in the left-hand column will provide:
- a designation of the exercise, which serves as its file name;
- a reference to the simulation file that will be active in the exercise;
- a title to be displayed when the unit is presented;
- instructional text to be provided in each item of the walk-through phase; and
- instructional text to be provided in each item of the practice and test phases.

The Introduction in the center will acquaint the student with the topic and the intent of the exercise. The section on the right establishes the conditions in which the practice phase is presented. The three radio buttons provide options for indicating whether the student will respond by selecting objects, by setting objects into particular states, or by making multiple choice selections. The text fields below the Select Choice button hold the labels of the multiple choice buttons, if any. The *Point to Object* check box indicates whether the instructional system should highlight objects in the model via a pointing hand, when they are mentioned in an item. The setting of this selection box allows some exercises to name an object but require the student to find it, while others will both name and highlight an object. An example of this screen after completion is shown in Figure 7-3.

117

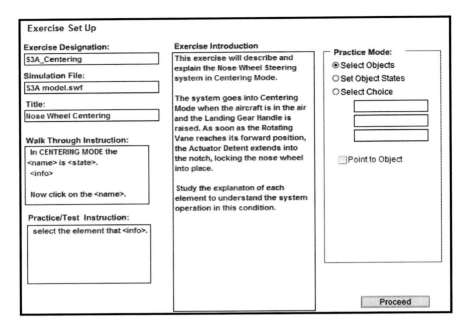

*Figure 7-3. A Completed Exercise Setup Screen.*

Here, the developer is establishing a simple exercise that will familiarize the student with the aircraft nose wheel steering system in Centering Mode via a series of items. In walk- through mode each item of instruction will highlight, name, and briefly explain the current state of an object in the functional model. In practice and test modes the student will be asked to locate elements from their functional descriptions.

The entries to the two instructional text fields serve as patterns for the instruction that will be presented in each item of the exercise. According to the pattern entered for the walk-through instruction, each item will display "In CENTERING MODE the", followed by the highlighted element's name (<name>) and state (<state>), followed by the instructional text entered for the item (<info>).

During instruction, the presentation system will fill in the pattern to create a complete sentence or paragraph for each item. Likewise, the text presented with each item in Practice or Test mode will start with "select the element that" followed by the functional description of the part (the automatic construction of the prompt prepends the term "First" or "Next" to each item, thus the phrase is not capitalized).

The developer has entered an Introduction that establishes the intent of the exercise as well as summarizing the system behaviors to be learned. Finally, the developer has left the *Select Objects* button in its default condition, to indicate that the student's response in practice and test items is to select objects and has left the

*Point to Object* in its unchecked condition, so that the system will not point to the correct object until the student has selected it.

*Model Initialization.* After completing the exercise setup, the developer sees the Model Initialization screen shown in Figure 7-4. The developer now manipulates the model to put it into the configuration in which it will first appear in the exercise. Depending upon the nature of the exercise, this initial configuration may persist throughout the exercise, or the system state may be changed any number of times thereafter as the exercise unfolds.

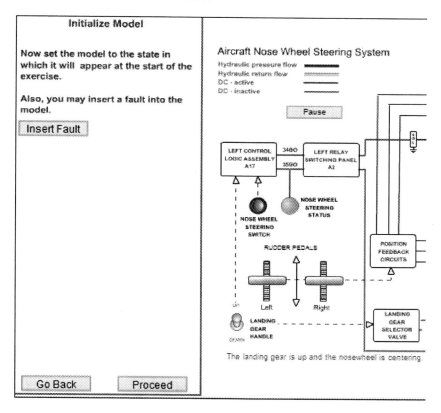

*Figure 7-4. Model Initialization Screen.*

In the example, the author has taken off and raised the landing gear, which drives the nose wheel to its centered and locked position. Now, all the object states in the model will correspond with the descriptions presented during the exercise.

Additionally, the developer may select *Insert Fault* then select the element to fail and any one of its fault modes. Exercises involving faults will be introduced in a later section and discussed in detail in Chapter 8.

*Item Creation.* After initializing the model, the developer sees the Item Specification screen shown in Figure 7-5, with which the exercise items are produced.

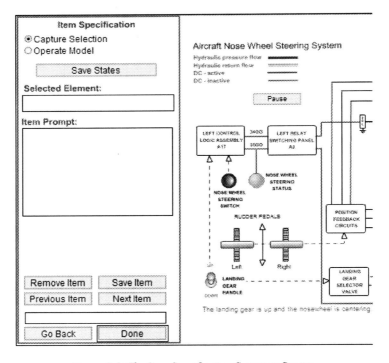

*Figure 7-5. The Item Specification Screen at Startup.*

If the developer needs to further manipulate the model prior to producing an item, he or she may select the *Operate Model* radio button, and then make any necessary changes before resuming object identification.

Now, for this particular exercise type, the developer selects an object, sees that object name and a hand pointing to the object, then enters a description of its function in the Centering mode. Figure 7-6 reflects the screen after identifying and describing the CENTERING SOLENOID VALVE.

The developer then selects *Save Item* and proceeds to produce the remaining items in the exercise in the same way. Selecting the *Done* button writes the data file, and all the information required to deliver the exercise is in place.

In this example the developer did not manipulate the model after initializing it, and he or she selected just one element per item. In other exercise types the developer might perform and explain a sequence of steps that change the model in significant ways and might also make multiple selections or actions that apply to a single item in the exercise. Examples of such applications will be given below.

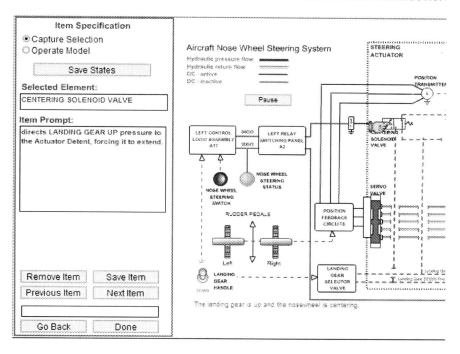

*Figure 7-6. A Completed Item Ready for Saving.*

## Chunking Content to Support Learning

Subject matter experts typically possess knowledge about the organization of the content that materially aids in recalling and understanding individual elements of information. For example, to a novice an aircraft cockpit might appear to be an overwhelming mass of knobs and dials, while the expert views that same interface in terms of functional groupings, each containing the panel elements that belong to the group. One group of elements might control and monitor propulsion, another set might deal with communications, and another might pertain to cabin environment. This chunking of information largely distinguishes an expert from a novice, and can materially aid learning if it is presented in an explicit manner.

Chunking is accomplished by presenting an explicit introduction prior to the elements that pertain to the description. This item is saved just as any other instructional item and is presented to assist the learner in forming meaningful structures of knowledge.

121

*Instructional Delivery*

Typically, lessons begin with the exercise introduction, followed by the relatively passive walk-through phase, followed by an active practice phase and possibly a test.

*Start Up.* At the start of an exercise, the learner sees the introduction to the lesson and the model, initialized as the author specified, as shown in Figure 7-7.

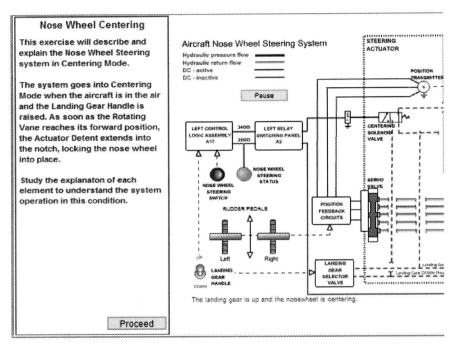

*Figure 7-7. Start of an Exercise.*

*Walk-through.* Upon selecting Proceed, the learner enters the walk-through phase, shown in Figure 7-8. The screen appears almost identical to the way it did when the author created the item, i.e., the object is named, described, and pointed out. The instructional text, however, has been expanded from the pattern provided in the exercise set up, i.e., the name and state of the selected element have been combined with the functional description to form a complete description of the element. In the first pass of this phase, the items are presented in the order in which they were created (Figure 7-8), and the learner selects each element discussed to move on the next. After completing one pass through all the items, the student may progress to the Practice phase or remain in the walk-through mode until ready to proceed.

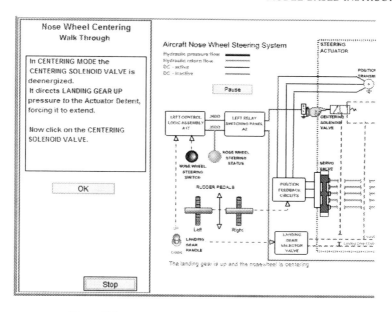

*Figure 7-8. An Item Presented in Walk-through Mode.*

*Practice Phase.* The practice phase, shown in Figure 7-9, prompts the learner to identify the objects from their functional descriptions only.

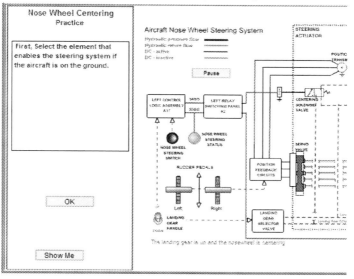

*Figure 7-9. An Item Presented in Practice Mode.*

123

In the practice phase, a correct response evokes a confirmation, while an incorrect one (Figure 7-10) evokes remediation in the form of an identification of the incorrectly chosen object and a repetition of the prompt. If the learner is unable to find the correct object, the Show Me button will reveal the correct element.

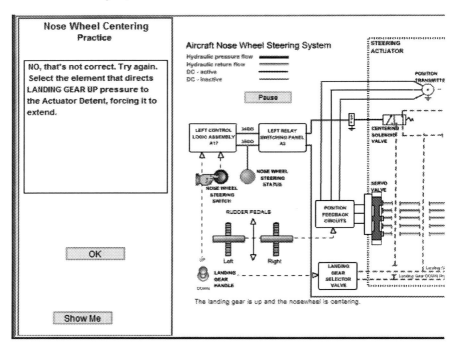

*Figure 7-10. Remediation of an Incorrect Object Identification.*

*Support of Multiple Choice Responses*

Suppose now we wish to exercise the student in making judgments about the normality of front panel indications using multiple choice responses. The set up for such an exercise, on a unit of a military EW system, is shown in Figure 7-11.

The walk-through instruction pattern is similar to that seen previously except that the correct answer (<choice>) is now worked into the instructional text. The prompt in each practice item asks the student whether the selected element is Normal or Abnormal and two corresponding buttons will appear with which to respond.

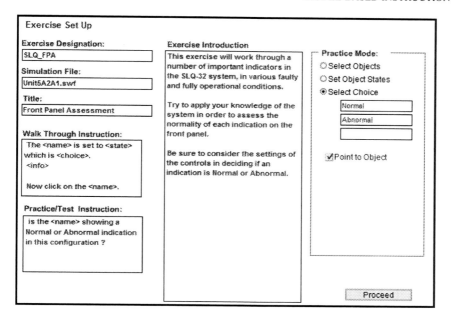

*Figure 7-11. Set up for a Front Panel Assessment Exercise.*

*Item Creation.* Figure 7-12 shows a multiple choice item ready to be saved.

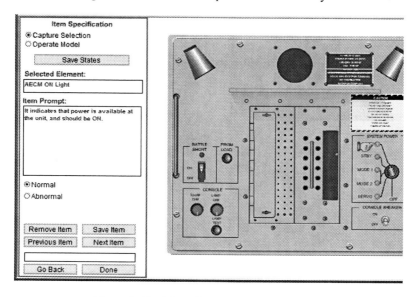

*Figure 7-12. A Completed Multiple Choice Item.*

125

*Instructional Delivery.*    Instruction in walk-through mode is shown in Figure 7-13, and Practice Mode is shown in Figure 7-14.

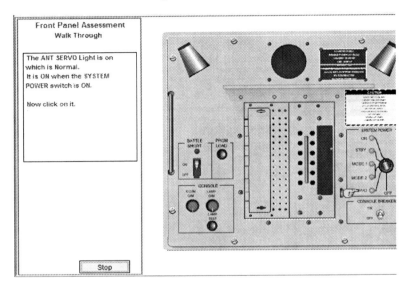

*Figure 7-13. A Front Panel Assessment Item in Walk-through Mode.*

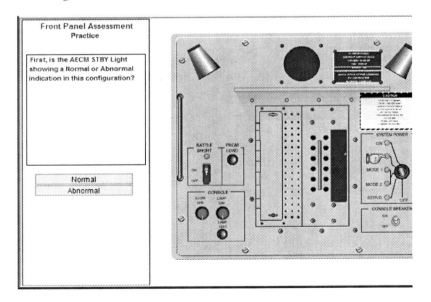

*Figure 7-14. A Front Panel Assessment Item in Practice Mode.*

*Instruction Involving Multiple Elements*

The previous examples have involved a single element discussed in each item. The first example addressed the function of each element in the aircraft steering system and the second dealt with the normality of each indication on a panel. Each item of these exercises was produced, in part, by selecting one element in the model or one multiple choice answer.

It is also possible, and highly useful, to create instruction in which a set of elements is identified by the developer and the student attempts to recreate that set or the states of the elements in that set. Suppose, for example, we wish to identify all the elements in a model that process a particular signal. The developer could create an item describing that condition, and then select all the elements that correspond to the description (multiple elements are captured by holding down the Shift key as they are selected).

In walk-through mode, the instructional system highlights all the elements in the list by setting each component to its highlighted state. In practice mode, the system displays an *OK* button and directs the student to select all the elements that correspond to the item description, and then select *OK*. When the OK button is selected, the instructional system compares the student's selection set to the correct set, and then generates remediation by first addressing omissions then commissions. When the student's selection set matches the stored set, the practice item is complete. In test mode, the student's selection set is simply compared to the correct one, and number of omissions and commissions is recorded.

A nearly identical situation obtains when the instruction is dealing with element states. If the exercise set up indicates that the student is to set object states, the system compares the states of the elements in the recorded set to those produced by the student. Thus, one can easily establish and save a total system configuration, and challenge the student to reproduce that configuration by manipulating the model, then selecting OK. A later section will outline some types of instruction in which sets of elements and their states are saved with an item.

We will now consider how the instructional delivery of exercises can be managed.

## MANAGING INSTRUCTIONAL DELIVERY

The manner in which an exercise is to be delivered is established in the Exercise Presentation Specification utility, shown in Figure 7-15. This routine allows the instructional developer to control such factors as the instructional modes in which an exercise is presented, the amount of assistance and remediation given, the time made available to complete the unit, whether items are given in a fixed or randomized order, and whether or not the student can operate the model during the exercise.

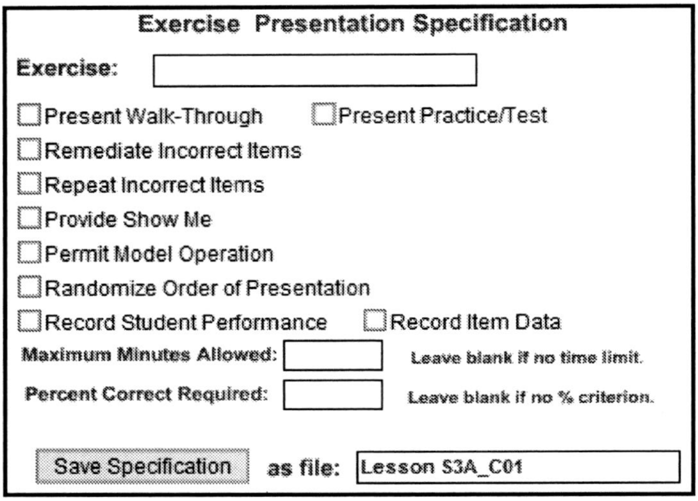

*Figure 7-15. Exercise Presentation Specification Screen.*

*Specifying a Practice Lesson*

Figure 7-16 specifies the delivery of exercise S3A_Centering, created in the previous example.

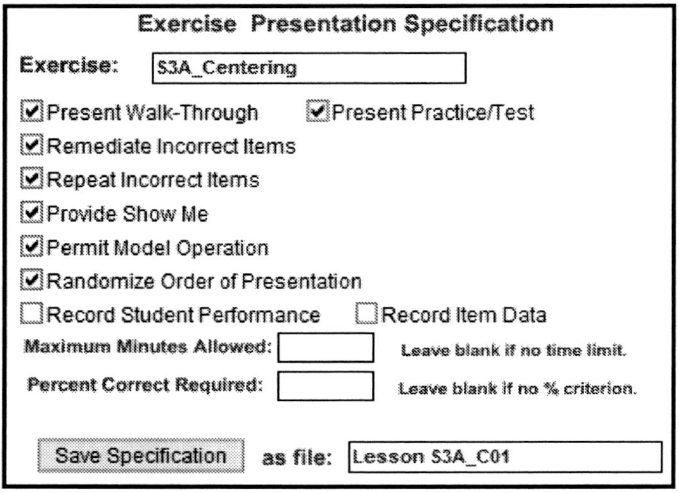

*Figure 7-16. An Exercise Delivered for Instruction and Practice.*

This particular specification establishes a practice lesson starting with a walk-through and providing full support in assisting the learner as needed. Furthermore, the sequence of item presentation will be randomized after the walk-through, the individual's performance will not be recorded, and no time or performance limits are to be enforced.

Notice that the specification for this lesson permits the student to operate the model in order to ascertain the behavior of an element or to confirm a belief about an element. This opportunity to learn by observation should not be confused with the discovery learning approach, in which the learner is tasked with formulating and conducting experiments to learn new concepts. The observations made in this well-controlled environment do not require the learner to manage his or her own learning regimen, and a student who does not choose to operate the model will still receive all the instructional content available in the exercise.

*Specifying a Test*

The same content, delivered as specified in Figure 7-17, produces a test for the record, with no assistance or remediation provided, and a fifteen minute time limit. When an exercise is administered as a test, the instructional delivery system asks for the student's name or ID at startup, and it converts the Show Me button into a Give Up button, so the student can declare an inability to make a response.

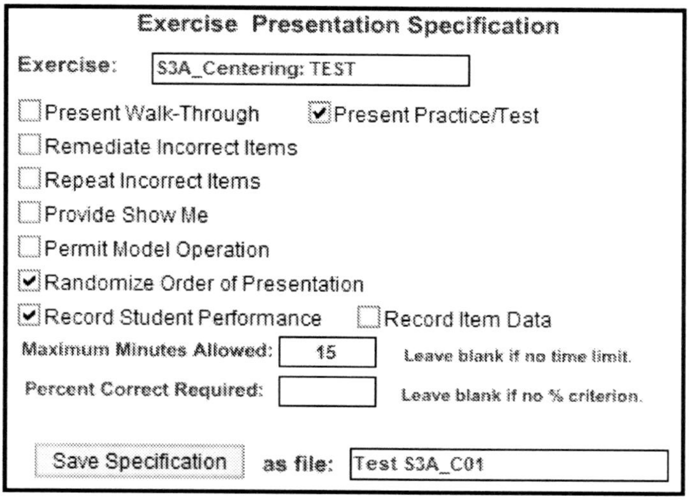

*Figure 7-17. An Exercise Delivered as a Test.*

The data written to file include number of items correct and incorrect, number of items on which the student gave up, and total time to complete. The option also exists to record student performance data by item, so that instructors can spot individual problems as well as general class difficulties.

## RANGE OF APPLICATIONS OF STRUCTURED METHODS

A rather wide variety of instructional topics can be addressed and instructional interactions can be implemented with the processes described above. The primary factors that determine the character of the instruction and the interactions are:
– the type of simulation used as the vehicle for the exercise, i.e., whether the model is a physical representation or a functional representation;
– the form of the textual prompts given; and
– whether the student response for an item in practice mode is to identify an object, to set an object state, to select a multiple choice answer, or to select multiple objects.
This section will briefly outline some of the possibilities.

### Front Panel Familiarization

A front panel familiarization exercise, as shown in Figure 7-18, deals with the abilities to identify and locate front panel elements by name and purpose.

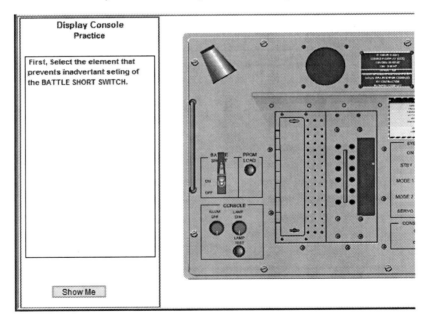

*Figure 7-18. A Front Panel Familiarization Exercise in Practice Mode.*

Obviously, finding named elements can be a trivial task for those elements that are clearly labeled in the model, however very little time is consumed passing through these elements, and the learner may benefit from the experience of locating them in the context of the less obvious system elements. A student's score in completing this exercise type reflects his or her ability to locate elements on the panel by name and to associate elements on the panel with descriptions of their purpose in the modeled system.

*Functional Familiarization*

As illustrated by the examples in the previous sections, this instruction type addresses the abilities to locate elements in a functional diagram and to identify elements from their functional descriptions. This exercise type has great potential for instructing how a complex system functions and for assessing the learner's understanding of that process.

*Procedures*

Exercises dealing with procedures demonstrate the required actions on the model and explain why those actions are performed and what those actions accomplish. A typical step in the walk-through phase is shown in Figure 7-19.

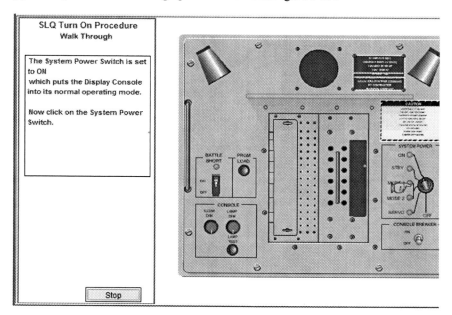

*Figure 7-19. Instructing a Procedure in Walk-Through Mode.*

*Practice and Test.* In general, two kinds of practice routines can be produced for any procedure: 1) one in which the student is shown the control to be set and is only required to learn the correct settings, and 2) one in which the student must both determine what control to set and what setting to make. For difficult procedures there may be considerable value in presenting the more guided exercise first, and progressing to the more realistic and challenging approach after the individual has successfully performed the procedure with guidance.

In Figure 7-20 a student is starting to practice the performance of a procedure under the former method. The unguided version of the procedure exercise is produced by simply changing the practice mode prompt to something like "Make the next setting" or "Perform the next action" and deselecting the *Point to Object* box in the set up screen.

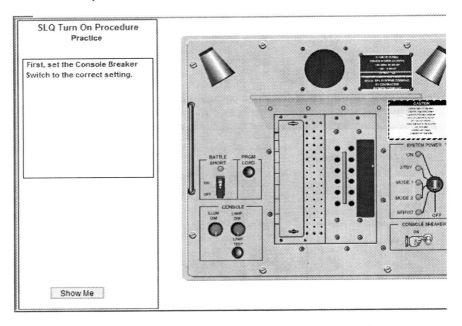

*Figure 7-20. A Guided Procedural Exercise in Practice Mode.*

## Complex Procedures

There are procedures that can be performed in so many different ways that it is extremely difficult to assess performance by examining the sequence of actions that was performed by the learner. While the methods for instructing procedures discussed in the previous section can effectively demonstrate one way of performing such a task, it may be unrealistic to expect and require that the student perform some complex tasks using the identical sequence of actions demonstrated.

One alternative for dealing with such tasks is to prepare one exercise presented in walk-through mode that demonstrates and explains one good way of performing the task and another exercise that deals only with assessment by examining the state of the model at the conclusion of the student's performance.

While even this approach may not always be possible, most complex tasks seem to have the character that there are certain critical objects in the model (and the real system) that assume certain particular states when a procedure is correctly performed. If this is the case, the instructional developer can perform the procedure in a correct way, then, as a practice mode exercise, select the critical object states that reflect the correct goal state. The instructional routine will then prompt the student to perform the task then select OK. At this point the set of element states produced by the student is compared to that captured and saved by the developer, and remediation or scoring follows, as appropriate.

*System Configurations*

Exercises that instruct setting systems into particular configurations are very similar to procedure exercises, except that the sequence of settings is unimportant. For a physical model, such as a front panel, the presentation of each item is identical to items in procedural exercises.

When applied to a functional model, the system configuration exercise addresses the particular states of normally unseen elements which are shown in the model. The walk-through phase of such instruction explains what state each element is in and why, and the practice mode requires that the student be able to recall or reconstruct that information. *In this case, the student clicks on the functional elements until they are in the correct states, since these elements are not traditional controls that are manipulated by mouse.* No modification of the model is required to support this option, since the instructional routine is capable of stepping any element through its states when selected in instructional modes[18].

Configuration exercises on functional models may require intensive study and thought by the student, in order to determine the condition of each of the internal elements, in the given mode of operation. For example, will the Servo Valve shown in Figure 7-21 move to its UP or DOWN position if the Right Rudder is pressed down? The answer is UP, but making this determination requires deep understanding of the system architecture and function (and possibly a deeper level of understanding than most maintainers actually require, but this complex system serves to demonstrate the possibilities).

---

[18] The instructional system simply sets the global variable userMode to a particular value, which is the name of a function in the instructional system that is notified when an element is selected. That function then steps the selected element to its next state (see Chapter 3).

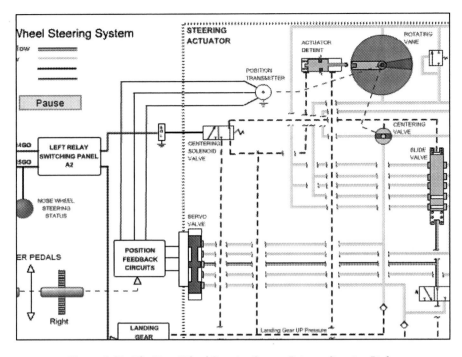

*Figure 7-21. The Nose Wheel Steering System Prior to Steering Right.*

*Practice and Test.* Two possible methods of supporting practice are possible here as well. In one, the student is permitted to operate the model to learn the correct answer, and in the second, this option is not available, and the student must mentally simulate the system operation.

*Fault Diagnosis Skills and Knowledge*

A number of lesson types can be produced with the structured method that address the skills and knowledge involved in conducting corrective maintenance. These sub skills include system state recognition (judging the normality of a set of indications), fault effect knowledge (predicting the impact of particular failures), and reasoning about possible causes of observed symptoms. These exercises are produced by specifying a particular fault to be inserted then interacting with the learner about the symptoms so produced and the possible courses of action that could be taken.

Instruction in applying these challenging abilities will be discussed in detail in the next chapter.

### THE STRUCTURED METHOD WITH CUSTOMIZED ITEMS

All of the structured exercises discussed above involve consistent kinds of items throughout the exercise. Whether the student was to select an object, produce a configuration, or answer a multiple choice question, the type of item and the kind of response in each item within any one exercise was consistent.

There are also situations in which one would like to produce an exercise consisting of a mixture of item types. For example, we might wish to explain a control, and then demonstrate a procedure involving that control, then present some multiple choice items, and conclude by setting the control to different settings to correspond with various described system uses. In this case, the developer would require complete control of the form of the exercise items, and there would not be a formal distinction between walk-through mode and practice mode. Instead, the exercise would be presented exactly as the developer creates it. This capability has been provided in the structured Instructional Development system as well.

*Creating Instruction with Customized Element Types*

To initiate development of an exercise consisting of customized element types, the instructional developer just enters an Introduction on the Exercise Set Up screen, leaving the remaining fields blank, as shown in Figure 7-22 (the default selection of the Select Objects button is ignored by the instructional system in this case).

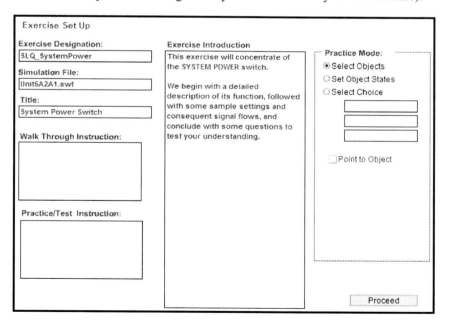

*Figure 7-22. Exercise Set Up for Custom Item Specification.*

Now, after initializing the model, the Item Specification screen appears as usual, but it now displays a *Set Up Item* button as shown here.

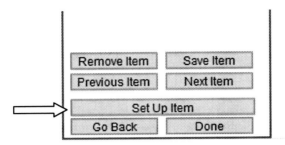

*Figure 7-23. Exercise Set Up for Custom Item Specification.*

When this button is selected, a new dialog box shown in Figure 7-24 appears, permitting the developer to establish the conditions of the current item.

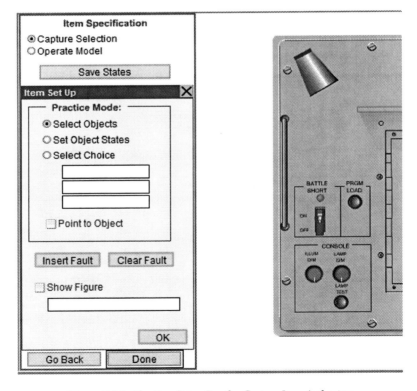

*Figure 7-24. The Item Setup Box for Custom Item Authoring.*

The entries made in this box now apply to the current item and all succeeding items, until a new set of entries is made. Thus, the developer can enter custom setup specifications for each item, or change the set up from time to time, as required.

After setting up an item, and dismissing the Item Set Up box, the developer creates the item as before by entering the textual content and manipulating the model, making object selections, or selecting the correct multiple choice.

*Specifying the Model or Figure to Present in an Item*

Also on the Item Set Up box of Figure 7-24 is an option, Show Figure, with which the developer may call up any existing graphical file (.jpg) or model file (.swf) for the current item. If a figure is specified, it will appear in place of the current figure or model as shown in Figure 7-25. This feature permits the developer to move through different levels of a complex, multi-screen model within an exercise, as when instructing such topics as signal flow, or supporting the instruction with associated technical drawings.

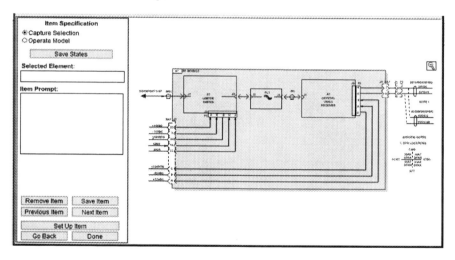

*Figure 7-25. A Figure Displayed for an Instructional Item.*

The next chapter will present examples of instruction of diagnostic skills and knowledge using the structured method with customized item types.

# INSTRUCTING FAULT DIAGNOSIS

Troubleshooting training typically follows the simple scheme shown here, starting with an instructional phase in the classroom centering on how the target system functions and behaves normally and terminating with a shorter practice phase on the real equipment.

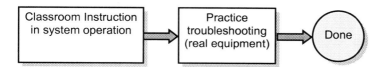

While this compartmentalized approach may ease the difficulty of managing hands-on practice in a highly complex and potentially dangerous environment, it provides little opportunity to address questions that arise during the troubleshooting phase, and it likely renders the initial instruction less effective and memorable.

With the availability of a model of the target system, however, troubleshooting practice can be integrated into the initial instructional phase, so that faults can be worked early in the course, either individually or as a class, while avoiding the complexity and dangers associated with operating on the real system. As shown here, the final hands-on phase can still be provided, but we would expect that experience to be considerably more productive than with the prior approach.

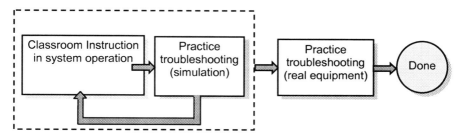

Of course, this design is predicated on the expectation that the same total course time can be maintained as a result of increased efficacy of the instruction and possibly some reduction in time practicing on the real equipment. This chapter will consider approaches 1) for presenting simulation-based instruction in fault diagnosis in this manner, and 2) for guiding learners as they practice applying their knowledge within diagnostic exercises.

## DOMAIN-INDEPENDENT INSTRUCTION OF FAULT DIAGNOSIS

The process of fault diagnosis has been cast in a number of different ways in an effort to arrive at some domain-independent structure that can be provided to novice maintainers to guide their performance. One such characterization, a five-step breakdown, is as follows:

1) system state recognition (determine the normality of the system);
2) fault localization (identify the faulty major unit or module);
3) fault isolation (identify the faulty replaceable unit);
4) repair/replace, and
5) confirm operation (repeat system state recognition)

This idealized list is intended to present the diagnostic process in a chronological fashion, starting with the broadest assessment of the system state and progressing to an identification of a particular fault, followed by actions to restore the system and then verify the efficacy of the work.

The utility of instructing this or any other such generic description is somewhat questionable, particularly since fault diagnosis is rarely so cleanly compartmentalized. For example, in some cases the faulty module or unit only becomes known when the faulty element is identified. And in other cases, a good troubleshooter might make a simple replacement as a diagnostic measure, rather than conducting further lengthy and possibly error-prone testing[19].

Some early research (Wiederholt, Norton, Johnson, & Browning, 1992; Johnson, Norton, Duncan, & Hunt, 1998) explored the utility of instructing the general process of fault diagnosis itself, rather than as an inseparable part of a specific target system, with limited results. Nevertheless, novices probably can benefit greatly from an introduction to fault diagnosis that emphasizes the needs to 1) tap into easily obtained information prior to making complex and time-consuming readings; 2) consider the possibility that some test results could be invalid due to human error, thus one should repeat and independently confirm readings if possible; and 3) defer replacement until the accumulated symptom information points strongly to a single suspected element, unless a suspected element is extremely easy and safe to swap.

## DOMAIN SPECIFIC INSTRUCTION OF FAULT DIAGNOSIS

The remainder of this chapter will deal with instruction of fault diagnosis within the context of a specific target system but in terms of generalized diagnostic abilities and processes. Toward those ends, we will describe two complementary

---

[19] The military rightly cautions trainees not to "Easter egg", i.e., mindlessly replace elements until the system is operational, but this does not mean that substitution is not sometimes a highly effective action.

approaches for addressing the skills and knowledge involved in performing diagnostic processes, the first of which employs the structured methods described in the previous chapter to present and apply the domain knowledge required to support diagnostic activity, and the second dealing with supporting the performance of complete diagnostic activity via automated expert guidance.

## PART TASK INSTRUCTION OF DIAGNOSTIC SKILLS AND KNOWLEDGE

From a performance viewpoint, the major components of diagnostic activity are these:
- assessing the normality of the target system (system state recognition);
- determining the effects that various faults would produce;
- identifying the possible causes of observed abnormalities and the implications of normal test results; and
- selecting a test that has high potential for discriminating among the current set of suspected system elements.

All of these abilities demand thorough knowledge of the inner workings of the system under test, and the first three can be practiced and tested within the structured method described in the previous chapter provided that the objects in the model specify their behavior in each fault mode, as described in Chapter 3.

The fourth diagnostic ability, test selection, presents complications that make this performance component a poor candidate for instruction via the structured method, and is instead directly addressed via the whole-task instruction method described in the second part of this chapter.

*Fault Insertion*

Most of the diagnostic training exercises are conducted with a fault inserted into the model, and the process for selecting faults demonstrates one use of the *type* value assigned to each object of a model. When the developer selects the Insert Fault button, the development system brings up the following dialog box and loads the upper drop-down selection box with the names of the all the failable elements in the model, sorted alphabetically.

When a particular RU is selected, the development system loads the lower box with all the faults for that RU, and the developer selects one, as shown here.

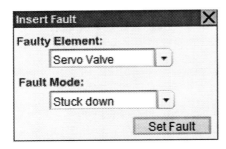

Now when the exercise runs, or the next item is presented, the specified fault will be introduced into the model, and the model will behave as the real system would in that condition.

In some of the exercises described below, the learner is advised that a particular fault has been introduced into the model so that the effects of that known fault can be considered. In other exercises, a fault is introduced "silently", i.e., the learner is only advised that a fault may be present, but the identity of that fault is not revealed until the exercise has presented all of the instructional items.

### System State Recognition

One of the critical functions of system operators and maintainers is recognizing when a system is fully operational and when it is in need of corrective maintenance. This ability requires that the individual thoroughly understand the underlying functionality of the system as well as the possible configurations into which it might be placed, including front panel settings as well as ancillary cabling and other connections. Novice technicians sometimes judge a normal indication to be abnormal, not recognizing that the indication is a proper consequence of the current system configuration. Similarly, they may fail to detect an abnormality that should initiate a maintenance action.

Two similar exercise types provide concentrated instruction and practice in performing system state recognition: 1) a guided exercise that assists the learner in setting the system to its various operational modes as normality judgments are made, and 2) an unguided exercise that corresponds more closely to the conditions on the job.

### Guided System State Recognition

In the guided exercise type, a fault is introduced into the model, and the learner is shown the abnormalities that result in various configurations. At the option of the instructional developer, the fault introduced may or may not be identified to the

142

learner. In walk-through mode the learner can observe and study the abnormalities pointed out. In practice mode, shown in Figure *8*-1, the learner attempts to identify the abnormalities produced by the fault.

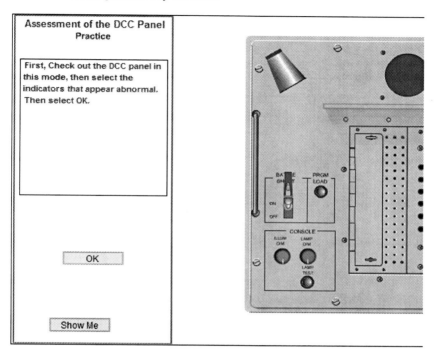

*Figure 8-1. System State Recognition Drill in Practice Mode.*

By randomizing the order in which faults are introduced and items are presented, the developer assures that the learner must reason about the indications rather than memorizing the abnormalities from the walk-through. Since the instructional system executes all of the system setups, however, the learner is spared this responsibility, and may instead concentrate on making the normality judgments.

*Unguided System State Recognition.* In the unguided exercise type, the learner checks out the system by placing it in its various configurations and identifying any abnormalities detected. If no abnormalities are claimed, but a fault is indeed inserted, then the system points out those abnormalities, and similarly the system corrects any incorrect judgments of abnormality.

*Fault Effects*

In this very challenging lesson type, a named fault is introduced in practice mode, and the abnormalities produced by that fault in various modes of operation are shown. A separate lesson presents the model in a fault-free condition, and the learner is challenged to identify what indicators would be abnormal if the named fault were indeed present. This kind of reasoning is exactly that which allows a diagnostician to eliminate certain elements from suspicion when normal test results are obtained. Figure 8-2 shows the practice mode of such an exercise in progress.

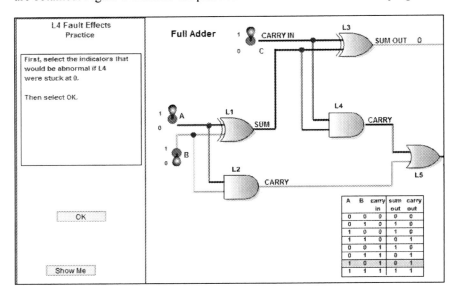

*Figure 8-2. Fault Effect Exercise in Practice Mode.*

*Possible Cause*

In this lesson type, a different fault is introduced silently into the model for each item. In walk-through mode, the instructional system identifies all the elements which, if faulty, could produce the symptoms seen. Note that the actual fault that is producing the abnormal symptoms is unimportant and never identified, since it serves merely to produce a symptom complex that may be shared by multiple possible faults. In practice mode, conducted with randomized items, the student works to identify those system elements which could produce the symptoms seen as a result of their failure.

This exercise type addresses the student's ability to interpret both normal and abnormal symptoms in terms of possible causes. Any element omitted from the correct set of possibilities is one which the student incorrectly believes does not affect the abnormal indicator(s). Any element incorrectly included in the set of possible causes is one which the student believes affects the abnormal indicator(s) when it does not. Figure 8-3 illustrates such an exercise in progress during the practice phase.

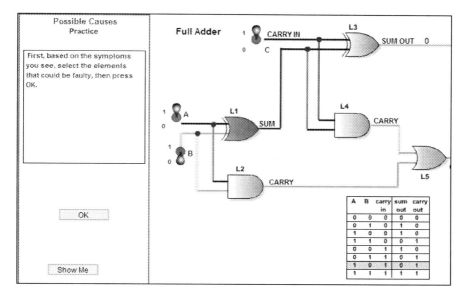

*Figure 8-3. Possible Cause Exercise in Progress.*

Here, the student has been directed to study the Full Adder circuit in a particular mode of operation and possible fault condition, and to indicate, based on the outputs, which of the system elements could produce the symptoms shown. In this case, L4 has been failed to produce a 0 output regardless of its inputs.

When the learner selects an element, the instructional system toggles its display between highlighted and not highlighted. In the figure, the student has (incorrectly) selected element L1 which now appears highlighted. Upon selecting OK, the student sees the correct elements highlighted and would thus learn that L1 cannot produce the symptoms shown (L1 stuck at 0 would produce an abnormality at the SUM OUT output as well).

Note that in this particular example, a truth table is provided in the lower right corner to assist the learner in determining the normality of the outputs. Thus, the student can determine by simple examination the normality of the two outputs, SUM OUT and CARRY OUT. A considerably more difficult exercise results by omitting the truth table.

## INTELLIGENT GUIDANCE OF TROUBLESHOOTING PRACTICE

Following successful completion of the part-task lessons described above, for any particular target system, the student would be prepared to begin practicing complete troubleshooting exercises in which faults are introduced into the model and the student performs diagnostic actions to identify and rectify them. This transition from accomplishing highly structured subtasks to managing and performing a complete diagnostic performance represents a formidable transition, however, and the guided troubleshooting method described in this section is designed to ease that learning process.

Experience shows that learners cannot effectively use simulations alone to practice fault diagnosis, since they often become stumped, and they typically require guidance to work through such impasses. Thus, the instructional method discussed here is to assist the learner in assessing symptom information seen, in making inferences about possible causes of those symptoms, and in identifying tests to perform to further discriminate among current fault hypotheses.

The system we have developed to carry out this guidance function is DIAG (Diagnostic Instruction and Guidance) (Towne, 1994, 1997a, 1998b, 2003). DIAG was developed to provide the support that allows conscientious learners to effectively practice fault diagnosis in a simulation environment. Students wishing to simply complete practice problems by exploiting the support features rather than thinking for themselves may do so, however the performance records captured by DIAG would clearly indicate that such individuals were simply "gaming" the system.

This section will describe the use of DIAG in supporting individualized practice of simulated faults, all in the context of the Full Adder model. While this subject is atypical in that it is by far the simplest DIAG application that has been made, it is one that is easy to follow since its functionality is totally apparent in the graphical model.

*System Overview*

DIAG is a stand-alone system that can administer exercises and support individualized practice on faults introduced into any simulation developed using the design presented in this volume. After a model is produced, a process within DIAG is executed that analyzes the effects that faults produce in the operation of the model. The data generated by this analysis represent DIAG's knowledge of the effects of faults in the system, and they permit it to interact intelligently with students as they work through practice problems. Thus, no traditional instructional authoring is involved, and additionally *no expert system need be developed*.

During guided practice, DIAG is available to assist in evaluating possible tests to perform, interpreting test results, and maintaining a set of possible failure hypotheses, all within the context of a particular system model and the tests the individual performs.

*Research Basis of DIAG Diagnostic Reasoning Process*

The diagnostic reasoning process within DIAG was originally developed as part of an effort to predict corrective maintenance workloads resulting from particular system designs (Towne & Johnson, 1987). After extensive analysis of captured diagnostic strategies, we produced a process that closely resembled the testing sequences of qualified technicians in resolving various faults in real systems.

The model of diagnostic reasoning, originally termed PROFILE, was produced by analyzing the detailed performances from two studies:
- 48 Navy electronics instructors, each working 8 faults in a computer system and
- 29 college students, each working 6 faults in a logical network.

The validity test involved generating PROFILE diagnostic strategies on 8 faults in a transmitter/receiver system, then collecting detailed data from 10 Navy instructors working those same faults. Since different experts carry out somewhat differing testing regimens, the test of validity investigated whether or not the artificially produced testing sequences could be distinguished from those produced by human technicians working the same faults, that is, application of the Turing test (Turing, 1950).

The two most pertinent findings were: 1) based on test selections and time to solution, the PROFILE solutions were essentially indistinguishable from those of the instructors, and 2) the performance of the less proficient technicians could be accurately projected by degrading the accuracy of the fault effect data used by the model, but not by degrading the rationality of the strategy rules. In other words, there was strong evidence that variation in individual diagnostic ability was a function of their system knowledge rather than in their generic diagnostic strategies.

*Development System*

Upon completing a system model the developer employs the selection box shown here to produce the necessary data to support intelligent diagnostic support.

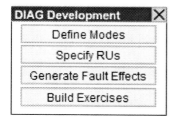

*Define Modes.* Complex systems can exist in an immense number of possible configurations, thus it is necessary to specify a reasonable number of valid operating modes in which DIAG guidance will be provided. The developer uses the

147

Mode Specification dialog box shown in Figure 8-4 to makes the settings in the model corresponding with each defined mode.

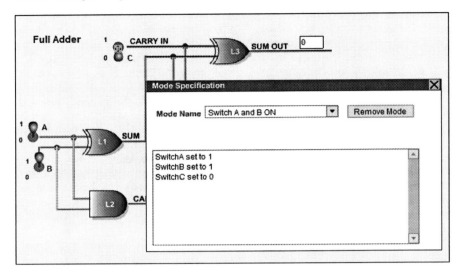

*Figure 8-4. Defining an Operating Mode in DIAG.*

*Specify RUs.* In order to make effective diagnostic decisions, DIAG requires two additional pieces of information about each Replaceable Unit (RU): 1) the approximate time to replace or fix it, and 2) its approximate reliability, *compared to the other RUs in the system.* Upon selecting *Specify RUs*, the developer uses the dialog box shown in Figure 8-5 to enter these data.

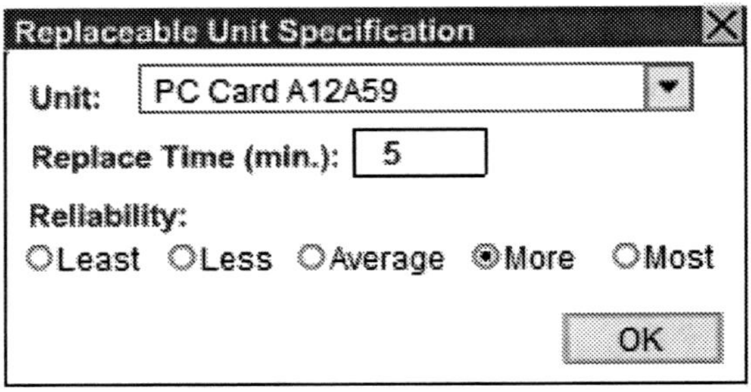

*Figure 8-5. Replaceable Unit Specification.*

The relative reliability assignments are used only to initially rank-order the RUs according to their level of suspicion, thus very subjective values suffice. The following table provides suggested reliability values for some types of failures.

*Table 8-1. Suggested Relative Reliability Assignments.*

| Failure Type | Reliability |
|---|---|
| Digital element | Most |
| Hydraulic actuator | More |
| Digital circuit | More |
| Analog circuit | Average |
| Electro-hydraulic part (e.g., servo valve) | Average |
| Switch or control | Less |
| Electro-mechanical part (e.g., relay) to function | Less |
| Mechanical element (e.g., interlock) to function | Less |
| Connector or plug, failed open | Least |
| Fuse or circuit breaker | Least |

*Generate Fault Effect Data.* The third step in producing DIAG instruction is to command DIAG to analyze the effects of all the faults that it can simulate in all the modes that have been specified. When the developer selects *Generate Fault Effects*, DIAG records the readings at all indicators in all modes under the no-fault condition, then inserts each fault into the system model and records the indications produced in each mode. The process to generate the raw fault effect data is as suggested by this pseudo-code:

```
for each operating mode:
        for each Replaceable Unit (RU):
                for each fault mode in the current RU, including no-fault:
                        clear previous fault
                        set fault mode of current RU to current fault mode
                        place model in current operating mode
                        record readings at all indicators
                end
        end
end
```

In order to make realistic suspicion updates, however, we found in the initial studies that the artificial reasoning needs to operate upon a less crisp representation of symptom information than the raw symptom data. To be both understandable to the learner and reasonably natural, DIAG automatically converts the raw symptom data file to a *fuzzy* form that is also far more compact than the original. For excellent discussions of fuzzy data and fuzzy reasoning, see Kosko, 1993 and Zadeh, 1992.

The process of producing the fuzzy fault effect data is shown in Figure 8-6. The developer only selects the Generate Fault Effects button, and the fault analysis functions within DIAG do the rest, including the conversion of the raw symptom data to the fuzzy form.

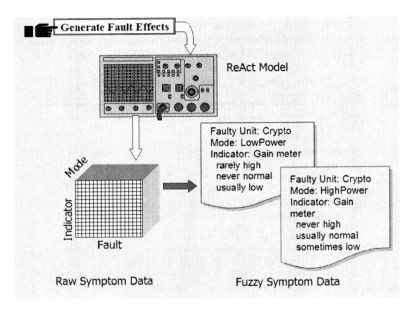

*Figure 8-6. Automatic Generation of Fuzzy Symptom Data.*

In the raw symptom data every fault mode of every RU carries a reading for every indicator in every defined mode, leading to a large data bank, mostly representing normal indications. After the data are made fuzzy, however, each RU fault mode carries just one assignment for each possible outcome of the indicator, in the particular mode, with values as shown in Table 8-2.

*Table 8-2. Fuzzy Symptom Likelihood Values.*

| Value Assigned | Likelihood | Ratio of Faults (Approx) |
|---|---|---|
| 1 | always | 1 |
| 2 | usually | .9 |
| 3 | very often | .75 |
| 4 | often as not | .5 |
| 5 | sometimes | .25 |
| 6 | rarely | .1 |
| 7 | never | 0 |

For example, if a circuit board has ten fault modes defined, then the fuzzy symptom data describing the impact of fault in that board upon a particular two-state indicator might simply be [2, 6], signifying that *usually* (value 2) faults in the board produce symptom 1, and *rarely* (value 6) faults produce symptom 2, where symptom 1 is reserved for normal, i.e., no impact, and symptom 2 is whatever the abnormal reading for that indicator happens to be. If our example indicator is a two-state light, then symptom 1 is normal, say ON, and symptom 2 is OFF.

It is important to understand that *working on this fuzzy form of symptom information does not cause loss of information.* The data still reflect rare and unlikely relationships as well as frequent ones, but now DIAG can present remarks to the learner such as:

| This result is not likely to be caused by a fault in the Power Amplifier. |
|---|

While no assumptions or claims are made that the fuzzy form of the symptom data corresponds to the way in which an experienced technician stores or represents such system knowledge, these data represent DIAG's experiential knowledge of the particular model's behavior in a large number of failure conditions, and they permit it to reason about observed symptoms in a manner that closely resembles experimentally observed human performance and to explicate that reasoning in a comprehensible fashion.

*Build Exercises.* The final step in creating the data for diagnostic support is to build a number of training exercises using the dialog box shown in Figure 8-7.

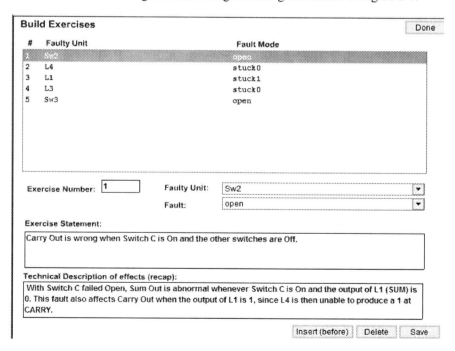

*Figure 8-7. Specifying DIAG Exercises.*

151

For each new exercise, the developer 1) enters an ordinal exercise number, 2) selects a unit to fail, 3) selects a fault mode for the faulty unit, 4) enters a short statement to be given the student prior to the problem, and 5) enters a technical description, or recap, of the fault to be presented to the student after the exercise is completed.

Exercises of very different levels of difficulty can be produced for the same fault simply by crafting the Exercise Statement to be helpful or not. In some cases the statement might provide a useful description of the problem, as if a skilled operator had reported the problem, but in other cases the statement can be vague or even misleading[20], to correspond with real field conditions.

## The Diagnostic Process

As noted above, at the start of each diagnostic exercise DIAG rank orders the RUs according to their relative reliability, forming the initial ranking of suspicion about the elements. Then, as the student performs tests on the model, DIAG silently processes the symptom information produced by the student's actions to update its suspicions about various fault hypotheses. Thus, at any juncture, DIAG stands ready to interact with the student concerning what elements are logical suspects, why that is so, and what the learner should do next to further home in on the fault.

## Updating Suspicions

For those interested in all the inner workings of DIAG's diagnostic reasoning, we now look briefly at its method for processing symptom information to update its suspicions. We will consider the simplest possible case, in which there are two possibly faulty RUs, RU1 and RU2, currently suspected equally, and the student obtains a reading at a two-state indicator. Suppose, further, that the fuzzy symptom data for RU1 and RU2 for some mode are as follows:

RU1: [3, 5]
RU2: [6, 2]

That is, 1) the majority (about three-fourths) of faults in RU1 do not affect the indicator, but some faults (about a quarter) do produce an abnormality, and 2) almost all of the faults in RU2 impact the indicator adversely.

Now, suppose the student throws a switch that puts the model into this particular mode, and the indicator shows an abnormal symptom. How shall we update our suspicions? The suspicion updating process within DIAG is an application of Bayes' theorem, which states that:

$Pr(A|B) = Pr(B|A) Pr(A) / Pr(B)$

---

[20] If misleading problem reports are to be given, the student should be advised of this possibility, to prevent a loss of trust in the training system.

If we designate A as the hypothesis that RU1 is faulty, and B as the observation of an abnormal reading at the indicator, then the terms in Bayes' theorem are as follows:

Pr(A|B) is the conditional probability that RU1 is failed, given that we
    have observed an abnormality at the indicator;

Pr(B|A) is the conditional probability of an abnormal reading at the
    indicator given that RU1 has failed;

Pr(A) is the prior[21] probability that RU1 is failed; and

Pr(B) is the prior probability that RU2 is failed.

Here, Pr(A) and Pr(B) are both about 0.5, and, applying the percentages from Table 8-2 above, Pr(B|A) is found to be about 0.25, thus

$$Pr(A|B) = 0.25 \times 0.5 / 0.5 = 0.25$$

So, the abnormal symptom causes us to significantly reduce our suspicion that RU1 has failed, and to increase our suspicion of RU2. *Note that the reassessment of suspicion can be conveyed to the learner without ever dealing with this quantitative process.* When called upon to give an expert's inference regarding the abnormal reading, DIAG uses the fuzzy quantifiers (e.g., *usually*, *rarely*, etc.) to reflect the strength of the conclusions that may be drawn.

*Exercise Administration*

The DIAG user interface provides a number of user-selectable functions that allow the student to observe known faults, start and stop exercises, make replacements of suspected elements, and, most importantly, confer with DIAG about an ongoing exercise. For maximum realism, DIAG exercises only end when the student has corrected the fault and declares the system restored (except for the *Stop* option which aborts an ongoing exercise).

The set of administrative functions, presented as a row of buttons across the bottom of the screen, provide these functions:
– See Instructions
– Insert ( or Remove) Fault
– Begin (or End) Exercise
– Replace Unit
– Consult
– Stop

The *See Instructions* option displays domain-independent meta-instruction to learners in the use of DIAG. This familiarizes the user with the intent and use of DIAG and the options for requesting guidance.

---

[21] That is, prior to the test, also termed *a priori*.

Except when an exercise is in progress the learner may select *Insert Fault* then choose a fault of interest and operate the model to observe the fault's effects. This fault is then removed with *Remove Fault*.

The student initiates exercises by choosing *Begin Exercise* and then selecting from a list of exercises, described by their level of difficulty or by any other useful description that does not reveal the identify of the fault. This method of problem selection permits instructors to assign certain exercises to be worked that will be appropriate to the progress of the individuals. The student selects *End Exercise* when he or she believes the system is operating correctly. The *Stop* option is used to terminate an exercise regardless of its status.

*Replace Unit* is used to call for a replacement of a particular suspected element. If the selected RU is the one currently failed in the model, DIAG removes the fault.

*Within-Exercise Consultations*

As the student performs tests within an exercise, DIAG silently assesses the symptoms produced and reasons about the possible fault just as an expert would. At any time, then, the student can call upon DIAG's Consult options, shown here, to compare suspicions, inquire about symptom implications, or get direction.

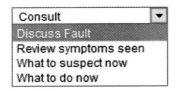

*Discuss Fault.* The Discuss Fault consultation type provides two alternate types of information about any selected fault: 1) the indicators affected by the fault, in each mode, and 2) the possibility that the selected fault could produce the symptoms already observed in the exercise. Thus, the first option is independent of the leaner's performance, while the second option relates the symptoms seen to the selected fault.

In Figure 8-8, the learner has selected the first option, and DIAG is displaying the indicators that the selected fault (L2 stuck at 0) affect and the modes in which those effects occur. If the student were suspecting the fault to be L2 stuck at 0, he or she could utilize this information to partially confirm or possibly deny that hypothesis. If, for example, the student had seen a normal *carryOut* indication with all three switches on, then he or she would learn from this that L2 could not be stuck at 0.

Discuss Fault
Fault
L1 failed stuck0
L1 failed stuck1
L1 failed stuckIn1
L1 failed stuckIn2
L2 failed stuck0
L2 failed stuck1
L2 failed stuckIn1
L2 failed stuckIn2
L3 failed stuck0
Select a fault from list above, then select the information you want below.
Fault Discussion
Summarize the fault's effects
Discuss fault's effects on tests performed
The fault L2 stuck0 affects these indicators:
carryOut
in mode All ON
in mode Sw A and B ON

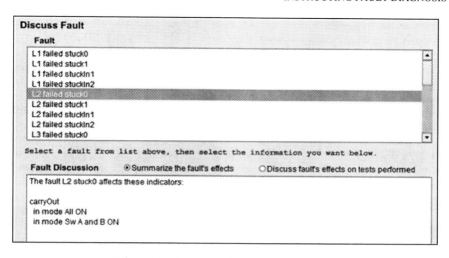

*Figure 8-8. Discuss Fault Consultation in DIAG.*

Review Symptoms Seen. This support function (Figure 8-9) lists the symptoms that have been displayed and the inferences that could be drawn from any one.

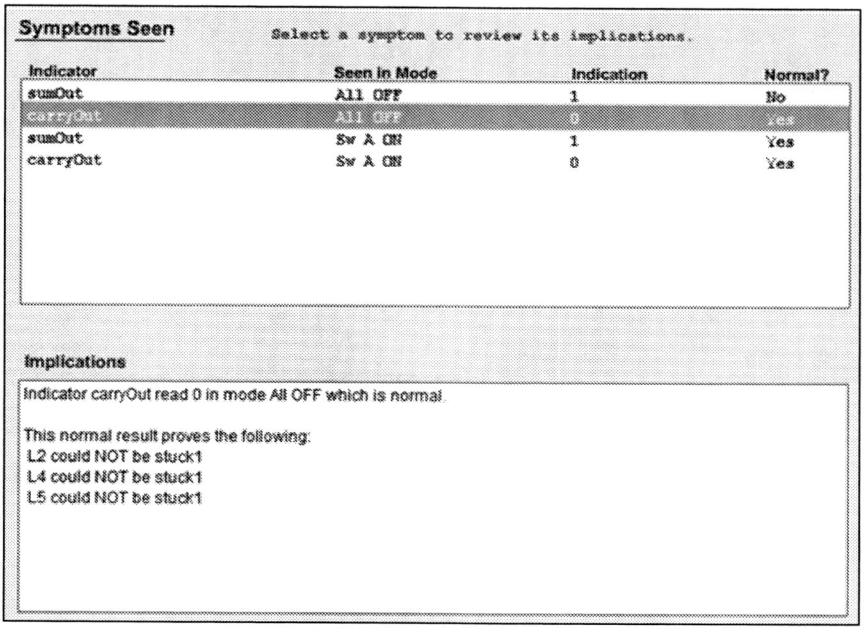

Symptoms Seen
Select a symptom to review its implications.
Indicator
Seen in Mode
Indication
Normal?
sumOut
All OFF
1
No
carryOut
All OFF
0
Yes
sumOut
Sw A ON
1
Yes
carryOut
Sw A ON
0
Yes
Implications
Indicator carryOut read 0 in mode All OFF which is normal.
This normal result proves the following:
L2 could NOT be stuck1
L4 could NOT be stuck1
L5 could NOT be stuck1

*Figure 8-9. Review Symptoms Seen Consultation in DIAG.*

This also serves to present symptoms that the student may have overlooked and to interpret the normality and implications of each.

In the figure, the student has selected the second significant symptom -- a normal indication of the carryOut indicator in the ALL OFF mode -- and DIAG has listed three fault hypotheses that this normal result eliminates. For example, an expert would know that the L2 element could not be stuck at 1 output, since this fault would produce an abnormality at the carryOut indicator, in the ALL OFF mode, and that is not the result that was seen.

*What to Suspect Now.* When this guidance type is selected, as shown below, DIAG lists the faults (RUs in particular fault modes) it most suspects, based on the symptoms that the user has seen in the exercise, and it lists the symptoms that cause DIAG to hold those suspicions.

In this example, just one symptom has reduced the suspected elements down to the three listed. Thus, there are only three RUs -- L1, L3, and SwitchA -- that could fail in a way that would produce an output of 1 at the sumOut indicator when all switches are off.

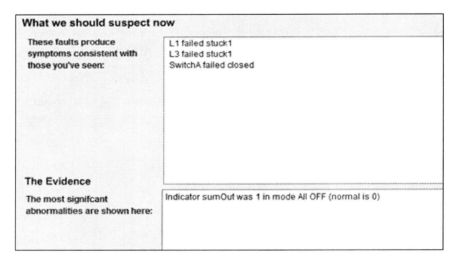

*Figure 8-10. Example DIAG Summary of Current Suspects.*

*What to Do Now.* When this guidance type is requested, DIAG executes its test-selection function to identify the best test to perform next, in light of the symptoms the learner has already seen, as shown here.

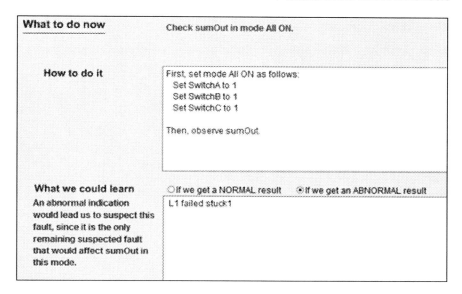

| What to do now | Check sumOut in mode All ON. |
|---|---|
| **How to do it** | First, set mode All ON as follows:<br>Set SwitchA to 1<br>Set SwitchB to 1<br>Set SwitchC to 1<br><br>Then, observe sumOut. |
| **What we could learn**<br>An abnormal indication would lead us to suspect this fault, since it is the only remaining suspected fault that would affect sumOut in this mode. | ○ If we get a NORMAL result   ⦿ If we get an ABNORMAL result<br>L1 failed stuck1 |

*Figure 8-11. DIAG Test Recommendation*

The learner can then opt to see what could be learned from a normal result or an abnormal result of that test. The intent of providing this option is to instill in the learner the concept of thinking through the possible outcomes of a test under consideration, in terms of the inferences that could be made for each of the possible outcomes. In the figure, DIAG is recommending that the student check the sumOut indicator with all switches ON, and it is listing the switch settings that must be made to accomplish this test. In this model, the switch settings are obvious from the name of the mode, but in more typical systems, the set of switch settings associated with a named mode might not be known to the less experienced student. Listed below the guidance in performing the test, is DIAG's analysis of what could be learned if the test is performed and an ABNORMAL result is seen.

The test selection process considers the expected value of performing each possible test in reducing uncertainty about the true fault, and it selects as its preferred test that one which produces the greatest *expected* reduction in system uncertainty, or entropy in information theory terms. This in turn is affected by the current levels of suspicion. Initially, all possible faults are rank ordered by DIAG, according to their relative reliability.

As symptom information appears, from the student's testing, DIAG silently updates its own internal suspicions regarding the fault and modifies the suspicion rankings. In general, the best test is that one which best splits the remaining suspicion into two approximately equal sets, each set having about the same total probability of failure. For a complete discussion of the test selection and hypothesis maintenance process, see Towne (2003).

*After-Exercise Guidance*

Two Consult functions are available after an exercise is completed, as shown here.

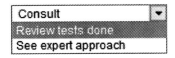

*Review Tests Done.* When this consultation type is selected, DIAG first reinserts the fault into the model so that the learner will again see the symptoms of that fault. DIAG then repeats each test the learner did by setting the model into the mode the learner established and pointing out the significant indications. One sample step of a review is shown in Figure 8-12.

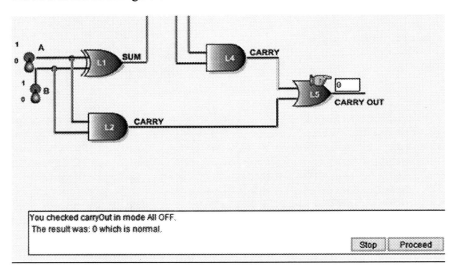

*Figure 8-12. Example DIAG Review Step.*

Upon selecting *Proceed*, the learner sees a review of what that observed symptom signifies, which is identical to the symptom interpretation screen shown in Figure 8-10. This review process permits the learner to see what inferences an experienced technician would draw from the tests that he or she performed on the just-completed exercise. One significant learning opportunity that this interaction affords is the capability to separate the contribution of symptom interpretation from test selection toward success on the exercise. One possible outcome of such a review is that the learner sees that the tests he or she performed were not sufficient to adequately discriminate the true nature of the fault.

Alternatively, the learner may discover from this review that his or her tests were indeed sufficiently informative, but that the learner did not adequately extract their significance and thus did not isolate the true fault. Finally, another very common possible outcome is for the learner to discover that he or she committed some type of error in performing one or more tests, e.g., a control may have been set incorrectly, thereby producing a mode that was not intended, often leading to catastrophically incorrect inferences.

*See Expert approach.* The interface for this guidance option is identical to that of the *Review Tests Done* consultation type just discussed, except that for this function DIAG generates and explains an *expert* diagnostic sequence, rather than using the learner's own work. As always, this expert approach is one generated by DIAG from its generic rules of diagnostic performance.

This debriefing function permits the learner to "look over the shoulder" of a virtual experienced technician working to solve the same fault just worked by the learner. The objective is to both demonstrate good generic diagnostic performance and to convey a wealth of deep domain-specific information about the target system's functionality.

## APPLICATIONS

The DIAG system has been used experimentally for a number of years, during which a relatively wide range of applications have been produced. These applications are summarized in the final chapter

# SCENARIO-BASED INSTRUCTION

A wide range of tasks in both the military and private sector involve a series of actions performed to manage, maintain, or resolve some sort of complex situation that changes over time. Examples of such tasks include leading a search and rescue operation, directing aircraft to safe landings, dealing with a civil disaster, and negotiating with a hostage taker. Included in just these few examples are situations in which the decision maker has high control (aircraft landings) to moderate or minimal control (negotiations). Also included are situations in which the decision maker is confronting natural forces and those involving hostile agents that may act to thwart or defeat the intentions of the decision maker.

## DYNAMIC, DISCRETE-ACTION TASKS

This chapter addresses a task type we term *dynamic, discrete-action*, signifying that the problem environment changes over the time during which the decision maker deals with it and that the observable actions of the decision maker are discrete.

### Comparison of Task Types

The dynamic, discrete-action task type differs from those involving a sequence of decisions to solve some static problem, such as fault diagnosis, and from those involving continuous motor-perceptual actions, such as tracking. The following table lists examples of the types of tasks in each possible category, with the dynamic, discrete-action examples appearing in the lower left cell.

*Table 9-1. Task Types by Problem Environment and Action Type.*

| Problem Environment | Observable Action Type | |
|---|---|---|
| | Discrete Action | Continuous Motion |
| Static | Troubleshooting Manufacturing Design Stock portfolio assessment | Not defined |
| Dynamic | Air traffic control Fire fighting command Tactical decision making | Space shuttle docking Aircraft landing Tank maneuvering |

While any such scheme for partitioning tasks is an imperfect and incomplete abstraction, this simple classification is helpful in explicitly defining the kinds of tasks that are addressed in this chapter.

*Common Characteristics*

One particular dynamic discrete-action task – tactical decision making – has been the subject of considerable research, including that of Tannenbaum, Beard, and Salas (1992). They provide the following list of attributes that often characterize this task:
– rapidly evolving scenarios
– time compression
– threat
– adverse physical conditions
– auditory overload/interference
– high workload
– ambiguity
– command pressure

These attributes apply as well to a great many of the tasks that we will address. Whether dealing with a natural threat or one caused by hostile actions, many of these same factors serve to complicate decision making, and they challenge the skill and experience of the decision maker.

*The Decision Making Process*

In the design of instruction of this task type, we make no assumption that there is a discrete decision made for each observable action. Furthermore, we recognize that some decisions may produce no observable activity whatsoever, as when one elects to wait for further developments or better information.

Zachary and Ryder (1997) provide a thorough discussion of modern decision theories, and aspects of the decision making process. In describing the naturalistic decision theory, they suggest:

> … human experts do not make decisions in an analytical manner, indeed or even in a conscious manner, but rather apply their accumulated experience and knowledge (collectively called their <u>expertise</u>) to identify and effect the most appropriate action.

They continue:

> There is no decision event, but rather a larger dynamic task in which decision makers take actions.

This characterization has profound implications both for designing training methods for such tasks as well as acquiring from experts their decision rules. The approach we have developed specifically avoids attempting to capture generalized decision rules from experts, but instead asks experts to perform prototype scenarios and to explain those actions that they can, but only in terms of the specific scenario situation that evoked the action.

We wish to provide a robust simulation-based environment for training the performance of such tasks while making virtually no assumptions about the nature of the decision making process that underlies the observable performance. That is, we wish to deal explicitly with the conditions that evoke particular actions while making no attempt to model the intervening decision making process.

## APPLICATION ISSUES

Instruction in this performance domain can be viewed in two relatively distinct parts: 1) a knowledge acquisition part, and 2) a knowledge application part. The former of these concerns the mastering of the domain knowledge that is prerequisite to performance of the task. The methods described in earlier chapters may be appropriate for addressing some of this content, and other methods are likely called for as well to address the conceptual and declarative knowledge involved.

The second part commences when the individual has acquired some proficiency in dealing with the individual components of the task and has at least received an introduction to the performance of the whole task. Typically, however, the learner we are targeting is already working in the environment in question and has performed as a subordinate to the kind of decision maker the learner wishes to become.

Within this knowledge application, or whole-task, phase are two primary application issues: 1) how to represent the problem environment, and 2) how to represent the task in a manner that supports explicit statement of expert performance explanations, assessment of learner proficiency, and remediation.

### Representing the Problem Environment

The ability to effectively represent the problem environment varies greatly across domains, and is highly dependent upon whether the decision maker acts upon the problem environment directly or indirectly. When the learner will be acting directly upon the environment, as shown here, representing the appearance and nature of the task environment is essential to performing in the simulated world.

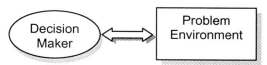

Examples of such tasks are apprehension of suspects in a building, leading disaster victims to safety, or searching for people after an avalanche. While virtual reality technology is achieving the capacity to cope with these requirements, our

163

simulation graphics and mouse-based input medium do not serve these needs very well.

A great many complex decision making tasks, however, involve indirect action upon the environment and indirect sensing of the environment, via either human or machine intermediaries, as shown here.

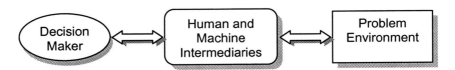

Oftentimes, the decision maker works out of a command center in which information is received via voice or data networks, and responses to the problem are carried out by those under the command of the decision maker. The decision maker's environment, which we term the *command interface*, is then represented by what the performer sees, hears and acts upon, and the *problem environment* may require little or no graphical representation at all.

The air traffic control (CIC) task described in Chapter 4 demonstrates this distinction between the operator's interface and the real world. The CIC operator sees an artificial rendering of the real world on the radar screen, and interacts with that world only via radio and intercom communication systems.

*Representing the Task*

As mentioned previously, the dynamic tasks we wish to instruct are often clouded with uncertainty and charged with high risks and threats. A key element of performance, therefore, is the continual evaluation of the situation and consideration of alternatives, including doing nothing for some period of time. Because of this, the decision maker's interface must always be available for use, and the instructional system must attempt to avoid directing attention to any particular facet of information or possible action. Except when presenting remediation or explicitly guiding the performer, therefore, we wish to maintain a situation where the learner is performing, rather than carrying on a dialog with the training system.

*Accommodating Variations in Approach*

Finally, we note that the kinds of tasks discussed here can usually be performed expertly in a number of different ways. Typically there are critical rules that apply to task performance that few experts would violate and many novices would, and those are rather easily dealt with. A major challenge in the design of the instructional approach is to represent expert performance in a manner that accurately accepts variations that accomplish the objectives, even though those variations may have not been explicitly expressed.

SYSTEM OVERVIEW

The system we have developed to meet these requirements is called D³M, for Dynamic Discrete-action Decision Making (Towne, 1998a, 1999, 2000). The major elements of the system (Figure 9-1) are 1) a *scenario generator* that produces customized scenarios for the individual learner, 2) a *simulation management system* composed of models and the ReAct simulation control system, and 3) a *training management system* that directs the production of customized scenarios and provides context-dependent tutoring, demonstration, and debriefing services to the learner.

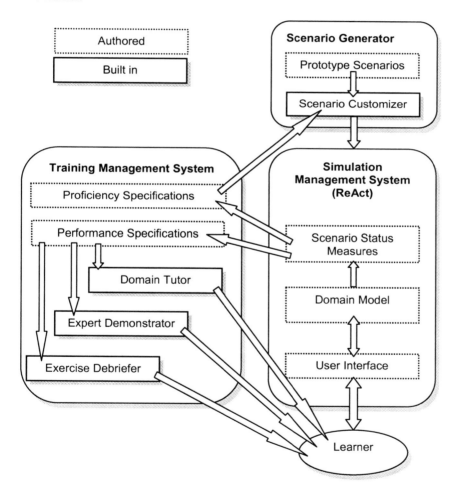

*Figure 9-1. Design of a Generalized Scenario Tutoring System (Towne, 1998a).*

165

*Instructional Approach*

Relying upon one or more domain-specific graphical simulations to represent the command interface and various internal domain-specific processes to maintain the problem environment, $D^3M$ manages the presentation of practice scenarios by:

- demonstrating exercises previously worked by experts and presenting those experts' explanations of particular actions as the demonstration unfolds;
- producing practice exercises at appropriate levels of difficulty;
- administering exercises in a manner that permits assessment of individual proficiency and presentation of expert performance explanations; and
- maintaining the status of learning objectives achieved by the learner.


## APPLICATION DEVELOPMENT

A $D^3M$ application is produced by one or more specialists and consists of these elements:

- a model of the *problem environment*, the situation to be managed;
- a model of the *command interface* with which the learner interacts with the problem environment;
- a set of *learning objectives* to be addressed by the application;
- a number of *prototype scenarios* to exercise the learning objectives;
- *scheduled events* that may happen during a scenario;
- task-specific *proficiency measures* that reflect good or poor performance and the relationships between proficiency measures and learning objectives.
- demonstrations of *expert performance* on each prototype scenario;
- a set of *exercises*, specifying the scenarios to present and the conditions of presentation.

The following diagram reflects the basic elements of a scenario-based instructional application. An additional element – the back-story – may also be developed (outside of $D^3M$) to introduce some types of scenarios. This element will be discussed along with exercise creation.

Like many such development processes, this one is iterative and not rigidly ordered. The following, however, discusses the individual elements of an application in the order in which they are typically initiated.

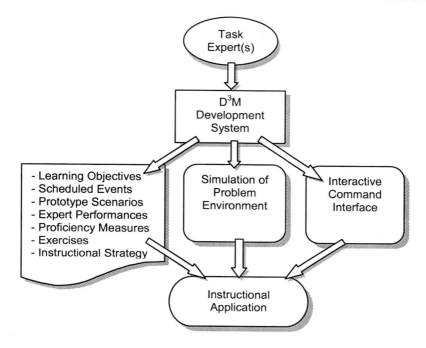

*Figure 9-2. Elements of D³M Scenario-based Instruction.*

## Sample Application

The figures shown in this chapter are taken from a D³M application dealing with command of forces fighting a fire in a high-rise office building. In this task, the first battalion chief that arrives on scene establishes a command center near the building, sizes up the situation, and calls for additional resources as required. This individual remains the Incident Commander (IC) of the operation, unless another chief arrives to assume that role.

Complete accounts of the responsibilities and tactical decision functions in high rise fire fighting have been documented by Coleman (1997), the Los Angeles Fire Department (1998), McAniff (1974), and the National Fire Service (1996).

## The Command Interface

The first step in producing an instructional application is to define the nature and components of the task to be trained in terms of the actions that the learner will be able to perform and the information that will be accessible. We term the elements that the learner observes and acts upon the *command interface*, distinguishing it from the simulation of the problem environment.

Among the action types that might be supported in a command interface are these:
- Interacting with virtual personnel via direct contact;
- Interacting with virtual personnel via telephone or radio;
- Referring to documentation or reference material;
- Changing virtual locations in order to observe conditions;
- Maintaining records of situation status and actions taken;

All of these action types are supported in the command interface of the IC task, starting with the reception of an alarm at the fire station, as shown here:

> **Alarm received at: 5:01 AM**
> **Location:   525 Hawthorne Blvd., Torrance.**
> **Dispatched: E-1   E-5   E-11   T-4   T-31**

The learner then travels virtually (via video) to the fire scene. On the way, the scenario in progress may produce a message from a virtual officer who has arrived first, and is assuming command. In this case, our student must take over in the prescribed manner when he or she arrives.

Upon arrival, the learner observes the conditions that are immediately evident. The following is a frame of a video showing one of the possible conditions seen upon arrival.

*Figure 9-3. Smoke and Fire Showing upon Arrival.*

From this point on, the actions that can be performed are accessed via the interface shown here.

| Transmit on : | Go to: | See: |
| --- | --- | --- |
| ○ OCD channel<br>○ fire ground | ○ fire control room<br>○ stairway<br>○ elevators<br>○ Command post<br>⊙ outside | floor plan<br>stair and elevator plan |

*Figure 9-4. Top Level View of IC's Command Interface.*

Selections in the left section lead to more specific menus of messages to be sent, the middle section brings up scenario-specific simulations of other locations in the building, and the right hand section produces static documentation concerning the building design.

Dealing With Speech Output. Typically some difficult compromises must be made to deal with spoken commands and advisories. If speech is deemed to be essential to the training environment, and the vocabulary is sufficiently constrained, then the speech recognition technology to process these utterances is available and surprisingly effective, but the cost and difficulty of development then increases dramatically.

The more manageable option is to provide menus and dialog boxes that allow the user to formulate messages, and then voice those messages with a text to speech (TTS) system. The menus shown in Figure 9-5 are a few of the menus provided to accomplish this.

Upon setting the options shown in Figure 9-5 and selecting *Send*, the user would hear this message.

> Engine 1 is on the scene of a 35 story office building, with fire and smoke showing. We're going fast attack. We have life hazard. This is a defensive fire. Engine 1 will be Hawthorne Command.

Clearly, there are substantive differences between actually voicing messages and making selections with a mouse. The critical issue is not that using a mouse is different than speaking, but that the method we used to accomplish transmission of messages necessarily displays the options, and this represents an artificial crutch that is not present in the real world. Nevertheless, this approach goes a long way toward creating a learning environment in which the decision maker has to formulate messages properly, and it does avoid offering any unrealistic reminders that certain kinds of transmissions should be sent at particular times.

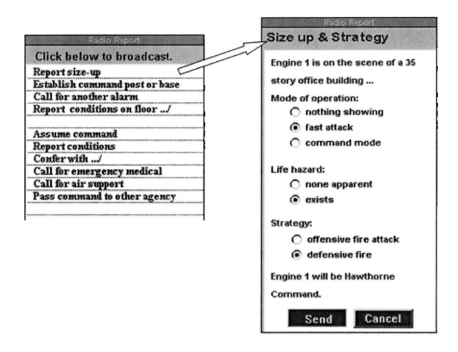

*Figure 9-5. Menus for Selecting Message Type (left) and Size up Report (right).*

*Dealing With Incoming Messages.*   Realistic incoming messages are more easily delivered to the trainee. After constructing a message from virtual agents in the problem environment, the system can either display them, as was done in the air traffic control task of Chapter 4, or voice them by a text-to-speech (TTS) utility, the approach taken here. A number of excellent off-the-shelf TTS systems are now available offering both male and female voices that can be controlled in pitch, rate, and other characteristics.

*Providing Documentation.*   Like many tasks dealing with emergencies, the fire fighting command task is performed in a setting that is unfamiliar to the decision maker, thus the IC can call up certain static documentation about the building involved, including floor plans, elevator layout, and the floors served by various stairways. The floor plan is as shown in Figure 9-6.

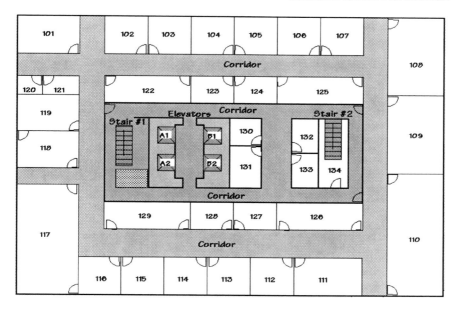

*Figure 9-6. Building Floor Plan.*

Making Observations at Other Locations.   In many tasks the decision maker may move about at the scene in order to obtain more information. In such applications we must provide context-specific views of conditions at those locations. The following table lists the locations to which the IC may move, the kinds of information available at each location, and the method used to represent the site.

*Table 9-2. Locations to which the IC May Move.*

| Location | Information Source | Depiction Media |
|---|---|---|
| Fire Station* | Advisory from central dispatch | text |
| Fire Station* | Audio alarm | sound (.wav) |
| Arrival at scene | External condition of building | Video |
| Arrival at scene | Aerial view of buildings and roads | Static graphics |
| Fire Control Room | Operator Interface Panel | Graphical simulation |
| Fire Control Room | Floor plan | Static graphics |
| Fire Control Room | Stair and elevator plan | Static graphics |
| Stairway | Door condition (temperature) | text |
| Hallway | Condition (clear, smoky, flames) | video |
| Elevators | None; just means for changing floors | Video, graphical simulation |
| Fire floor | Status of rooms/offices | Video |
| Command Post | Current assignments and status | Graphical simulation |
| All locations | Incoming voice reports & dispatch | Text and Text-to- speech |

* Initial location

171

For example, the IC may go to the fire control room in the building involved to interrogate the Operator Interface Panel, as shown in Figure 9-7.

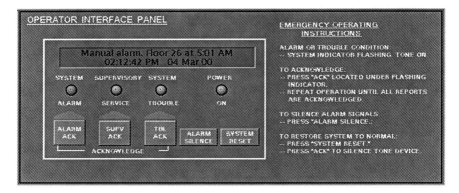

*Figure 9-7. Information Available at the Fire Control Room.*

This unit reflects current conditions in the building as well as the history of alarms that arose in the recent past. Since this is an active device model, it was not difficult to hand it values of scenario variables, causing it to provide accurate information about the situation at any time.

*Maintaining Records and Assignments.* The interactive status/assignment board shown in Figure 9-8 is provided on screen to both reflect the current status of people and equipment and to issue orders to those resources. As units arrive on scene, their status is automatically changed from En route to Base, which is where they would report upon arrival (in reality an assistant makes this change to the status board).

| ASSIGNMENT/STATUS | Alarm 1 | | | | | | Alarm 2 | | | | | |
|---|---|---|---|---|---|---|---|---|---|---|---|---|
| | E-1 | E-5 | E-11 | T-4 | T-23 | BC-1 | E-4 | E-9 | E-21 | T-5 | T-14 | BC-2 |
| En route | | | | | | | | | | | | |
| Base | | | | | | | | | | | | |
| Command Post | | | | | | | | | | | | |
| Staging | ✓ | | | | | | | | | | | |
| Search | | ✓ | | | | | | | | | | |
| Evacuate occupants | | | | | | | | | | | | |
| Determine fire floor | | | | ✓ | | | | | | | | |
| Attack | | | | | | ✓ | | | | | | |
| Backup | | | ✓ | | | | | | | | | |
| Lobby control | | | | | ✓ | | | | | | | |
| Elevator control | | | | | | | | | | | | |
| Ventilation | | | | | | | | | | | | |
| Return to service | | | | | | | | | | | | |

*Figure 9-8. Interactive Status/assignment Board.*

Now, the IC can assign any unit that is on scene by clicking the mouse in any box. If the IC calls for a second alarm, a second set of units appear on the *En route* row, and they change over time to *Base* as they too arrive on scene. With each assignment, a corresponding verbal report is automatically evoked. In the figure above, the IC has just assigned Truck Unit 23 (T-23) to Lobby control, and the following is voiced:

| Truck 23, you will handle lobby control. |
|------------------------------------------|

*Modeling the Fire*

To model the spread and intensity of the fire over time, we used a very simple scheme in which each room on a floor contained a specified amount of combustible fuel (e.g., papers, wooden furniture, etc.) expressed in terms of minutes of combustion, and each partition provided a specified level of containment, also expressed in minutes. The consumption of fuel in all spaces currently combusting was then updated continuously, and the fire would spread depending upon the duration of fire in a compartment and the properties of the adjoining walls. Similarly, the fire would be exhausted in some spaces when all the fuel was consumed, as determined by the total time of combustion in a space.

Thus, at any time during an exercise, the internal model of the fire was available to influence the Operator Panel shown previously, as well as reports coming in from virtual fire fighters.

*We must emphasize that this model of fire in no way allows one to analyze building design, the suitability of various building materials, or the adequacy of various fire codes.* Since the learner does not know the exact contents of each space on a floor, or the exact construction of all partitions, the simple fire model used here generates a reasonable change of conditions over time that is sufficient for training purposes.

*Specifying Learning Objectives*

Learning objectives are statements expressing specific actions that the learner will or will not perform under specific conditions or specific outcomes that the learner will or will not produce when he or she attains the criterion level of expertise. In general, therefore, there may be objectives that state desired conditions as well as conditions to be avoided. An example learning objective is as follows:

> The officer relieves crews when their fatigue or air supply conditions would hamper further safe and effective performance.

Learning objectives are entered on a dialog box as shown below.

173

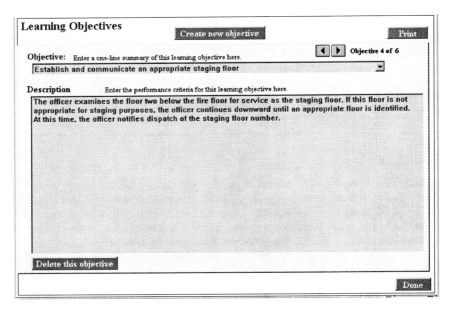

*Figure 9-9. Dialog Box for Composing Learning Objectives.*

These verbal statements of the learning objectives are not processed or analyzed by the instructional system. Instead, proficiency rules refer to the objectives by number, thus both an instructor and the instructional system know at any time which objectives have, and have not, been met by each student. As will be described shortly, the particular learning objects remaining to be achieved directly determine which scenarios are presented to an individual.

Any ambiguity or vagueness in these statements is likely to be detected when the instructional developer creates specific scenarios to involve these learning objectives and devises specific scoring rules designed to measure whether each objective has or has not been attained. Inevitably, therefore, the learning objectives receive repeated attention to attain relatively unambiguous statements.

*Scheduled Events*

A scenario can be affected by scheduled events that are typically changes in conditions that are beyond the control of the decision maker and are also difficult to anticipate with any certainty. Such events might include changes in natural conditions and actions by a hostile force. Scheduled events are specified via the dialog box shown here.

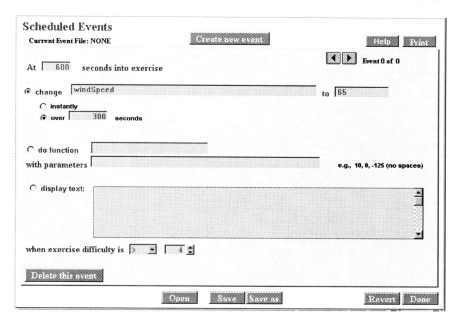

*Figure 9-10. Specification of Scheduled Events.*

Three different types of events may be specified:
- *change* a simulation attribute instantaneously or over a period of time;
- *do* (execute) a developer's function; or
- display some *text message* to the user.

The first of these change types is shown in the figure; the *windSpeed* property will start changing 600 seconds into the scenario and will achieve a final value of 65 (MPH) after 300 seconds. The second type of change, executing a developer function, is provided to produce more complex effects than are built into the simulation. We could, for example, introduce an explosion into a situation, even though the simulation has no provisions for such an event. The third type of scheduled event simply displays some text to the performer, thereby opening up many opportunities for enriching the flow of communications to the learner while not complicating the basic simulation of the problem environment.

*Specifying a Difficulty Level for Event Occurrence.* The entry at the bottom of the Scheduled Events dialog box specifies the difficulty levels at which the event will be executed. Thus, novices can be insulated from these complications while more advanced learners will have to confront them.

## Prototype Scenarios

With the learning objectives in mind, a subject matter expert now creates a set of prototype scenarios, using a *domain-specific* dialog box, as shown in Figure 9-11.

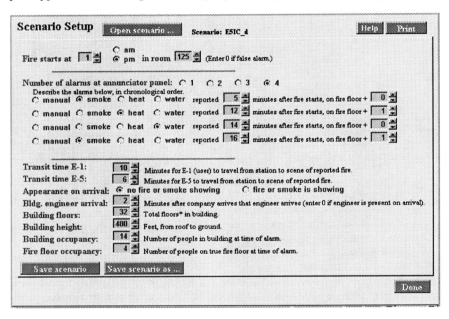

*Figure 9-11. Dialog Box for Defining High-rise Fire Scenarios.*

While a prototype scenario could be specified by entering a list of object properties and associated values, we have found that the modest effort required to produce a domain-specific dialog box, as shown in the figure, is rewarded with fewer errors, much easier ability to review existing scenarios, and reduced development time.

This admittedly busy dialog box lists all the attributes of a high-rise fire scenario that can be set. The scenario specified in Figure 9-11 calls for a fire to start in room 125 at 1:00 PM of a thirty-two floor building, with no smoke or fire showing on arrival, along with other details concerning the types of alarms raised.

For each prototype scenario, the subject matter expert defines two instances: 1) an extremely easy instance that presents the simplest set of conditions that still retains the essence of the situation, and 2) an extremely difficult instance that presents the same situation under the worst possible conditions for a decision maker. As will be explained in a later section, the instructional system uses these two extreme cases to generate a scenario instance of the desired level of difficulty.

*Measures of Proficiency*

The task expert then develops a set of scoring rules that reflect positive or negative evidence of proficiency. These are entered on the dialog box shown here.

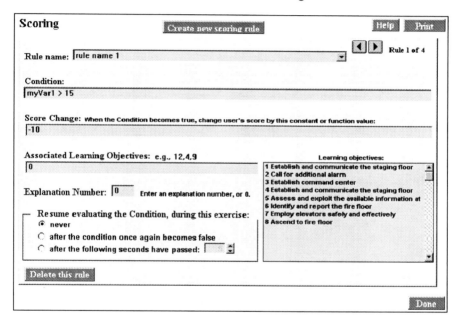

*Figure 9-12. Specifying Scoring Rules.*

Each rule contains four parts:
– a *condition* describing some desirable or undesirable situation;
– a *value,* possibly negative, that is added to the learner's current score;
– a set of *learning objectives* which are directly related to the task condition; and
– an optional *explanation* that expresses the expert's assessment of the situation.

The conditions are expressions composed of variables maintained in the domain simulation, thus this step requires access to the simulation. For example, in the CIC task, the simulation process maintains a value called *nearestApproach*, which is the closest that any unidentified aircraft comes to the operator's ship, in miles. One could therefore develop a rule that uses this value to measure the proficiency of the CIC controller.

*If a variable required to measure proficiency is not already maintained in the simulation, then the model developer would have to add one or more statements to the model to do so.* This is the one case where instructional development may create the need to modify the model of the target system.

The following table lists some of the score changes associated with various performance conditions of the IC. In this case, all the scoring rules represent performance faults, i.e., evidence of a performance error. Some of these are actions that are performed that should not be performed, and others are actions that should be performed but were not.

*Table 9-3. Score Changes Associated with Performance Conditions.*

| Condition | Score Change |
|---|---|
| Failure to call additional alarm | -50 |
| Calls an unnecessary additional alarm | -15 |
| Failure to issue size up in a timely fashion | -20 |
| Selects inappropriate command option during size up | -40 |
| Failure to issue adequate periodic status reports during ascent | -20 |
| Failure to report fire floor | -40 |
| Failure to check door before opening | -50 |
| Failure to close a door | -30 |
| Failure to determine status above fire floor | -30 |
| Failure to report staging floor during ascent | -20 |

*Expert Performance*

With the scenarios and proficiency rules specified, the task expert now performs each scenario two times, once performing as well as possible, while providing explanations for the actions and judgments, and a second time performing the scenario in a manner that approximates that of an acceptable student performance.

For the expert demonstrations, the task expert pauses the exercise when desired to enter an explanation for why something was done or not done. In this mode of performance, the system automatically records each action performed and the time at which it was performed. If different experts have different approaches to a particular scenario, the different performances may be captured and demonstrated. An example remark entered to explain one expert's decision is as follows:

> Now, my first crew has been working under oxygen masks for over 15 minutes, and I need to get them some relief. I'll bring up the people from staging as soon as I hear that we have the line connected in the second stairway.

Note that commentary given during the learner's work is triggered by the existence of a condition which the expert specified, and is not keyed to any particular exercise or scenario. Thus, the domain expert needs only specify a particular task situation one time, and D$^3$M will watch for that situation over all exercises.

For the student-like performances, one or more experts perform the scenario to the minimum level of proficiency that is deemed acceptable considering the training environment. When a reasonably reliable mean can be computed from the resulting proficiency scores on these performances it may then be used as the criterion for assessing individual progress.

*The Curriculum of Exercises*

The curriculum is a set of exercises, each specified via the dialog box shown in Figure 9-13.

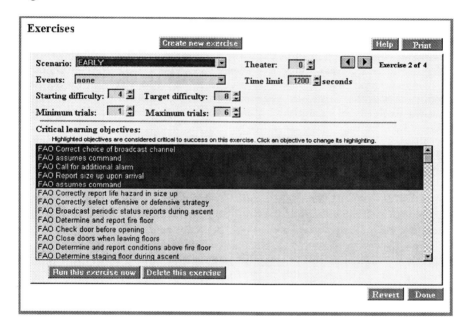

*Figure 9-13. Exercise Specification.*

With this form, the developer specifies exercises in terms of:
- a particular scenario to present;
- a theatre of operation in which the exercise occurs;
- zero or more scheduled events to occur during the scenario;
- the time limit in which to complete the exercise (or none);
- the initial difficulty level of the scenario (on a scale of 10);
- the target difficulty that signifies mastery of the scenario;
- the minimum and maximum number of trials permitted; and
- the particular learning objectives that the exercise involves.

In the figure, the developer has highlighted five learning objectives, to indicate those that are critical to the performance of the particular scenario specified. Note, too, that the scenario specification does not include any reference to the back-story, which is produced externally to the system.

*The Back-Story.* A back-story is a verbal account of general conditions that have preceded a particular exercise. While a back-story was not provided for these fire fighting exercises, such verbal accounts can provide background information that makes exercises more realistic and possibly more instructive. If a learner were managing the assault on a forest fire, a back-story could provide the kind of information that local officials might supply, such as the tendency for high winds to come up in the afternoon. This might be a more fair way to present a scenario that did then involve such conditions.

In other kinds of tasks, such as the military air traffic control task, the back-story can possibly set up expectations in a manner that could be dangerous to rely upon in the real world. For example, a back-story might advise the learner that conditions are very tense and that hostilities are likely. Then, when given a scenario involving innocent aircraft following accepted procedures, a learner might overreact and fail to follow the procedures being taught, ultimately learning the consequences of allowing expectations to impact behavior in that fashion. Conversely, the back-story could describe very tranquil and friendly conditions, testing the individual's vigilance in performing per the rules of engagement.

*Theater of Operation.* Some tasks can be specified in a manner that they can be presented in multiple settings. In the fire fighting application we developed just one floor plan and building design, but multiple buildings could have been produced. In the military air traffic control task, CIC, the background on the radar display can be set to show the Persian Gulf or any other geographical profile. Thus, the theater of operation can affect the problem environment in some ways that quantitative variables cannot.

*Sample Exercises.* By combining scenarios with various scheduled events, a rich set of conditions can be produced, as shown in Table 9-4.

*Table 9-4. Exercises Defined for the IC Task.*

| *Exercise Condition* |
| --- |
| Simple false alarm |
| Pranksters set manual alarms; no fire |
| Telephone call received warning of bomb in building; none found. |
| Telephone call received warning of bomb in building; bomb discovered. |
| Simple fire with smoke showing, no problems |
| Simple fire with smoke showing, dangerous toxins encountered |
| No smoke showing, smoke alarm identifies higher floor |
| Night time fire, building engineer unavailable, janitor has heart attack |

As outlined next, the instructional system selects exercises from the curriculum according to the proficiency level of the individual, the achievement of learning objectives, and the Instructional Strategy.

## The Instructional Strategy

The final step in developing an application is to specify the instructional strategy to be administered by D$^3$M. The instructional strategy specifies the very highest criteria concerning the presentation and selection of exercises, and is set up via the dialog box shown in Figure 9-14.

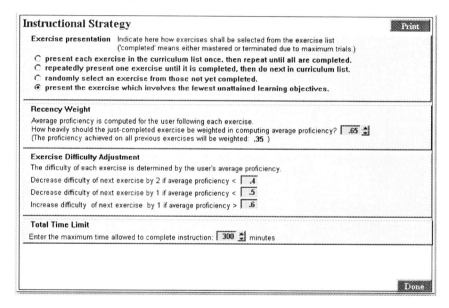

Figure 9-14. Specifying the Instructional Strategy.

The *Exercise Presentation* section presents alternatives for selecting exercises. For some types of problems, such as locating a lost hiker, there is no point in repeating the same exercise multiple times in a row, while other types might be repeated until some level of proficiency is demonstrated by the learner. In the figure, the instructional planner has called for exercises to be selected in a manner that involves the fewest unattained learning objectives. The *Recency Weight* section allows the instructional planner to control how heavily performance on the just-completed exercise is regarded, compared to performance on all the prior exercises. The *Difficulty Adjustment* section is used to specify how exercise difficulty is modified as a function of the learner's average proficiency. Judicious entries here can enable the system to increase problem difficulty appropriately as the individual gains proficiency and to decrease difficulty if performance is poor. Finally, the *Time Limit* can be set to any number of minutes to complete the curriculum.

## INSTRUCTIONAL DELIVERY

D³M operates in a demonstration mode, a practice mode, and a replay mode. The demonstration mode replays an expert's performance, along with commentary, and the replay mode repeats the learner's work, also with retrieved remarks related to conditions produced. The practice mode, shown in Figure 9-15, provides the guided instruction using all of the resources described previously.

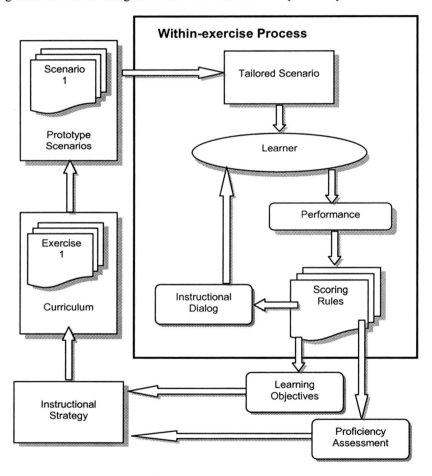

*Figure 9-15. D³M Instructional Delivery in Practice Mode.*

The process begins with presentation of a particular designated exercise, at it minimum level of difficulty. Upon completion of the initial exercise, the system computes the learner's demonstrated proficiency level, marks any learning objectives achieved, and selects and tailors the next exercise, as outlined next.

### Computing the Learner's Proficiency

The learner's proficiency level on a completed exercise, $P_L$ is computed as the score earned on the exercise divided by the score achieved by the expert performing the same exercise at the same level of difficulty. If possible, actual expert scores for each difficulty can be obtained and used as the baseline for normalizing student scores. If this is not possible, an interpolated score can be computed from the expert's scores on the two extreme prototype instances.

The learner's *average proficiency*, $P_A'$, is then computed as:

$$PA' = Wr\ Pp + (1 - Wr)\ PA$$

where:
  $W_r$ is the *recency* weight, a value from 0 to 1 expressing the weighting of the most recent exercise proficiency;
  $P_p$ is the proficiency computed for the student's prior exercise, and
  $P_A$ is (prior) average proficiency.

The key parameter here is the recency weight, $W_r$, which is set by the instructional developer to reflect the importance given to recent performance versus earlier performance.

### Maintaining the Status of Learning Objectives

There are two independent mechanisms available within $D^3M$ for specifying when a learning objective has been mastered: 1) when an exercise to which the objective has been linked is performed successfully, and 2) when a particular proficiency condition to which the objective has been linked is achieved by the learner.

In some cases, it may be difficult to define specific conditions that indicate mastery of particular learning objectives, yet feasible to specify the learning objectives that are met when the learner succeeds on a particular exercise. Conversely, some tasks may offer straightforward opportunities for defining proficiency conditions, in which case the applicator may elect to exploit this means of expression alone, or may use a combination of the two.

Regardless of the performance that leads to an updating of the status of learning objectives, the process may reverse the setting of a learning objective that has been previously marked as satisfied. This seems wholly consistent with what we know about learning and human performance; a novice might recall and correctly apply a particular principle while performing a task and later fail to apply it, particularly in a more difficult situation involving other considerations and distractions.

*Exercise Selection*

Upon determining the learner's proficiency level and satisfied learning objectives, the system selects the next exercise according to the settings of the Instructional Strategy. Upon making an exercise selection, the system:
– computes the difficulty level at which the exercise shall be presented;
– tailors the scenario in the exercise to the computed level of difficulty;
– presents and records the scenario along with any remarks or warnings; and
– assesses the learner's proficiency and mastery of learning objectives.

*Computing the Difficulty Level of the Upcoming Scenario*

Upon computing the learner's average proficiency, the instructional system determines the difficulty level at which the upcoming scenario will be presented. As seen in Figure 9-14, difficulty may be decreased by 2 or 1, it may be increased by 1, and it may be unchanged, all depending upon the individual's average proficiency. In general, exercise difficulty can be reduced significantly if the learner performs poorly, but it moves up more gradually, so as not to overreact to a single positive outcome.

*Tailoring Scenario Difficulty*

The final step before presenting a scenario is to tailor it to produce the desired level of difficulty. The general process of tailoring a scenario is to interpolate all the attributes of the scenario between the very easy and very difficult versions, using 1 as the difficulty of the easy version, 10 as the difficulty of the difficult version, and the desired difficulty level as the selector value. This also has the convenient effect of maintaining all values that are common between the two extreme versions.

More specifically, the formula for computing the value, a', of a property at a specified level of difficulty is:

$$a' = a_e + ( a_d - a_e) (D - i_e) / (i_d - i_e)$$

where
  a' is the adjusted value of the attribute
  $a_e$ is the value of the attribute in the easier instance
  $a_d$ is the value of the attribute in the more difficult instance
  D is the difficulty level of the scenario being produced
  $i_d$ is the difficulty level of the more difficult scenario instance (here, 10)
  $i_e$ is the difficulty level of the easier scenario instance (here, 1)

For example, suppose we wish to adjust the value of some scenario property to correspond to a difficulty level of 7, when the easy scenario has that property at 50 and the difficult scenario has it at 20. The value, a', of the property in the tailored scenario would be:

$$a' = 50 + (20 - 50)(7 - 1)/(10 - 1) = 50 + (-30)(6)/9 = 50 - 20 = 30$$

The identical computation is made to tailor scheduled events to a desired difficulty level, but the easy and difficult values are expressed differently. For each value entered to a scheduled event definition the developer may instead enter a range, e.g., 45-85, and the system computes the appropriate value from that range.

*Scenario Presentation and Maintenance of Score and Learning Objectives*

The instructional system now presents the tailored scenario and its tailored event, if appropriate, and it maintains constant watch over the scoring rules. When a scoring rule fires, the instructional process updates the ongoing score, it issues any associated remarks or warnings, and it marks associated learning objectives as learned or not learned.

*Replay Mode*

At the conclusion of an exercise, the learner may request to run a replay of his or her performance, at which time the instructional system presents the replay in real time, with any provided instructional commentary. This replay is recreated from a data file written as the learner originally worked. During a replay, the learner may pause the simulation in order to study any external documentation or instructions or to confer with others about the situation.

*Accessing Learner Performance Data*

An instructor may review and print the performance data recorded for any learner, as shown in Figure 9-16. The upper portion of this report lists the number of trials, the difficulty level, and the proficiency achieved for each exercise worked. The lower section lists the learning objectives involved in the exercises that have been worked, and their current status.

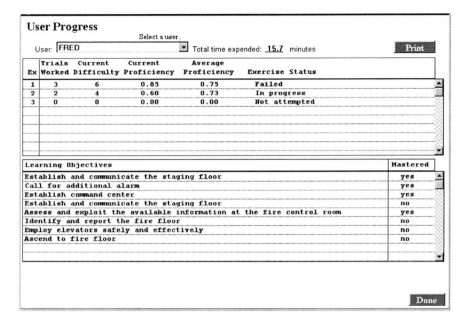

**User Progress**

Select a user .

User: FRED     Total time expended: **15.7** minutes     Print

| Ex | Trials Worked | Current Difficulty | Current Proficiency | Average Proficiency | Exercise Status |
|----|---------------|--------------------|--------------------|--------------------|-----------------|
| 1 | 3 | 6 | 0.85 | 0.75 | Failed |
| 2 | 2 | 4 | 0.60 | 0.73 | In progress |
| 3 | 0 | 0 | 0.00 | 0.00 | Not attempted |

| Learning Objectives | Mastered |
|---------------------|----------|
| Establish and communicate the staging floor | yes |
| Call for additional alarm | yes |
| Establish command center | yes |
| Establish and communicate the staging floor | no |
| Assess and exploit the available information at the fire control room | yes |
| Identify and report the fire floor | no |
| Employ elevators safely and effectively | no |
| Ascend to fire floor | no |

Done

*Figure 9-16. Example User Progress Data Display.*

## SUMMARY AND CONCLUSIONS

### Concerning Expert Systems

There is a crucial difference between the highly context-specific performance explanations that we ask the expert to provide and the general rules of expertise that conventional expert systems require. While it appears that experts have considerable difficulty expressing what they do and why they do it *in generalized terms*, experts seem to have little difficulty composing instructive practice situations and explaining their performance *in those particular situations*.

### A Development Alternative

As the fire fighting application was being developed, it became increasingly clear that virtually identical functionality could have been achieved by exploiting the scheduled event element within $D^3M$, in place of the simulation of the fire. A modest series of scheduled events could have produced the same progress of fire over time as does the fire simulation, all transparently to both the end user and other elements within the instructional environment.

It appears that this alternative is equally viable for many other domains, such as hostage negotiation, response to natural disasters, and forest fire fighting. Such tasks as air traffic control or CIC functions, however, probably are better implemented via object-oriented simulation of the numerous elements in the problem environment.

Use of Video

While static photographic images may have sufficed to represent the fire and smoke conditions, the motion and sound of video adds considerable realism. If nothing else, that increased realism seems to heighten the tension of the presentation, possibly better preparing learners to work in the real environment. Even with use of video, some aspects of the task, such as sensing temperatures, nature of smoke, and directions of drafts were either done via textual substitutes, or not provided at all.

Use of Text-to-Speech

As noted, text-to-speech resources were used to convey spoken messages to the learner, and to voice the messages and orders composed by the learner. While voice quality was generally acceptable, the realism of spoken messages, in terms of voice tension, background noise, and static was quite low. Surprisingly, in the fire fighting application, realism would have been greatly enhanced had there been a way to degrade the quality of the incoming messages, while maintaining the realism of the pronunciation. This is not infeasible, since the synthesized speech is first written to file, then played through the standard utilities for handling .wav files. There may be filtering resources that could degrade the quality of the speech file, making it resemble that which is heard over cell telephones or radio sets in an environment of high background noise and high tension.

Scenario Adaptation Issues

The described method for tailoring scenarios and scheduled events applies to variations that are linear and monotonic. There are cases, however when difficulty does not vary in this fashion. An example of a non-continuous property is the difficulty of getting fire fighters up to various floors in a building. In general, higher floors are more difficult to reach, however safety policy allows fire fighters to use elevators if the elevator terminates at least five floors below the fire floor. Thus, getting to a fire on floor 28 is actually easier than getting to floor 15, *if there is an elevator that terminates at floor 20.*

The following chart illustrates how difficulty and fire floor are related in such a building for fires in even-numbered floors from 14 through 32.

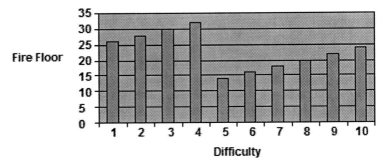

*Figure 9-17. Example of a Non-linear Difficulty Relationship.*

A mechanism is provided, therefore, by which the developer can explicitly state the difficulty levels associated with any variable.

A broader question concerns how one assigns particular difficulty levels to the two prototype scenarios, for if these assignments are inaccurate the interpolation method becomes irrelevant. The instructional system places no constraints on how this assignment is done. Four possible approaches are:

− Obtain subjective judgments of scenario difficulty from a single expert;
− With a panel of experts, use quantitative methods to arrive at consensus;
− Use the proficiency scores experts achieve in performing the scenarios to represent their difficulty; and
− Use the proficiency scores that novices achieve in performing the prototype scenarios.

Of these, the fourth alternative appears to be the one most justifiable. There does arise the question of whether or not relative difficulty across scenarios is consistent as learner expertise increases, and the most likely belief is that it is not. If this is a concern, then learners of varying levels of expertise could work the prototype scenarios, and measures of difficulty would result that could be used across the range of proficiency. Ultimately, a method might be devised in which the difficulty of the prototype scenarios is first established according to the individual's ability, prior to generating one to be delivered to that individual.

Secondly, there is the issue of independence of scenario variables. The current method of manipulating variables within $D^3M$ assumes independence, varying each one to produce the desired exercise difficulty. An alternative approach would have the applicator specify interactions or at least relationships among the individual variables. At the simplest, this could be a set of weights expressing the impact of each variable upon scenario difficulty. If this were done, then some of the variables could be automatically set more difficult than called for by the desired exercise difficulty, and some set easier, with the final result that the exercise difficulty is as desired. This approach would yield the benefits of 1) removing the independence assumption, which is probably not true in general, and 2) producing a richer, more varied, set of practice conditions. This comes, of course, at the cost of considerably greater development effort due to likely difficulties in specifying interactions among variables.

## Scoring Systems

$D^3M$ accepts virtually any scoring system one wishes to specify. The system used in the fire fighting application awards 100 points at the start of an exercise, and deducts for errors. Other scoring systems could award points for achieving various objectives, and could permit the number of points to vary according to the outcome achieved.

An ideal system might use real-world measures such as loss of property and loss of life to score the performance, however this then 1) forces the applicator to confront highly difficult questions about the value of property and life, and 2) forces the developer to carry through the simulation to accurately reflect the consequences of all actions. In a CIC setting, for example, this approach would require a much more powerful simulation of weapons effectiveness and range, so that the consequences of all decisions could be determined. Similarly, for the fire fighting domain, the simulation would have to more accurately reflect true fire propagation than is currently required.

### Normalizing Student Scores

$D^3M$ also imposes no constraints upon the manner of obtaining expert proficiency scores, for normalizing raw student proficiency scores. Perhaps the most legitimate way of doing this is to have a panel of experts perform the task in $D^3M$ to the level of proficiency they deem to be acceptable. Given sufficient agreement in the resulting criterion scores, those can be the basis for increasing and decreasing exercise difficulty, and therefore the basis for grading exercises as failed or mastered.

# SIMULATION-BASED PERFORMANCE SUPPORT

Simulation-based resources can significantly enhance some types of performance on the job. In recent years the military services have been placing increased reliance upon the ability of on-job support systems to both improve field performance and permit a significantly reduced investment in training. While the expectations may be unrealistic, there are some areas where performance aiding can offer considerable benefits. This chapter will look at three such areas: 1) support of diagnostic reasoning tasks, 2) support in performing complex procedures; and 3) supporting the conduct of documented diagnostic procedures.

## SUPPORT OF DIAGNOSTIC REASONING TASKS

Chapter 8 outlined the diagnostic reasoning functions performed by DIAG in its role as a collaborative tutor during instruction. The same functions provided to support the learner – selecting effective tests, drawing inferences about the implications of a just-completed test, and maintaining levels of suspicions about the various system elements – can be provided to the maintainer in the field with just a slight modification to the user interface. As a performance aid, DIAG recommends the tests to perform at each step of the process, the technician performs the tests and reports the symptoms seen, and DIAG processes the reported result to arrive at revised suspicions and further recommendations.

### Test Recommendations

The test recommendation computation made by DIAG in performance aiding mode is identical to that made in the instructional setting, but it is executed at each step of the aiding process. In Figure 10-1 we see the first test recommendation in troubleshooting the Full Adder circuit. The top portion of this display advises the technician what test to perform, in terms of the indicator to observe and the mode in which to observe it, and the middle section lists the settings required to carry out the test.

### Symptom Analysis and Suspicion Level Modification

Upon performing the recommended test, the technician reports whether or not the result matches the normal result given (Figure 10-1). DIAG then processes this reported result against its fault effect knowledge and advises the technician of its conclusions, as shown in Figure 10-2.

Stop
What to do
Check carryOut in mode Sw C ON.
How to do it
First, set mode Sw C ON as follows:
Set SwitchA to 0
Set SwitchB to 0
Set SwitchC to 1
Then, observe carryOut.
Report the result
Is carryOut giving its normal result in this mode of 0?
Yes
No

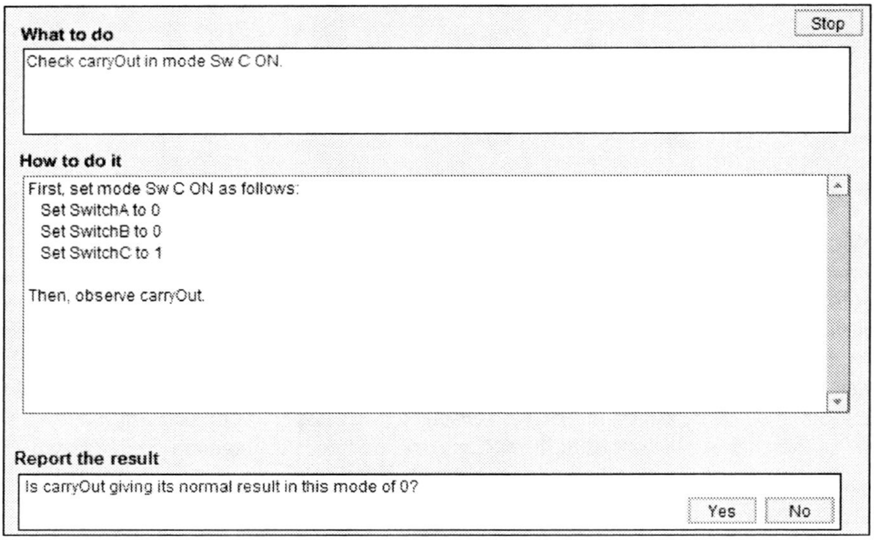

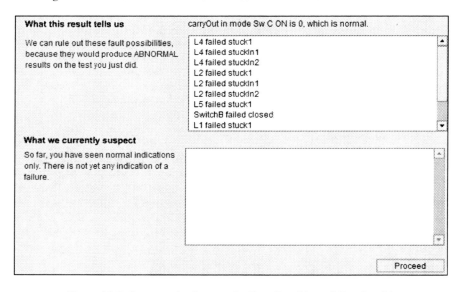

*Figure 10-1. Initial DIAG Test Recommendation to Troubleshoot the Full Adder.*

What this result tells us
carryOut in mode Sw C ON is 0, which is normal.
We can rule out these fault possibilities, because they would produce ABNORMAL results on the test you just did.
L4 failed stuck1
L4 failed stuckIn1
L4 failed stuckIn2
L2 failed stuck1
L2 failed stuckIn1
L2 failed stuckIn2
L5 failed stuck1
SwitchB failed closed
L1 failed stuck1
What we currently suspect
So far, you have seen normal indications only. There is not yet any indication of a failure.
Proceed

*Figure 10-2. Symptom Analysis on the First Test (Normal Test Result).*

The symptom analysis following the first test is somewhat atypical, however. If the technician reports a normal result, as shown above, the analysis just lists the faults that can be eliminated from consideration, as they all would impact the test. While

all other possible faults might theoretically exist, there has not yet been any abnormality observed, so it would be incorrect to suspect any of them. Conversely, if the first test result is abnormal, as shown in Figure 10-3, then DIAG simply lists the faults that could produce them.

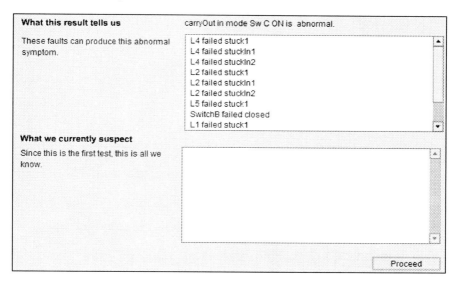

*Figure 10-3. Findings Following a Reported Abnormal Symptom on the First Test.*

In this circuit, there are four fault modes defined for each of the five logical elements and two for each of the three switches, yielding a total of 26 possible faults. A normal reading on DIAG's first recommended test eliminates 12 possibilities (9 of which can be seen in the figure), while an abnormal symptom eliminates 14.

## Subsequent Testing and Fault Isolation

Following all tests after the first, DIAG's fault analysis lists those previously suspected faults that can be eliminated from consideration based on the latest test result, and it lists the suspected faults that are still consistent with all symptoms seen[22]. The second recommended test, after an initial normal, is shown in Figure 10-4.

---

[22] There are some special cases: 1) sometimes a test result may provide no new information, even though the *expected* gain was positive, and 2) sometimes no fault matches the body of symptoms seen, as when a fault is encountered that was not represented in the device model.

193

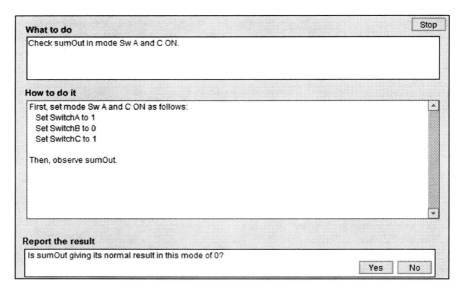

*Figure 10-4. Second Test Recommendation, Following a Normal on the First.*

Figure 10-5 shows the fault analysis given if the second test yields an abnormal symptom.

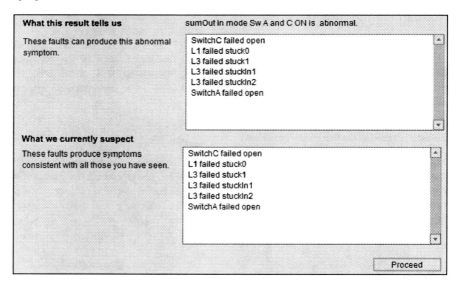

*Figure 10-5. Second Symptom Analysis, Following an Abnormal Report.*

*Value of the Symptom Analysis*

It could be argued that the symptom analysis screen could be eliminated, providing just the test recommendation screen at each step of the process. We believe, however, that the symptom analysis is a crucial part of performing the task, for at least two reasons. First, this information may enlighten the technician, making him or her a better diagnostician in general, and better informed about the behavior of the particular system under test.

Secondly, and possibly of most importance, the symptom analysis may serve to make the aided process less *brittle*, i.e., it may provide important intelligence about the ongoing diagnostic effort that could be of use in those cases when DIAG cannot resolve the fault. As mentioned above, DIAG may fail to identify a particular fault if the symptoms of that fault mode differ substantially from the symptoms produced by the faults included in the device simulation. In this case, the analysis of diagnostic reasoning may assist the technician in completing the diagnostic task unaided.

*Conclusion of the Diagnostic Process*

The aided diagnostic process continues until DIAG has reduced the suspected elements to the smallest possible set, considering the available tests. If this set contains just one RU, DIAG recommends making a replacement, as shown in Figure 10-6, else it advises the technician that it cannot further discriminate among the remaining suspects.

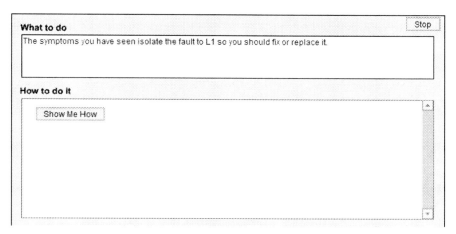

*Figure 10-6. Example Termination of a DIAG-aided Troubleshooting Task.*

The Show Me How button appears in those cases in which there is performance support available for completing the recommended replacement, repair, or adjustment. Methods to develop and present such support are covered in the next section.

AIDING PERFORMANCE OF COMPLEX PROCEDURES

Many procedures carried out on complex systems are difficult to accomplish correctly unless the individual has been well trained and either has performed the operation relatively recently or has access to robust aids to support that performance. By robust we mean an aiding capability that goes far beyond that found in most technical manuals. The procedures documented there are often given as check lists that are quite usable by domain experts but quite inadequate to support those who do not already know the names and locations of the elements to be manipulated, the possible conditions encountered during performance of the procedure, and the results that are sought.

A good example of a complex procedure is the energizing and check out of a major electronic system such as a shipboard radar system. Here, the process of energizing the system is combined with assessing its operation, to ensure that it is fully functional, thus it is termed a diagnostic procedure.

As with the training resources described in earlier chapters, our goal is to exploit existing system models and preprogrammed interactive processes to produce these aiding products at a high benefit to cost ratio. As will now be outlined, the two key elements for developing and presenting aiding of complex procedures are 1) a template for specifying a step of a procedure, and 2) a procedure presentation system that accepts and delivers any set of developed steps.

*Definition of a Complex Procedure*

We define a complex procedure as a series of *steps* to be performed and zero or more conditional branches that can either skip some of the specified steps or include some steps not in the main sequence. This definition accommodates simple step sequences, such as assembly and most component replacement, as well as more complex operations such as calibration, repair, and even procedural diagnostics. It even applies to procedures in which the order in which steps are performed may vary from one requirement to another, since any variation in sequence can be represented as a conditional path, although the implementation of such variations can become somewhat untidy.

The typical procedures requiring performance support involve some assessment of conditions and some manageable number of conditional branches to accommodate those conditions.

*Scope of a Procedure Step*

The only constraint we place on the scope of a procedure step is that it must always be performed in exactly the same way. If, for example, there are five closely related actions that are always performed as a unit, and are conceptually useful to

present together, they could constitute a step. From a practical viewpoint, a step is also a chunk of performance that can be described and documented on just a few screen-sized displays. A number of benefits are realized by developing and presenting steps as individual units, including these:
- Steps may be developed by different individuals, working in parallel.
- Conditional branches are easily supported.
- Procedures may be easily modified by reordering, adding, or deleting steps.
- Variations of procedures may be produced without modifying individual steps.

## *A General Purpose Template for Step Development*

Steps are produced with little or no programming in the Flash Development System, starting with the template shown in Figure 10-7. (Towne, 2005b).

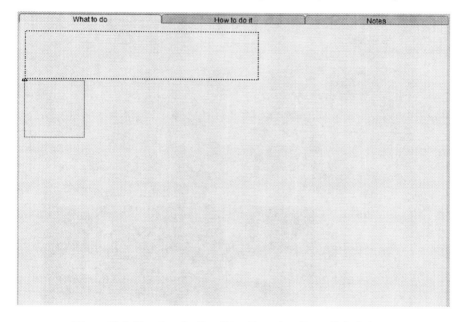

*Figure 10-7. Template for Specifying Procedure Steps (default form).*

This template is much more than a graphical pattern; it also contains functionality that supports interactivity and various model-maintenance operations, such as persistence of state. In its default form the template provides three topic tabs along the top, one text field below the tabs, and one placeholder below the text field for presenting any existing device model developed according to the design presented in earlier chapters. The template provides a separate screen display for each of the topic tabs, and the applicator has almost total control over the content and layout of each screen.

197

Almost all steps involve some changes to the default design. The following lists some of the modifications the applicator may make in producing a step:
– Text fields and model placeholders may be added, deleted, moved and scaled.
– Topic tabs, and associated screen displays, may be added, deleted, and named.
– Computer graphics and photographic images may be added.
– Interactive elements may be dragged from the Library to any topic screen.

*Example Steps*

Figure 10-8 depicts a simple step with just one topic tab but some added elements for highlighting[23], manipulating the model, and presenting a photographic image.

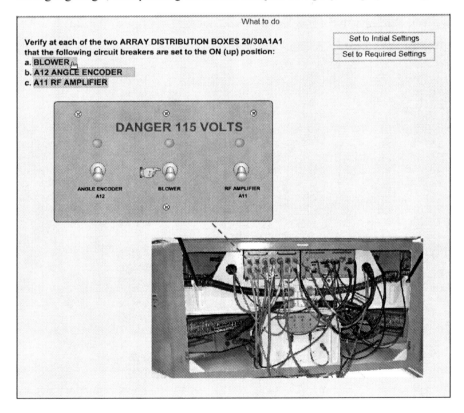

*Figure 10-8. A Simple Step.*

---

[23] In the figure, the user has moved the cursor over the term "Blower" in step a, and the Blower breaker is being pointed out.

The interactive elements support hyperlinking to other steps, highlighting various elements of the model, and manipulating the model. This last capability is crucial for both demonstrating the goal state of an action and for allowing the user to operate the model prior to operating the real system.

Almost all customization is done by entering values to dialog boxes or extracting objects from the Library, however buttons that manipulate the model are assigned program statements to set the states of the controls.

*Steps in Diagnostic Procedures*

Steps in diagnostic procedures typically provide three topic tabs, one to direct performance of the step, one to illustrate a normal outcome and one to address abnormal outcomes. Figure 10-9 shows such a step with the first tab selected.

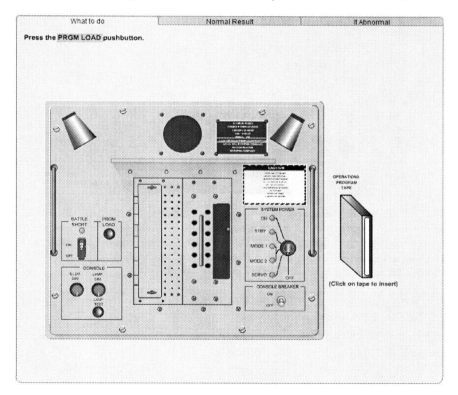

*Figure 10-9. Initial Screen of a Diagnostic Procedure Step.*

The *Normal Result* screen shown in Figure 10-10 illustrates the desired result of the action.

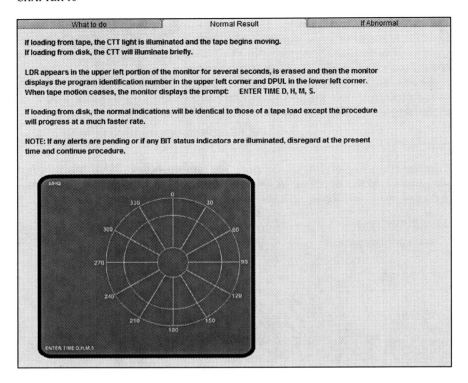

| What to do | Normal Result | If Abnormal |
|---|---|---|

If loading from tape, the CTT light is illuminated and the tape begins moving.
If loading from disk, the CTT will illuminate briefly.

LDR appears in the upper left portion of the monitor for several seconds, is erased and then the monitor displays the program identification number in the upper left corner and DPUL in the lower left corner. When tape motion ceases, the monitor displays the prompt: ENTER TIME D, H, M, S.

If loading from disk, the normal indications will be identical to those of a tape load except the procedure will progress at a much faster rate.

NOTE: If any alerts are pending or if any BIT status indicators are illuminated, disregard at the present time and continue procedure.

*Figure 10-10. A Normal Result of a Diagnostic Procedure Step.*

The screen shown when an abnormality is encountered typically directs the individual to conduct other procedures, such as calibrations, replacements, or further diagnostic actions on a subsection of the system. Figure 10-11 shows the presentation when the example step outcome is abnormal, leading to two different procedures depending upon the particular symptom observed.

| What to do | Normal Result | If Abnormal |
|---|---|---|
| If nothing is displayed on the monitor go | Here | |
| If monitor display is abnormal or distorted, go | Here | |

*Figure 10-11. An Abnormal Result of a Diagnostic Procedure Step.*

Upon completing a step, the developer saves and compiles it. The compiled step files are then assembled into a procedure, as described next.

*Assembling and Presenting Procedures*

Procedures are created by the applicator, and presented to a user, via the Procedure Presentation System, in the general format shown in Figure 10-12.

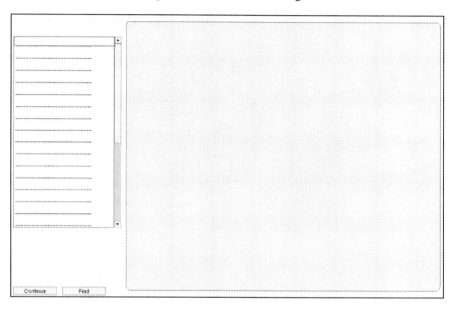

*Figure 10-12. Procedure Presentation System Screen Layout.*

The scrollable and selectable text field on the left lists the steps of a procedure textually, and the area on the right displays the currently selected step of the procedure.

To produce a new procedure, the applicator enters a list of steps and a name for the procedure, and then runs the Procedure Presentation System in file creation mode. The result is a data file that contains all the information necessary to 1) provide the scrolling list of step descriptions on the left; 2) display the models and other content associated with each tab of each step; and 3) support finding and identifying elements in the procedure models and step descriptions.

In Figure 10-13 we see the presentation when a user selects a step from the scrolling list (the next to last step displayed, which is also the step discussed above). The user may advance to the next step by pressing the *Continue* button, or by selecting it from the scrollable list.

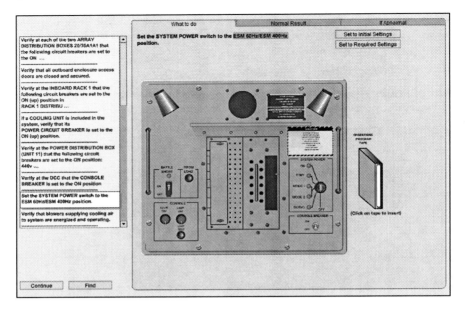

*Figure 10-13. A Step Shown in Presentation Mode.*

## Persistence of Model States

Although the individual steps of a procedure are created and stored as individual compiled files, the Presentation System maintains persistence in the states of the model elements as a procedure is shown and acted upon by the user. Thus, any action performed on a device model on one step is reflected in any other steps that show that model. In this way, a user can perform the documented steps on the model prior to doing so on the real equipment, and compare what is seen in the real world with what is being described and shown.

## Finding Content by Keyword

In the process of producing the data file for a procedure, the Presentation System also compiles a list of the names of all elements in the models, and all the technically interesting keywords that it encounters in the step text fields. Upon selecting the Find button at the bottom of the screen, the user sees the display shown in Figure 10-14 (Towne, 2007).

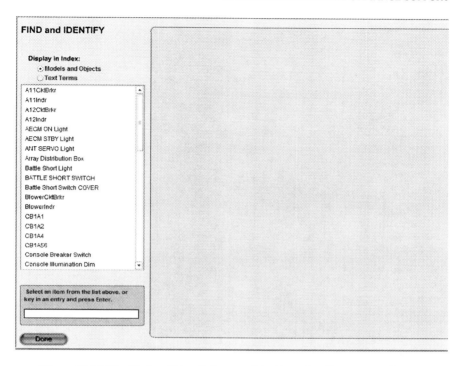

*Figure 10-14. The Find and Identify Screen of the Procedure Presentation System.*

Via the radio buttons at the top left corner, the user can control whether the names of the Models and Objects are listed, or the Text Terms that are present in the procedure. Suppose, for example, the user is performing a procedure that mentions CB1A2, but he or she does not know where that element is or what it looks like. Upon selecting CB1A2 in the list of Models and Objects, the learner would see the presentation of Figure 10-15. In this case, the pointing hand makes it clear that CB1A2 is a toggle switch on the Distribution Box, which is the top unit in Rack 1.

Alternatively, suppose a user is trying to locate the indicators related to coolant "flow", but cannot find an entry in the Models and Objects list that starts with "flow". By entering "flow" to the Search box, the user sees the presentation of Figure 10-16, which identifies an object whose name includes "flow". In this case the system has highlighted the LOW FLOW PORT indicator, both by displaying a pointing hand on the model as well as by highlighting the object name in the Models and Objects list (the sixth name in the scrolling list). Now, the user can rapidly step through all the parts whose name include "flow" by repeatedly pressing the Enter key.

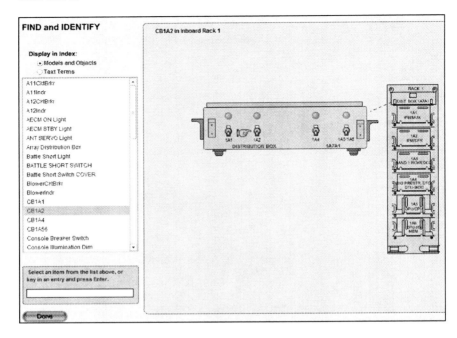

*Figure 10-15. Finding and Locating CB1A2 from the Index.*

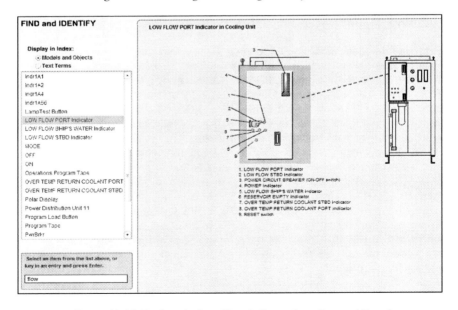

*Figure 10-16. Finding the Low Flow Indicator by a Keyword Search.*

In a similar fashion, the user may search for textual terms in the steps of a procedure, either by selecting from the automatically produced list of interesting technical terms or by keying in entries to the keyword search box. Suppose a technician knows what the Cooling Unit is and what it looks like, but wants to locate the steps in the procedure that deal with the cooling system. By entering "cooling" to the keyword search box, with Text Terms listed in the Index, the user sees the display of Figure 10-17, showing the first step involving this term, and each time he or she subsequently presses the Enter key the next step that references "cooling" is shown.

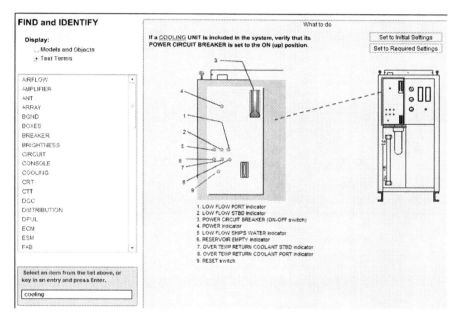

*Figure 10-17. Finding a Text Term ("cooling") in the Procedure Steps.*

## Identifying Model Elements

The finding functions described above serve the user who knows an element name but does not know its location or appearance; the user supplies the name and the system locates and highlights the element.

The converse requirement arises when a user wishes to identify an element seen in the presentation. In the front panel of the EW system, for example, there is a tiny element near the center of the unit that is unlabeled, and would be difficult to identify. As shown in Figure 10-18, the user may move the mouse cursor over the element (near the right side of the figure), and that element's name is displayed at the bottom of the screen.

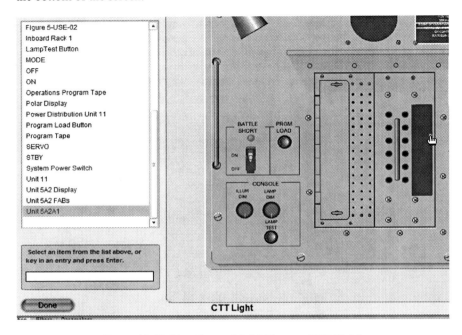

*Figure 10-18. Identifying a Model Element (CTT Light).*

AIDING SYSTEM-LEVEL DIAGNOSTIC PERFORMANCE

Throughout the system turn-on and checkout procedure are links that exit the main procedure when abnormalities are seen, as shown in Figure 10-19.

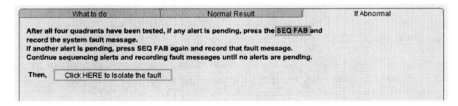

*Figure 10-19. A Link to a Separate Diagnostic Routine.*

The abnormality encountered in this step happens to arise from faults in a section of the system termed the Band 2 Direction Finding Receivers, or DFRs. Since there are four identical DFRs, the procedure first determines which receiver is faulty, and then it proceeds to identify the faulty module in the receiver. The remainder of this section will focus on how troubleshooting is supported in carrying out this process.

## Procedures for Fault Localization

With this target system, and many others, there are documented strategies that the technician is to follow to localize the fault to a major unit in the system. This procedure is tightly bound to the extensive built-in test (BIT) capabilities that constrain the diagnostic procedure. Thus, this level of diagnostic performance is much more proceduralized than the diagnostic reasoning required in lower (depot) level troubleshooting, as covered in Chapter 8.

## Supporting Performance of the Strategy

The functions for supporting the technician in performing the preexisting diagnostic routine are similar to those described in the previous section, with the additions that the overall diagnostic strategy serves as the basis for selecting steps, and the diagnostic steps typically include explicit identification of system elements that are suspected or confirmed as operational, similarly to the way in which the DIAG system enumerates these findings.

The main screen of the DFR fault-localization process presents the diagnostic strategy, with the first step, *Identify Faulty Quadrant*, selected, as shown in Figure 10-20.

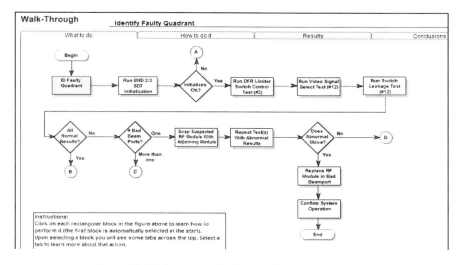

*Figure 10-20. Overview of DFR Troubleshooting Strategy.*

This strategy screen, with the currently selected step highlighted, appears whenever the *What to do* tab is selected, for all steps.

*How to do it.* The screen shown in Figure 10-21 is presented when the user selects the How to do it tab for the step.

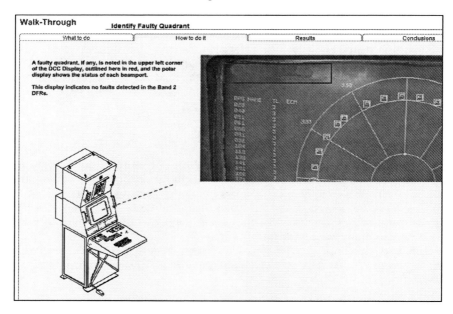

*Figure 10-21. Supporting Performance of a Diagnostic Step.*

This advises the technician where he or she should look for the outcome of the test and how a normal result would appear (in this case, the absence of an alert is normal, as indicated by the highlight on the photograph).

*Results.* The Results tab leads to the screen shown in Figure 10-22. This screen shows a sample of one abnormal result, it lists the four possible abnormal outcomes that could be seen, and it prompts the technician to select the symptom seen on the actual system.

When the technician indicates the symptom actually seen, the step determines what system units could be the cause, in preparation for the Conclusions portion of the step, as described next.

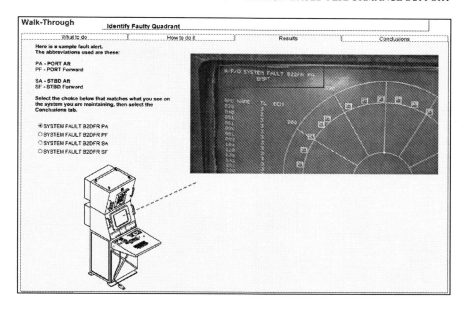

*Figure 10-22. A Listing of Possible Test Results.*

Conclusions.   The *Conclusions* tab for this first step presents (Figure 10-23) a top-level system diagram for the entire EW system with the suspected elements (DFR A7, in the Aft section of the ship on the port side) highlighted in red and the confirmed good elements -- both DFRs on the starboard side of the ship and DFR A8, at the forward section of the ship on the port side – highlighted in green.

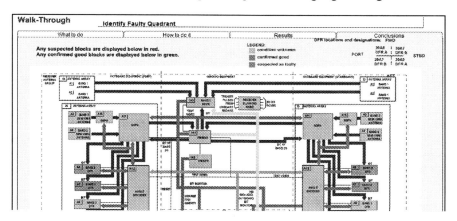

*Figure 10-23. Conclusions from the Reported Test Outcome.*

The technician would now select the *What to do* tab again, select the next step in the procedure, and continue in that fashion until either the fault is isolated to a replaceable board or a symptom leads out of the current procedure.

*Possible Termination Conditions*

In those cases in which the course of testing leads to identification of a faulty board, the replacement step provides all the information required to locate and remove the board and install a known good spare. Figure 10-24 shows the removal topic of the replacement step, a procedure that requires identifying certain cables. Consequently, tables are provided as topics in the step with which to make these identifications.

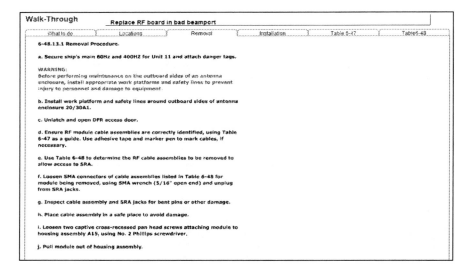

*Figure 10-24. The Removal Portion of the Board Replacement Step.*

If the symptoms seen do not implicate a particular board in a particular DFR, the strategy either leads to fault isolation strategies for sections outside of the DFRs (exits A, B, and C in Figure 10-20) or it advises the technician to adopt conventional troubleshooting methods in portions of the DFRs not covered by the BIT system (exit D). It is under this latter condition that the rich symptom implication information already provided is of vital use, since this serves as the starting point for further troubleshooting, possibly supported by DIAG.

*Extensions to the Default Template*

The examples have demonstrated that the default step template can be condensed or extended as required. Figure 10-8 illustrated a step with only one topic tab, while the step of Figure 10-24 uses six. Thus, there is no built in constraint that limits what technical issues can be addressed in a step. In general, a step will document what is to be done and where in the target system that activity is to occur, and the placement of the step in the sequence implies when the step should be performed. If a developer feels that the technician will need additional information, however, such as why a step is performed, how it is done, or under what conditions it should, or should not, be performed, those are perfectly legitimate topics that can be addressed in the step.

# INTERACTIVE TECHNICAL DOCUMENTATION

The technical documentation accompanying complex systems can have a significant impact on the effectiveness with which the system is employed and maintained. Even when conventional user manuals are developed with the user's projected experience and needs in mind, which too often is not the case, the ways in which their fixed hard-copy form can serve the end user and the options for representing complex system behaviors are extremely limited. Even the textual content provided in hard-copy manuals is often difficult to interpret, as the conceptual connections between the text and accompanying graphics are rarely indicated.

In this chapter we will review an approach for producing highly interactive technical documentation using device models combined with other text, computer graphics, and video media. The end product is an example of an Interactive Electronic Technical Manual (Fuller, Rainey, & Post, 1996), or IETM, that can be viewed on any platform capable of executing Flash applications.

This development and delivery system, PKS (for Personal Knowledge Source) (Towne, 2001, 2002b), was briefly introduced in Chapter 6. Given one or more device models, developed in conformance with the design of earlier chapters, one can rapidly develop the kinds of demonstrations and explanations that are appropriate to the purposes of an IETM. Moreover, if those models were already produced to meet training and/or performance aiding requirements, the marginal cost to produce a truly effective technical manual can be quite modest.

## SYSTEM OVERVIEW

PKS can be viewed as a massively empowered version of MS PowerPoint. Like PowerPoint slide presentations, PKS IETMs are created via direct manipulation of media, including text, graphics, sound, and video, following the WYSIWYG (What You See Is What You Get) principle. Also, both systems employ a screen view as the basic unit of an application. PowerPoint, however, is primarily oriented toward presentation of those screens in a sequential fashion, whereas PKS offers a number of options for navigating to different sections and for locating particular content of interest.

### Screen Layout of User Mode

A view of a sample PKS IETM, as seen by the user, is shown in Figure 11-1.

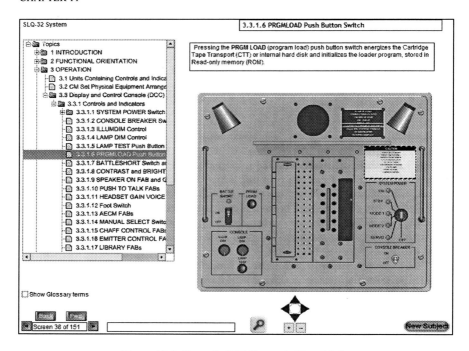

*Figure 11-1. Example PKS Screen in User Mode.*

The subject name is displayed in the upper left corner and the number and title of the current screen is given on the upper right side.

The selectable list of topics positioned along the left side is produced automatically by PKS. This list, which can be expanded and collapsed by the user, serves to explicitly reflect the organization of the content as well as providing one way for finding and viewing particular topics of interest.

The majority of screen real estate is devoted to the content for the selected topic. This area may contain any number of text fields, interactive ReAct models, graphical overlays, GUI controls, and other media elements. At the discretion of the developer, models on any screen may be operable by the user or restricted to configurations set up by the developer.

Below the Topic list is a check box with which the user may control whether glossary terms are highlighted or not, and below that are the buttons for navigating through the user's History (Back and Fwd) or through the default sequence of screens (left and right arrow).

At the bottom center is a magnifying glass icon used to search for keywords in the textual content. To the right of that is a control used to zoom in to complex figures or models and to drag figures that are too large to display at one time.

Near the lower right corner is the *New Subject* button that brings up a list of available PKS IETMs.

214

*External Media Files*

In addition to the built-in capabilities for presenting text and graphics, various external media files may be incorporated into an IETM, as listed in Table 11-1.

*Table 11-1. External Media File Types Usable in PKS*

| Source media | Source file type |
|---|---|
| Digitized images | .jpg |
| Digitized video | .avi |
| Flash animation | .swf |
| ReAct simulation | .swf |

When a PKS IETM is saved, only the references to the external files are stored, thus the application files are quite compact. Additionally, this approach permits media files to be modified independently of the application files, so that all presentations of the application reflect the latest media updates.

The developer may choose the controls to provide for playing digitized video. In the figure below, a video is shown with controls for Stop and Play.

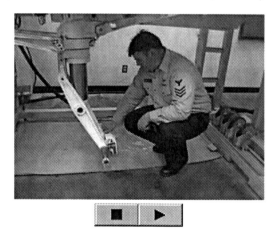

*Figure 11-2. A Digitized Video with Stop and Play Controls.*

IETM DEVELOPMENT

In development mode, shown in Figure 11-3, additional command buttons appear at the bottom of the screen.

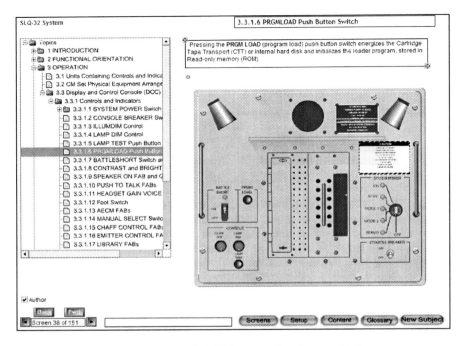

*Figure 11-3. Example PKS Screen in Development Mode.*

Briefly, the development functions are as given in Table 11-2.

*Table 11-2. Summary of PKS Development Functions.*

| Function | Purpose |
|---|---|
| Screens | Add, move, remove, or duplicate screens. |
| Setup | Specify characteristics of the current screen, e.g., background color and provision of the image zoom control and the Topic List. |
| Content | Select and place content elements on the current screen, e.g., text fields, ReAct models, model control buttons, jpg images, hyperlinks, GUI elements (radio buttons, tabs, etc.). |
| Glossary | Add a glossary term with definition, or remove an existing glossary term. |

*Creating a New IETM*

When a new IETM is created, the developer specifies the name of the IETM and the default setup of the screens in that application. The setup options include the background screen color, and the presence or absence of the Topic list, the image zoom control, and the navigation buttons. While the default layout would normally provide these three elements, the developer may elect to omit any that are not desired, and can override this default setup for any particular screen. The new IETM is initialized with ten screens, ready for populating with content.

*Populating a Screen*

Each screen of the IETM is populated with content by selecting the Content button, then dragging elements from the resulting dialog box to the display area and customizing those elements as desired. As seen in Figure 11-4, the dialog box used for this purpose is organized into three sections:
- Static elements such as basic graphical shapes, icons, text fields, and jpg images;
- Active elements such as models, buttons to control models, and hyperlinks; and
- GUI elements: radio buttons, tabs, and checkboxes.

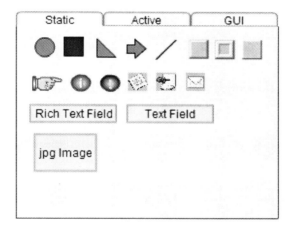

*Figure 11-4. Dialog Box for Adding Content to PKS Screens (Static tab selected).*

The customization that follows the placement of an element depends upon the type of element. All of the graphical shapes and icons may be scaled and rotated; models and text fields may be scaled; and elements that overlay others may be scaled and made semi-transparent.

*Static Graphical Elements*

The static elements include geometric shapes, beveled rectangles, icons, text fields, and jpg images. Two types of text field are provided: 1) a field for Rich Text, with no limitations on formatting, and 2) a simple text field, typically used for labels and other short descriptions. The formatting of Rich text includes most of the options available in standard word processors, including font style, font size, bold,

217

italic, underlined, text color, background color, border color, text alignment, and bullets. The simple text field provides most of these options as well, but the selected formatting is applied to all the text in the field.

*Active Elements*

The active elements (Figure 11-5) are those that are operated upon by the end user, and include graphical overlays (cover links), textual hyperlinks, buttons that modify the screen, vector graphic files (ReAct models and Flash files), and controls that operate models.

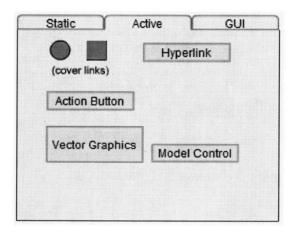

*Figure 11-5. Active Screen Content Elements.*

The *cover links* and hyperlink elements navigate to another screen in the current IETM or to one in another IETM.

Action buttons are used to modify the presentation on the screen, primarily by adding or removing other elements. With such buttons, for example, a screen could step through a procedure, adding step-specific information with each actuation of the action button.

The *Vector Graphics* selection evokes a list of all ReAct models and Flash files available for placement on the current PKS screen. A number of options are available for controlling how models are presented and used. With these the developer may control whether or not the user may operate the model and how, or if, a model is initialized each time it is shown, as opposed to maintaining its state between presentations. In addition, the *Model Control* buttons may be set up to put a model into a designated condition when selected by the user.

*GUI Elements*

Four GUI elements – radio buttons, check boxes, scrolling fields, and tabs -- may be selected from the dialog box shown in Figure 11-6 and assigned appropriate labels and content.

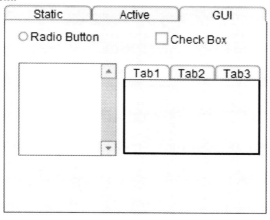

*Figure 11-6. GUI Screen Content Elements.*

*Maintaining the Topic List*

The Topic list (Figure 11-7) is generated automatically by PKS each time an application is started in development mode.

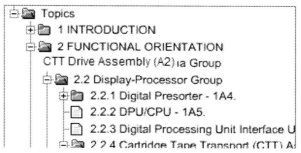

*Figure 11-7. Example Topic List.*

Thus as the developer adds, removes, and reorganizes screens as an application evolves, the Topic list is automatically kept current. Additionally, there is no need to develop hyperlinks between the topics and the content, as PKS takes care of responding to mouse clicks on topics by navigating to the associated screen.

*Establishing a Glossary*

As an option, a list of glossary terms may be entered along with definitions. The dialog box for doing this is shown in Figure 11-8.

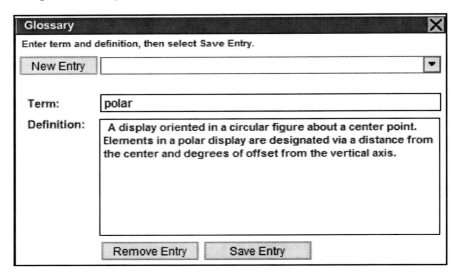

*Figure 11-8. Dialog Box for Defining a Glossary Term.*

PKS manages all highlighting of glossary terms and the presentation of the Glossary definitions when selected by the user, as described below.

### USING A PKS IETM

The user can navigate to different screens as desired, operate upon the active screen elements, view the definitions of Glossary terms, search for textual terms, manage the view of complex figures and models, and change IETM topics. These user actions will be discussed next.

*Navigating to Screens*

Navigating from one screen to another can be accomplished in four ways:
1) by selecting topics from the Topic list;
2) by moving through topics in sequence, using the forward and back arrows;
3) by moving through the individual's History of screens viewed, using the Back and Fwd buttons; and
4) by following hyperlinks provided within the screen content.

Navigation by screen sequence and user History is accomplished with the button group at the lower left of the screen, as shown here.

The appearance and response of hyperlinks is established by the developer. In Figure 11-9, a hyperlink is provided at the bottom of a text field, linking to a screen that shows a detailed view of the Pilot Instrument Panel Assembly. Hyperlinks can also be placed over any text or graphical elements.

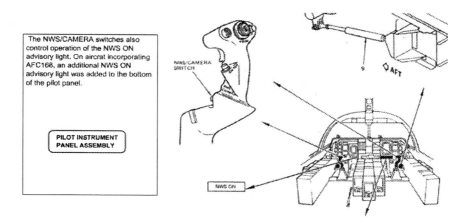

*Figure 11-9. A Hyperlink within a Text Field.*

*Operating Models*

If allowed by the developer, the user may operate a model directly. In most technical documentation applications, however, the model is presented in particular conditions that the developer wishes to show, possibly accompanied with buttons that produce specified changes. In Figure 11-10, for example, the *Panel ON* and *Panel OFF* buttons allow the user to compare an energized configuration to a de-energized configuration.

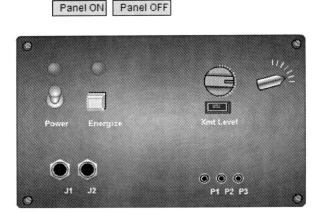

Figure 11-10. A ReAct Model With Configuration Controls.

### Operating on Active Screen Content

The active elements provide linkage between the text and the graphic presentation. In Figure 11-11, the user has selected "Cooling Unit" in step d, and the corresponding unit is being highlighted in the graphics.

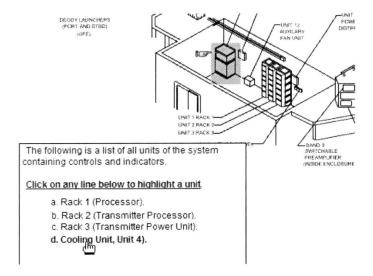

Figure 11-11. A User Selection Producing an Action on a Diagram.

*Finding Terms on PKS Screens*

Just as a *Find and Identify* function was implemented within the procedure presentation system of Chapter 10, PKS includes such resources designed specifically to search through the content of IETM screens. This section will outline the finding of textual terms, and the next will describe how one locates parts of systems in graphical views.

To find textual terms, the user selects the magnifying glass icon and keys in a term of interest and the types of media to be searched. In Figure 11-12 the user is searching for "angle" in text, and PKS has brought up the next screen whose text includes that term. Each subsequent actuation of the *Find Now* button produces the next instance of the term of interest. The user may also search for terms that appear in the Topic list and within figures and models.

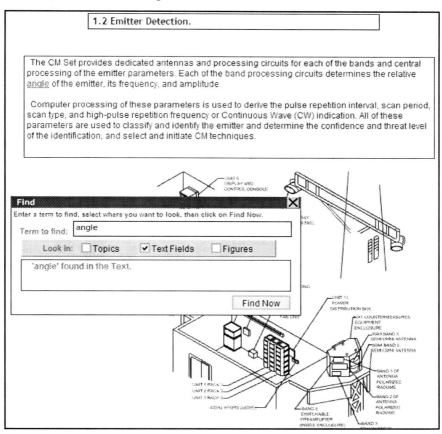

*Figure 11-12. Example Keyword Search ("angle").*

*Finding and Identifying Parts of Systems*

Because PKS IETMs typically incorporate many preexisting drawings and figures, in addition to simulations and models, a facility is provided (Towne, 2002a) that permits the IETM developer to identify parts on those types of drawings. In general, a part is identified by 1) dragging the mouse across the area of a figure and entering the name of the elements shown there, and 2) indicating whether the figure reflects the location of the part or just its appearance.

While involving some development effort, as opposed to the automatic part identification resources described in Chapter 10 for models, this approach provides a powerful way for the developer to encode static figures with part identifications.

When this facility is provided, the user interface includes an additional button, labeled *Find Part*, the actuation of which produces an alphabetic list of system elements, as shown in Figure 11-13.

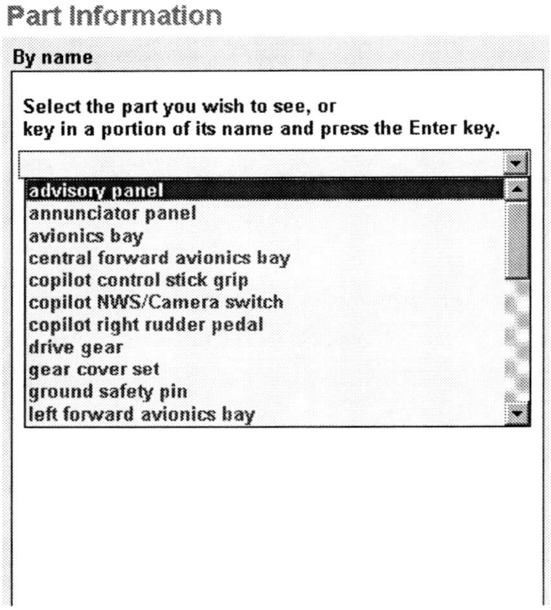

### Part Information

**By name**

Select the part you wish to see, or
key in a portion of its name and press the Enter key.

- advisory panel
- annunciator panel
- avionics bay
- central forward avionics bay
- copilot control stick grip
- copilot NWS/Camera switch
- copilot right rudder pedal
- drive gear
- gear cover set
- ground safety pin
- left forward avionics bay

*Figure 11-13. Alphabetic Listing of Parts.*

When the user selects a part from this list, the first diagram containing this part is presented, the part is highlighted, and a list of the other types of figures containing the part is shown.

In Figure 11-14, the user has selected "drive gear", and that part is highlighted via a red (on-screen) rectangle.

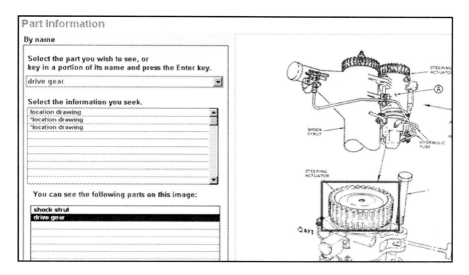

*Figure 11-14. A Diagram Identifying "shear pin".*

Two lists are presented at the left of the diagram. The upper list itemizes all the diagrams that include the searched part, listed by the type of information available. In the example there are three diagrams in which the *location* of the drive gear is apparent, and the user may select any of these. In other cases, the term "appearance" might be given, indicating a diagram that shows the part, but does not provide information about its location.

The lower list itemizes all the parts that are identified on the current diagram. As the user moves the mouse through this list, PKS highlights the part in the diagram, thus one can also determine the name of a part from its appearance and location. In the figure, the shock strut is also identifiable.

*Viewing Glossary Definitions*

When the Show *Glossary Terms* checkbox is set to checked, all terms that are in the Glossary are highlighted on each screen as it is viewed. When any such term is then selected, its definition is shown. In Figure 11-15, the user has selected the term "polar" (the highlighting of the term on the computer screen is very evident, but less obvious in the black and white figure).

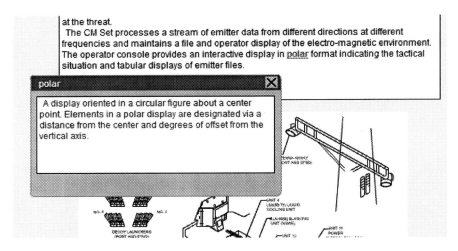

at the threat.
  The CM Set processes a stream of emitter data from different directions at different frequencies and maintains a file and operator display of the electro-magnetic environment. The operator console provides an interactive display in polar format indicating the tactical situation and tabular displays of emitter files.

polar ☒

A display oriented in a circular figure about a center point. Elements in a polar display are designated via a distance from the center and degrees of offset from the vertical axis.

*Figure 11-15. A Glossary Term (polar) Selected.*

## Managing the View of Complex Models

Frequently, technical documentation involves diagrams that are far larger and more detailed than one would like. While such diagrams can be decomposed into smaller independent sections, this can conflict with viewing the diagram as a whole, and can actually exacerbate the problem of comprehending the content. Often, a better option is to present the entire diagram, and allow the viewer to control the scale at which it is rendered. PKS provides the control shown here to do this.

The plus and minus buttons increase and decrease the scale of the diagram under the control, while the four arrow heads can be selected to reposition the diagram. In Figure 11-16, the user is viewing a complex signal diagram, but cannot read the signal designations. In Figure 11-17, the user has zoomed into the area of interest and can easily make out the smallest details. (When the higher scale causes a diagram to obscure the navigation controls, as it does here, the user can either zoom back out or simply drag the figure to the right until the Topic list and navigation buttons are again revealed.)

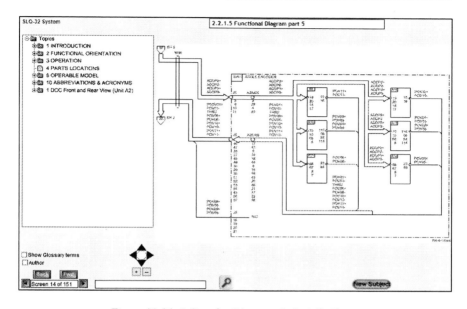

*Figure 11-16. A Complex Diagram As Initially Seen.*

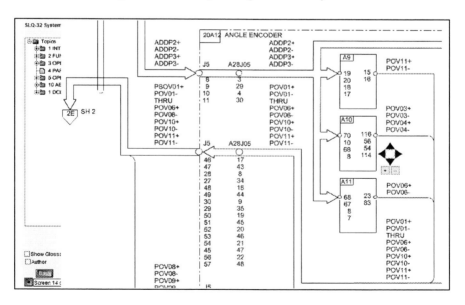

*Figure 11-17. A Diagram Viewed at a Higher Scale.*

*Changing Topics*

The New Subject button near the lower right corner presents a list of the PKS IETMs available for view, the same list that is presented each time PKS is started. With this button a technician could choose to leave a manual covering a particular radar system and review one on radar fundamentals, returning to the prior manual via the Back button.

*Documentation of Procedures*

Chapter 10 presented a system for supporting the performance of complex procedures, using a system dedicated to that purpose. Procedures can also be documented in IETM format as a series of steps and screens associated with each step. Unlike the dedicated approach discussed previously, a PKS step consists of one screen containing the textual explanation and the associated graphics.

When the user selects the procedure from the Topics list, the step explanations are assembled into a scrollable list presented on the left, and the graphics associated with the current step is shown on the right. The user may then work through the steps in sequence, or may select particular steps as required. In Figure 11-18, the user is viewing a step in a procedure for removing the Gear Cover Set from the aircraft nose wheel.

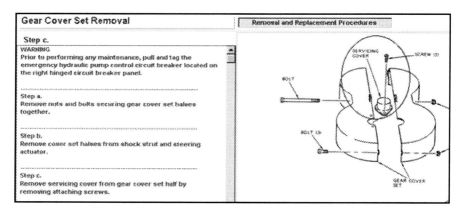

*Figure 11-18. PKS Presentation of a Procedure.*

RANGE OF APPLICATION

PKS IETMs have been produced for specific hardware systems, such as the EW system used in the previous examples; for technical fundamentals, such as theory of digital systems; and for software systems, such as the DIAG, ReAct, and PKS development and delivery systems. Figure 11-19 presents a sample screen from the ReAct Developers' Manual, developed in PKS.

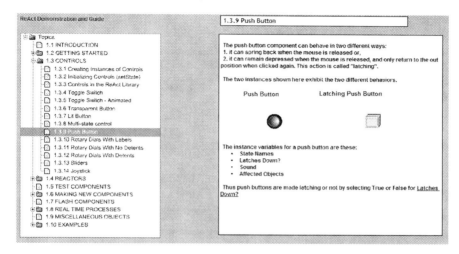

*Figure 11-19. A Screen From the ReAct Developer's Manual.*

Figure 11-20 presents a sample screen from the PKS Developers' manual, developed in PKS.

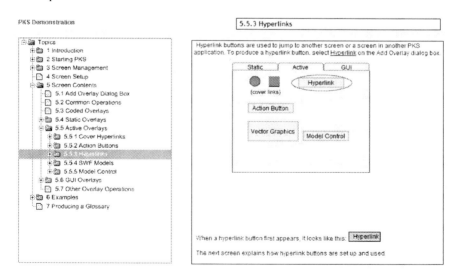

*Figure 11-20. A Screen from the PKS Developers' Manual.*

## SUMMARY OF PKS IETM APPLICATIONS

Table 11-3 lists the PKS IETMs that have been produced.

*Table 11-3. PKS IETMs.*

| Topic | No. Screens |
|---|---|
| Aircraft Nosewheel Steering System: Principles of Operation | 35 |
| Aircraft Nosewheel Steering System: Removal and Installation Procedures | 99 |
| Radio Principles of Operation * | 25 |
| Transistor Theory * | 34 |
| Amplifier Theory * | 41 |
| Power Supply Fundamentals * | 19 |
| Digital Theory * | 67 |
| Development of ReAct Models | 75 |
| Development of DIAG Applications | 19 |
| Development of PKS IETMs | 80 |

* Developed by Instructional Science and Development, Inc., Pensacola, FL

# SIMULATIONS IN MULTIPLE USES

The primary intent of this final chapter is to present an application that provides a full complement of technical services for a particular domain, the aircraft nose wheel steering (NWS) system. The chapter concludes with a summary of domain simulations and training and aiding applications produced for each.

## A COMPLETE TECHNICAL SUPPORT APPLICATION

The intent of this application is to provide the technical support required by the operator or maintainer, from the training school to the job site. The main user interface for the application is provided as a PKS screen, as shown in Figure 12-1.

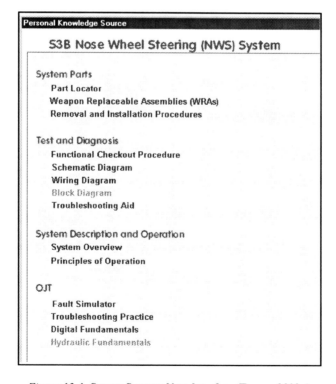

*Figure 12-1. System Support User Interface (Towne, 2002a).*

*Support Functions*

Of the subsections shown, two – the block diagram and hydraulic principles – have not yet been developed, and two – WRAs and wiring diagram – are static figures extracted from an existing technical manual and offering no interaction with the user. Each of the remaining topics involves some level of interactivity and most involve the model of the NWS system.

*Topics Presented From Within the PKS IETM*

The following five topics are presented from within the PKS application itself:
- Part Locator
- Removal and Installation Procedures
- Functional Checkout
- Schematic Diagram
- System Overview

Examples of the first four topics may be found in Chapter 11. An example screen from the System Overview is seen in Figure 12-2.

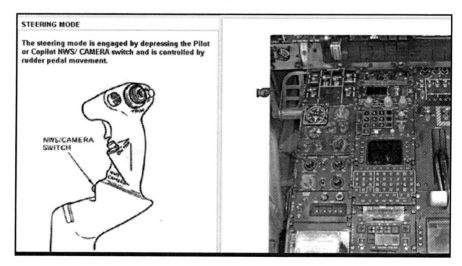

*Figure 12-2. System Overview, as Presented in PKS.*

*DIAG Aiding*

The Troubleshooting Aid topic links to DIAG in its performance aiding mode, as covered in Chapter 10, in which the technician performs tests according to the

DIAG recommendations and reports the symptoms observed. The first test recommendation is shown in Figure 12-3.

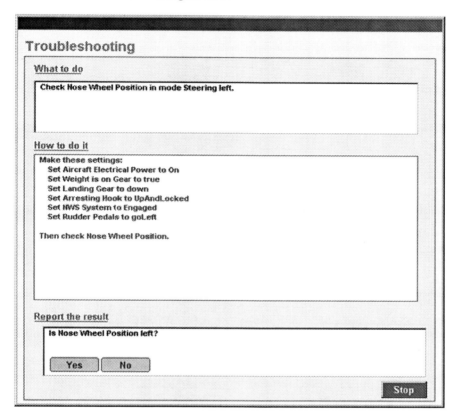

*Figure 12-3. DIAG Test Recommendation for the NWS System.*

After performing the recommended test and making the observation as advised, the technician reports whether the test outcome was normal or abnormal. If the nose wheel successfully repositions to the left, as it normally should, the technician would select *Yes* and DIAG would determine the significance of that result, as shown in Figure 12-4.

233

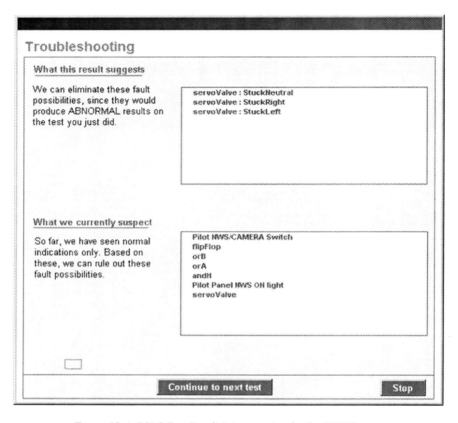

*Figure 12-4. DIAG Test Result Interpretation for the NWS System.*

*System Demonstration*

The Principles of Operation are demonstrated via the methods for interacting with the system model described in Chapter 6. Figure 12-5 is presented here as a reminder of the demonstration application.

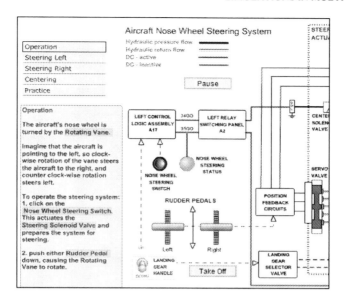

*Figure 12-5. Interactive Demonstration of NWS System Operation.*

## Fault Simulator

The Fault Simulator allows the learner to insert known faults into the system model and observe the fault effects. Figure 12-6 displays a partial list of available faults.

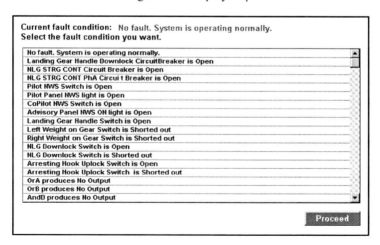

*Figure 12-6. Fault Insertion Choices for the NWS System.*

*Troubleshooting Practice*

The Troubleshooting Practice topic links to DIAG in its instructional mode. Figure 12-7 displays the DIAG guidance option that discusses a possible fault in light of the symptoms that have been observed on a current exercise.

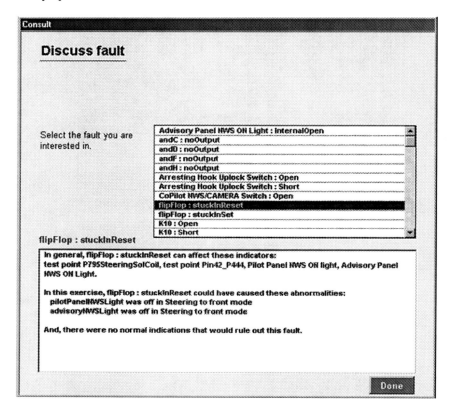

*Figure 12-7. DIAG Troubleshooting Practice (Discuss Fault).*

This practice environment includes a working model of a multimeter, in association with a schematic diagram containing "live" test points, thus the learner can make readings at this circuit level, as shown in Figure 12-8.

*Figure 12-8. Troubleshooting Practice with Working Meter.*

## Digital Fundamentals

Selecting Digital Fundamentals takes the user to a PKS application covering digital fundamentals, a screen of which is shown in Figure 12-9.

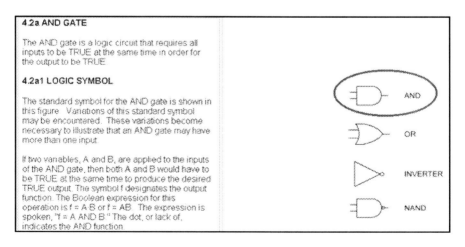

*Figure 12-9. Screen From Digital Theory Course.*

237

## SUMMARY OF MULTIPLE-USE APPLICATIONS

Table 12-1 lists the various models produced using the methods described in this volume and the kinds of applications in which they were used, not including their presentation within PKS IETMs.

*Table 12-1. Models and Their Applications.*

| ReAct Model | Functional Demo' | Procedure Aiding | Diagnostic Training | Diagnostic Aiding |
|---|---|---|---|---|
| Home Heating System | | | √ | √ |
| ES-3A Power Dist'n System | | | √ | √ |
| Generic Warning System | | | √ | √ |
| Oscilloscope Usage | √ | | | |
| Fluke Multimeter Usage | √ | | | |
| Aircraft Nose Wheel Steering | √ | √ | √ | √ |
| CIC Operations | √ | √ | | |
| Full Adder Circuit | √ | | √ | √ |
| Electronic Warfare (EW) system | √ | √ | | |

The simulation of fires in high-rise office buildings was employed only in scenario-based training, as delivered by $D^3M$.

# REFERENCES

Bhangal, S. (2004). *Flash Hacks.* Sebastopol, CA: O'Reilly.

Booch, G. (1991). *Object oriented design with applications.* Redwood City, CA: Benjamin/Cummings.

Coleman, J. F. (1997). *Incident management for the Street-Smart Fire officer.* Saddle Brook, NJ: PennWell Publishing.

Collins, A., Brown, J. S., & Newman, S. E. (1989). Cognitive apprenticeship: Teaching the crafts of reading, writing, and mathematics. In L. B. Resnick (Ed.), *Knowing, learning, and instruction: Essays in honor of Robert Glaser.* Hillsdale, NJ: Lawrence Erlbaum.

de Jong, T., van Joolingen, W., Scott, D., de Hoog, R., Lapied, L., & Valent, R. (1994). SMISLE: System for multimedia integrated simulation learning environments. In T. deJong & L. Sarti (Eds.) *Design and production of multimedia and simulation-based learning material.* Dordrect, The Netherlands: Kluwer Academic Publishers.

Franklin, D. & Makar, J. (2004). *Flash MX 2004 actionscript.* Berkeley, CA: Macromedia Press.

Forbus, K. D., & Whalley, P. B. (1994). Using qualitative physics to build articulate software for thermodynamics education. In *Proceedings of AAAI-94*, August, 1994, 1175-1182.

Forbus, K. (1984). *An interactive laboratory for teaching control system concepts.* (Tech. Report 5511). Cambridge, MA: Bolt Beranek and Newman.

Fuller, J. J., Rainey, S. C., & Post, T. J. (1996). *Maintenance and logistic system-support benefits resulting from introduction of IETM-based technology (NSWCCD/TSS-97/02)*, Carderock Division 97/02, Naval Surface Warfare Center. Bethesda, MD.

Harel, D. (1987). Statecharts: A visual formalism for complex systems. *Science of Computer Programming*, 8, 231-274.

Harel, D (1997). Executable object modeling with statecharts. *IEEE COMPUTER*, *30*(7), July, 31-42.

Hollan, J. D., Hutchins, E. L., & Weitzman, L. (1984). STEAMER: An interactive inspectable simulation-based training system. *The AI Magazine, 2.*

Johnson, W. B., Norton, J. E., Duncan, P. E., & Hunt, R. M. (1998). *Development and demonstration of an intelligent tutoring system for technical training (MITT)* (AFHRL-TP-88-8). Brooks AFB, TX: The Air Force Human Resources Laboratory.

Kaye, J. M. & Castillo, D. R. (2003). *Flash MX for interactive simulation.* Clifton Park, NY: Delmar Learning.

Kosko B. (1993). *Fuzzy thinking: The new science of fuzzy logic.* New York: Hyperion.

Los Angeles Fire Department (1998). *Emergency high rise operations.*

McAniff, E. P. (1974). *Strategic concepts in fire fighting.* Saddle Brook, NJ: PennWell Publishing.

REFERENCES

Moock, C. (2003). *ActionScript for Flash MX*. Sebastopol, CA: O'Reilly.

Munro, A., Johnson, M. C, Surmon, D. S., & Wogulis, J. L. (1993). Attribute-centered simulation authoring for instruction. In *Proceedings of AI-ED '93 — World Conference on Artificial Intelligence in Education*.

Munro, A. (1994). Authoring interactive graphical models. In D. M. Towne, T. de Jong, & H. Spada (Eds.), *The use of computer models for explication, analysis and experiential learning*. Berlin: Springer Verlag.

Munro, A., Johnson, M. C., Pizzini, Q. A., Surmon, D. S., & Wogulis, J. L. (1996). A tool for building simulation-based learning environments. In *Proceedings, Simulation-based Learning Technology Workshop, ITS'96*. Montreal: Canada.

National Fire Service (1996). *Model procedures guide for high-rise fire fighting*. Fire Protection Publications, Oklahoma State University.

Rigney, J., Towne, D. M., Moran, P. J., & Mishler, R. A. (1978). *Field evaluation of the generalized maintenance trainer-simulator* Technical Report ONR-90). Los Angeles, CA: Behavioral Technology Laboratories, University of Southern California.

Tannenbaum, S. I., Beard, R. L., & Salas, E. (1992). Team building and its influence on team effectiveness: An examination of conceptual and empirical developments. In K. Kelly (Ed.), *Issue theory, and research in industrial/organizational psychology*. Amsterdam: Elsevier.

Towne, D. M. (1994). Model based simulations for instruction and learning. In *Proceedings, Delta '94 Conference: Telematics for Education and Training*. Dusseldorf.

Towne, D. M. (1995). A *configurable task environment for learning research* (Technical Report No. 115). Los Angeles: Behavioral Technology Laboratories, University of Southern California.

Towne, D. M. (1997a). Approximate reasoning techniques for intelligent diagnostic instruction. *International Journal of Artificial Intelligence and Education, 8*(3-4), pp. 262-283.

Towne, D. M. (1997b). *A configurable task environment for learning research* (Technical Report 117). Los Angeles, CA: Behavioral Technology Laboratories, University of Southern California.

Towne, D. M. (1998a). *Development of scenario tutors in a generalized authoring environment: Feasibility Study* (ONR Final Report No. 119). Los Angeles: Behavioral Technology Laboratories, University of Southern California.

Towne, D. M. (1998b). *Diagnostic instruction and guidance* (Technical Report 120). Los Angeles: Behavioral Technology Laboratories, University of Southern California.

Towne, D. M. (1999). Automated production of instructionally appropriate scenarios. In *Proceedings, Eighth Conference on Computer Generated Forces and Behavioral Representation*. Orlando.

Towne, D. M. (2000). *Intelligent instruction of discrete dynamic decision making tasks* (ONR Final Report 121). Los Angeles: Behavioral Technology Laboratories, University of Southern California.

240

Towne, D. M. (2001) *An integrated environment for technical training and aiding* (NAWCTSD Scientific Report, Year Two). Los Angeles: Behavioral Technology Laboratories, University of Southern California.

Towne, D. M. (2002a). *Use of device models in supporting maintenance performance: Final report.* Los Angeles, CA: Behavioral Technology Laboratories, University of Southern California.

Towne, D. M. (2002b). Advanced techniques for IETM development and delivery. In *Proceedings Human Factors and Ergonomics Society, 46th annual meeting.* Baltimore, MD.

Towne, D. M. (2003). Automated knowledge acquisition for intelligent support of diagnostic reasoning. In T. Murray, S. Blessing, & S. Ainsworth (Eds.), *Authoring tools for advanced technology learning environments.* Dordrecht, The Netherlands: Kluwer Academic Press.

Towne, D. M. (2004). *Aiding performance via advanced technical representation systems* (NAVAIR Annual scientific report, year one). Los Angeles, CA: Behavioral Technology Laboratories, University of Southern California.

Towne, D. M. (2005a). *Aiding performance via advanced technical representation systems* (NAVAIR Annual scientific report, year two). Los Angeles, CA: Behavioral Technology Laboratories, University of Southern California.

Towne, D. M. (2005b). *Aiding performance via advanced technical representation systems* (NAVAIR Annual scientific report, year three). Los Angeles, CA: Behavioral Technology Laboratories, University of Southern California.

Towne, D. M. (2007). *Retrieving and explicating elements of model-based system representations* (NAVAIR Final report). Los Angeles, CA: Center for Cognitive Technology, University of Southern California.

Towne, D. M., de Jong, T., & Spada, H. (Eds.) (1994). *The use of computer models for explication, analysis and experiential learning.* Berlin: Springer Verlag.

Towne, D. M. & Johnson, M. (1987). *Research on computer-aided design for maintainability* (Technical Report No. 109). Los Angeles: Behavioral Technology Laboratories, University of Southern California.

Towne, D. M. & Munro, A. (1988). The intelligent maintenance training system. In J. Psotka, L. D. Massey, & S. A. Mutter (Eds.), *Intelligent tutoring systems: Lessons learned* (479-530), Hillsdale, NJ: Erlbaum.

Towne, D. M., Munro, A., Pizzini, Q. A., Surmon, D. S., & Wogulis, J. L. (1990). *Intelligent maintenance training technology* (Technical Report No. 110). Los Angeles: Behavioral Technology Laboratories, University of Southern California.

Turing, A. (1950). Computing machinery and intelligence. *Mind, LIX* (236), pp. 433-460.

Watrall, E. & Herber, N. (2004). *Flash MX 2004.* San Francisco: Sybex.

REFERENCES

Wiederholt, B. J., Norton, J. E., Johnson, W. B., & Browning, E. J. (1992). *MITT Writer and MITT Writer advanced development: Developing authoring and training systems for complex technical domains* (Final Technical Report AL-TR-1991-0122). Armstrong Laboratory, Brooks Air Force Base, TX.

White, B. Y., & Frederiksen, J. R. (1989). Causal models as intelligent learning environments for science and engineering education. *Applied Artificial Intelligence, 3*(2-3), 83-106.

White, B. Y., & Frederiksen, J. R. (1990). Causal model progressions as a foundation for intelligent learning environments. *Artificial Intelligence, 42*, 99-157.

Williams, M. D., Hollan, J. D., & Stevens, A. L. (1981). An overview of STEAMER, an advanced computer-assisted instruction system in propulsion engineering. *Behavior Research Methods and Instrumentation, 13*, 85-90.

Zachary, W. W., & Ryder, J. M. (1997). Decision-support systems: Integrating decision aiding and decision-training. In M. G. Helander, T. K. Landauer, & P. Prabhu (Eds.), *Handbook of Human-Computer Interaction* (2nd Edition) (pp. 1235-1258), Amsterdam: Elsevier.

Zadeh, L. & Kacprzyk, J. (Eds.). (1992). *Fuzzy logic for the management of uncertainty*. New York: John Wiley & Sons.

# INDEX

# GLOSSARY OF TERMS

**abstraction** A distilled, or simplified, expression of an element that distinguishes that element from all other types of element. An essential feature of an effective abstraction is the suppression of information that is not essential to describing the particular element.

**animation** In the computer graphic context, animation is the display of movement or other visible change of graphical elements over some period of time. Typically, an animated sequence is fixed in the programming statements that achieve it, rather than being under some higher level of control that can compute the changes required to reflect current conditions in a model.

**back-story** In scenario-based instruction, a verbal account of the events and conditions that precede the current exercise, providing the learner context that may be crucial to effective performance. The back-story can also tempt the learner to disregard rules of engagement, thereby demonstrating to the learner the importance of maintaining perspective.

**base class** In object-oriented programming, a base class defines the methods and properties of an element, possibly of a simulation, in parameterized terms, so that particular instances belonging to the base class can be constructed and those instances inherit the methods and properties defined in the base class.

**Bayes' theorem** A mathematical expression that can be used to update the strength of an existing belief of some hypothesis in the light of new evidence. Adherents to the Baysian theory believe that the theorem provides a good prediction of expert decision making, while others put more faith in pure frequency of occurrence, as a predictor of human assessment of evidence.

**chunking** In organizing the presentation of content, chunking refers to the method of collecting and presenting related information and identification of that common relationship, as an aid to learning. Thus, in introducing an aircraft cockpit, all elements related to communications might be presented before proceeding to the next group.

**class** In object-oriented design, a set of objects that share some common purpose, behavior and structure, typically in relationship to some hierarchy of functions.

**command interface** In scenario-based instruction, the collection of elements that provide information to the decision maker and respond to the decision maker's actions. Often, the command interface provides information coming in from the simulated problem environment and it offers some means with which the learner can issue orders and requests.

**component** In the Flash development system a component is a flexible graphical element that carries some defined functions that are sensitive to values of parameters. When instances of components are created to serve a particular simulation, each instance is assigned specific values for those parameters, and the instance serves as one version of the component.

**concurrency** In the more general sense, concurrent objects are those elements that are active within a simulation as opposed to static elements or ones which only respond to discrete events. Concurrency also refers to the apparent simultaneous change of multiple elements over time, an effect achieved by rapidly changing each active element by a small amount in each brief time slice.

**constraint-based system** A system designed so that a change in any element of the system automatically propagates to all the directly affected elements, and those in turn trigger additional waves of change. A system that is purely constraint-based has the limitation that it does not accommodate programmatic changes such as those that might express a sequence of actions.

**control** One of the two fundamental types of ReAct components (the other being "reactor"). A ReAct control object responds to actions of the user, typically mouse actions. Some few ReAct objects are both controls and reactors.

**D$^3$M** The acronym for the Dynamic Discrete Decision-Making system, a scenario-based instructional system.

**demonstration** As used here, the use of a simulation to illustrate some facet of behavior of the modeled system. A demonstration may serve a critical instructional requirement, but it alone does not satisfy the more intensive requirements of instruction, practice, and evaluation of learning.

**DIAG** The acronym for the Diagnostic Instruction and Guidance system, an intelligent diagnostic training and performance aiding system based upon an experimentally-derived and validated diagnostic decision making process.

**diagnostic reasoning** The process of modifying suspicions about possible faults in a system from symptom evidence. Initially, in a diagnostic event, experts appear to rank order suspicions according to relative reliabilities, then modify those suspicions via a process that considers frequencies of cause-effect relationships, in a fuzzy fashion.

**discovery learning** An instructional approach that emphasizes learner controlled performance of experiments to determine how and why a system behaves as it does. Discovery learning is based on the belief that such experimental results are more memorable than dictated facts. While that premise may be true, studies indicate that lacking strong support, the majority of learners have difficulty carrying out their own learning regimen.

**discrete-state object** An element, such as one in a simulation, that exists in some finite number of distinct conditions. This object type is distinguished from one that in reality can exist in an infinite number of different conditions, and in a simulation seems to exist in any of those possible states.

**emulation** Causing an element, or a system of elements, to appear to behave in a manner that corresponds to reality, typically with the minimum necessary effort to achieve the immediate objectives. Emulation is distinguished from true simulation in that the latter also attempts to express fine details about the underlying system behavior in order to learn more about the system. Much of simulation-based training is actually emulation-based training, with considerable attendant savings in development effort.

**encapsulation** A critical constituent of object-oriented design, in which implementation details about an element are hidden from the applicator, so that the applicator only deals with those parameters that impact the behavior of the element being instantiated. Encapsulation is an essential design approach that protects applicators from inadvertently modifying built-in functions, and it simplifies their task by focusing on essential behavioral aspects of the element.

**expert system** An approach to implementing intelligent training systems, in which training is based upon a set of highly context-specific rules provided by one or more domain experts. Generally, expert systems are extremely costly to produce and they are difficult, if not impossible, to test in all possible situations.

**fault diagnosis** The process of inferring the possible causes of observed symptoms in a system that might be faulty. In general, fault diagnosis includes decisions concerning what test to perform next, to further reduce the set of possible faults.

**fault effects** An expression of the manner in which particular faults will be evidenced in a particular system under various specified conditions, particularly modes of system operation. In the DIAG system of diagnostic training and aiding, fault effects are produced automatically by a process that inserts faults into the system model and records the symptoms at the various indicators and test points.

**fault simulator** A system that inserts faults, under programmatic control, into a model of a target system, so that the system model then operates as the real system does when failed in that fashion. A fault simulator can provide instructional benefits, particularly when a learner or a training system uses it to recap a completed exercise and to distinguish the effects of one fault from another in a well-managed learning environment.

**Flash** A software product of the Adobe (formerly Macromedia) Corporation. Originally developed as an animation development tool for Web-based presentations, the Flash product has become a full-fledged, object-oriented, product development system. The latest version of Flash is Flash MX 2004.

**fuzzy logic** A method of dealing with reasoning about data that is qualitative and imprecise in nature, as opposed to quantitative and precise. While imprecision might seem to be universally undesirable, some types of human reasoning are better emulated with fuzzy logic than any other process.

**global variable** A variable whose value is accessible by all of the individual software modules that may be executing. By posting the values of key variables globally, as in a blackboard system, one software module can be assured that all others can access that value if needed.

**GUI** Graphical User Interface, an on screen presentation with which a user of a system obtains information and acts upon the system. Elements of typical GUIs include buttons, scrolling text fields, selection lists, and radio buttons. In addition, the GUI may provide an abstraction of the target system, such as the depiction of a nuclear reactor within the control room.

**hierarchy** An expression of relationships among system elements. Systems may be expressed via "part of" hierarchies, in which subsystems are elements within parent elements, and "kind of" hierarchies, in which functions or objects are related by their purpose.

**IETM** Interactive Electronic Technical Manual, a general term for any technical documentation that is provided via computer. In general, most IETMs today closely resemble their hard-copy originals, with some added content-acquisition and linking features. The PKS system is a type of IETM, but one that is based upon, or at least exploits, interactive system models.

**instance** A particular active element, the structure and behavior of which are inherited from some base class definition. An instance, or object, carries some expression of its state and various functions that determine its behavior.

**instructional management** The process of selecting, tailoring, delivering, monitoring, and recording the results of instruction to an individual. Lacking instructional management, the possible uses and effectiveness of simulation systems become much more dependent upon the individual employing the system.

**instructional strategy** A particular method by which instruction will be delivered. Depending upon the system, the strategy may specify how exercises are selected for an individual, how those exercises are modified to suit the individual, and what types of guidance and remediation are provided during and after an exercise.

**intelligent guidance** The provision of computer-generated support that is sensitive to the particular context in which it is generated, possibly including past performance of the individual learner. Intelligent diagnostic guidance can be generated from the specific symptom information that has been seen by the learner and the possible symptoms that the system might produce, combined with generic (i.e., not domain-specific) diagnostic reasoning.

**knowledge acquisition** As used here, knowledge acquisition refers to the phase of learning in which content is first encountered and learned at a non-operational level, i.e., the phase in which one gains the ability to restate the content but not necessarily the ability to apply it effectively. This phase of learning is a necessary but insufficient stage to ultimate effective task performance.

**learning objectives** Statements of observable and measurable student behaviors that are the objectives of instruction. Also termed "performance objectives", these statements include what the learner will do and the conditions under which he or she will do them. In simulation-based instructional systems, the particular conditions in which exercises will be delivered are derived directly from the learning objectives.

**library** In the Flash development system, and the software products that exploit this software environment, the library serves as the storehouse of simulation elements, such as components. Instances of components – objects – are produced by dragging components from the library and entering specific values for the parameters carried by the component.

**logical element** A system element that carries out any of the Boolean operators, e.g., AND, OR, NOR, etc. Inputs to and outputs of logical elements are binary, and may be expressed as high/low, 1/0, or any other two-state specification.

**meta instruction** Instruction about the instruction. Meta instruction is crucial in simulation-based training systems, to ensure that the user understands what actions are possible and necessary to effect the various actions and what types of support are available. The need for meta instruction can be minimized by designing the operable elements to respond in ways that most users would expect.

**method** An operation performed on an object. Defined within a base class, or component, the methods specify what operations are performed and how the values of parameters affect those operations. In ReAct, the simulation developer only deals with the method that specifies how the specific instance will respond to changes in other objects, while all the other methods that affect its graphics and other behaviors are encapsulated in other methods.

**model** As used here, a model is an emulation of a target system. The term "model" is a particularly accurate description in that it suggests that the simulation of the target system is not attempting to characterize all the deep principles that produce the system behavior, but rather to duplicate the observable system responses.

**model progression** An instructional strategy studied by White and Frederiksen that begins with a highly simplified representation of a target system and then proceeds with a series of progressively more accurate and detailed representations.

**modularity** In general, the division of a complex program or application into a number of relatively independent units that can communicate and interact with one another in some way. In the development of large simulations, modularity is one key option for reducing the apparent complexity and facilitating parallel development and reuse of the parts of the application.

**navigation** In the use of computer-based user interfaces navigation refers to the change of focus from one element of the application to another, particularly when a user is moving from one schematic presentation to another, but also when passing through alternative representations of the target system.

**object** In object-oriented design, an instantiation of a more general specification of a type of element. An object has behaviors, state, and some form of identification. In ReAct, an object is an instance of a Flash component.

**object-oriented design** A process based upon object-oriented decomposition, modularity, encapsulation, and other fundamental methods for facilitating development and reusing the resulting products.

**parameter** A variable set by an applicator to specify an instance of a general class, or component. A parameter differs from a variable by being visible and controllable by the applicator, while non-parametric variables are not.

**performance support** A resource that works to assist one in accomplishing a task. Software-based performance support systems may monitor the performance in an ongoing fashion, injecting warnings or suggestions as they sense a need, they may be available as intelligent, context-dependent on-demand advisors, or they may offer static information that can be accessed in various ways.

**persistence** A characteristic of objects by which their existence and state is maintained over time, during a session, and over changes in point of view. Persistent objects behave the way real world objects do when attention is diverted then returned, however a persistent object may be reinitialized when a session is started anew.

**PKS** The Personal Knowledge Source, a model-based technical documentation system. PKS is necessarily electronic and interactive, thus it may be termed an IETM, however very few IETMs provide the functionality and information-accessing features found within PKS.

**property** A named and settable characteristic of an object. If the object is graphical it will carry some built-in properties, such as location, scale, and rotation, and it typically will carry some additional properties that affect its behavior.

**ReAct** The object-oriented simulation development and delivery system constructed within the Flash MX software development environment. Simulation applications produced in ReAct are guaranteed to be compatible with all the instructional and performance support methods described here.

**reactor** One of the two basic types of ReAct classes, or component types (the other being "control"). A ReAct reactor object responds to changes in other objects or in time. Some few ReAct objects are both reactors and controls.

**scenario** In training terms, a situation serving to provide the context of dealing with some specified set of conditions. In $D^3M$, a scenario is specified in terms of the elements involved in the exercise, their initial conditions, and scheduled events that will occur regardless of the actions of the decision maker.

**scenario-based instruction** Instruction delivered in the course of performing a task within a specified problem environment, an environment that may include uncertainty about some conditions.

**scheduled event** In $D^3M$, a change to the problem environment that will be simulated as occurring, without regard to the actions of the learner. Example scheduled events include changes to weather, a hardware failure, an error by a virtual team member, or a decision by a virtual hostile agent.

**setState** In ReAct, setState is a critical function present in all component definitions, responsible for establishing and maintaining the value of the *state* variable as a consequence of those factors that impact the object, and for maintaining the appearance of the object as a result of the value of *state*.

**simulation** In general, any synthetic representation of a real world system or phenomenon. A simulation is capable of reflecting some of the responses of the target domain to outside influences and is the more appropriate term, compared to "model", when describing a representation that generates behaviors from low-level principles.

**simulation engine** The software process responsible for maintaining the status of a simulation in response to user actions and the passage of time. In ReAct, the simulation engine calls the *setState* function of each object directly affected by an external event and those calls trigger changes to those objects consequently affected.

**SMISLE** System for Multimedia Integrated Simulation Learning Environment, a system for managing a learner's use of a simulation to encounter, discover, evaluate, and apply simulated behaviors of a target system or phenomenon.

**speech output** The automated generation of speech with some degree of flexibility beyond completely pre-recorded statements. At one extreme speech output systems operate with pre-recorded words, while at the other the basic elements are very elemental speech sounds with options for controlling pitch, rate, and other characteristics.

**state property** The critical property that distinguishes all objects. State may be of any type, including numerical, textual, color, array, and Boolean.

**statechart** A formal method for representing a complex process. The statechart is an extension of the more generic state-transition diagram, and as such is capable of representing hierarchy, concurrency, and communication. The statechart is one way to specify a model of a target domain in non-programming terms.

**STEAMER** An early object-oriented and graphical model of a shipboard propulsion system that inspired considerable simulation and training efforts in other domains.

**structured exercise** As used here, an exercise produced by interacting with a model of a target system. In general, a structured exercise may be delivered in a presentation (information acquisition) mode, an exercise mode, and a test mode, all under the control of a simple instructional management specification.

**system state recognition** The initial phase of system maintenance in which the maintainer is only concerned with determining whether the target system is fully operational or not.

**tactical decision making** The decision making process required to carry out various operations possibly involving hostile forces or threats. The factors associated with tactical decision making include high stress, high risk, uncertainty, and possible involvement of agents working to intentionally thwart the operation.

**text to speech (TTS)** The process that produces human-sounding speech from a text source, via a combination of hardware and software.

**theater of operation** In scenario-based training, the theater of operation specifies the environment in which the task is performed. Typically, the theater of operation is not modified to provide exercises of differing difficulty, but rather other variables such as weather and configurations of assets and threats are.

**timeline** In the Adobe Flash application development system, and hence the ReAct application development system, the timeline serves to specify the existence of different model elements at differing times and to order the objects in the Z-axis, i.e., visual layering order.

**Turing test** An early proposal by Alan Turing devised to address the question of whether or not computers could think, by asking whether or not a computer's responses to questions can be distinguishable from those of a human being.

**tweening** A special form of animation in which one graphical element is converted relatively smoothly into another via a series of small changes in each brief time increment. The process may be generalized to non-graphical subjects, e.g.., the values of an original vector, may be modified over time toward a predetermined outcome vector.

**type** In object-oriented programming, the possible values that an object may acquire. In ReAct and DIAG, object type such as "test point", "indicator", and "operable control" are used to support intelligent performance aiding.

**userMode** A key global variable used by the software systems described here that allows objects to respond appropriately to user actions, depending upon the particular instructional process that is in control. Thus, if an object-identification exercise is in progress, the setting of userMode causes objects to report their names when selected, rather than responding by changing state.

**vector graphics** A powerful and flexible method for expressing a graphical element, such as a line or an arc, via some descriptor and associated parameters. Vector graphics are distinguished from raster graphics, in which graphical elements are described via the pixels that form the element.

**virtual reality** A special type of simulation in which the objective is to produce, via hardware and software, the impression of the real world as the user moves about or operates various controls. Generally virtual reality (VR) goes well beyond flat-screen display and the emulation of a 3-D world.

**WYSIWYG** The acronym for What You See Is What You Get, describing a user interface in which the end product of a user's actions is virtually identical to what is seen throughout the development process.

Printed in the United States
137411LV00002B/6/A